D1740431

Traders of the New Era:

Interviews with a Select Group of Day and Swing
Traders Who Are Still Beating the Markets in the Era of
High Frequency Trading and Flash Crashes

Fernando Oliveira

First Edition

Revised and Improved

2014

ISBN 13: **978-85-916713-0-4**
Cover design by Leandro Oliveira. 2014 All rights reserved.

To Nathaniel Branden, David Sklansky and Kelly McGonigal. The most practical and helpful teachers I've had in my life.

Table of Contents

Introduction		1
Chapter 1	The Fundamentals of High Frequency Trading	5
Chapter 2	Flemming Kozok: The Big Bet Sniper	13
Chapter 3	Dennis Dick: The Base Hit Trader	45
Chapter 4	Jeffrey Goldman: Market Maker Turned Prop Firm Trader and Manager	97
Chapter 5	Eric Scott Hunsader: The Market Structure Expert	127
Chapter 6	Mitch Semon: The Veteran Stock Operator	165
Chapter 7	Wayne Kulcheski: The Trend Fighter	193
Chapter 8	Anonymous: The Former Winner	241
Chapter 9	Anonymous: The Secrecy of the Bot Destroyer	259
Chapter 10	atticus: The Options Expert	271
Chapter 11	Additional Advice, Resources and Tips	299
	The Boost Your Discipline Mini-Course	306
Chapter 12	The Core Principles of Good Short-Term Trading	323
Conclusion		339

Introduction

It was April 15, 2011. I was in my desk checking out some news and threads in a poker forum when all of a sudden a rumor broke out: the FBI had seized a number of major online poker websites. A few minutes later, I realized it wasn't a rumor at all when I tried going to these sites and found a message on each explaining that the domain names had been seized by the FBI pursuant to an arrest warrant obtained by the US Attorney's Office for the Southern District of New York.

I immediately logged on to my poker platform in a panic and tried to withdraw my funds. My logic was that the news might create a run on the bank on these sites and that they might not have all the money they needed to pay their players. I figured I could withdraw all my funds and then wait until things were settled before depositing again. But I soon realized my effort was futile. Posters on the forums were talking about how these sites bank accounts had been frozen. Supposedly these poker websites had been breaking all kinds of financial regulations, and there was no way they could process the withdrawals.

I was outraged. I thought "I'm not American. Why am I being dragged into this?" It was questionable whether poker was even gambling anyway. Why were US taxpayers' dollars being used to stop people from playing a skill game they played voluntarily? But it was a waste of time to complain. I had no idea if I was ever going to see any of the money I'd deposited with those sites, and Americans had been effectively banned from playing online poker.

Eventually I was able to get access to my funds, but the poker games were never the same. Instead of playing against mostly recreational American players, now I had to go up against tougher and harder-working Europeans and Asian players. My playing was still profitable, but my income had gone down. To make matters worse, in early 2012 the poker site I used made a major change to its bonus system, which cut my income even more. At that point, I decided that poker had had its run in my life. It had been a good job over the years due to all the freedoms it gave me, but now I had to move on to bigger and better things.

I didn't want a nine-to-five job, so I thought, "I'd better get into day trading". Trading was a natural transition for me because I'd been a "position" trader since 2007. I would make trades based on macroeconomic trends, buy and hold or short stocks I felt were incorrectly priced, etc. I had made some good profits off my macro account over the years, sometimes even more than in poker, so diving deeper into markets and trading felt completely appropriate to me. The issue was that in 2008, during my first try at day trading, I struggled with profitability. I would make some and give it back. Commissions would add up. Overall, I posted a small loss after a month or two. When I came back to day trading in late 2011, I wanted a solid strategy that I could rely upon so I wouldn't struggle like I had in 2008. I decided to go with a popular NYSE opening imbalance strategy.[1] Essentially, you would provide liquidity against opening imbalances and take the other side, along with the specialist. You would get in long or short on a stock that was away from its theoretical "fair value," and you would profit as the stock approached its fair value.

I started to use this strategy every day; however, I began to notice all kinds of strange things in the stocks that I traded. For instance, I would short a stock in the opening print, and if I put in a

---

[1] This strategy is explained in more detail in Chapter 3.

limit order to buy a stock at, for example, $20.15, sometimes the stock would trade down to right above my price, say $20.17 or $20.16, and it would stop there. If I did get hit, it would then drop another 10 cents very quickly, which means I left money on the table. There was also a situation in which I sent a market sell order for 600 shares, I got filled at the exact low of the day, and then the stock proceeded to rally a lot. Before I sent the order, I saw in the Level 2 that the bid wasn't that low. The quotes moved as soon as my order was sent.

After months of trading with this strategy, I had almost no profits. I'd made about $2,000 and then gave all of it back. At that point, I realized that I had to improve my trading by learning from other traders that were already doing it well. I wanted to understand these markets so that I could develop sounder strategies. I wanted to make a living off this business and was willing to do whatever it took to get there.

I decided to pay for subscription services, day trading chat rooms, and interview and learn from as many traders as I could. I wanted to talk to the best guys I could possibly find and try to learn how they were able to extract profits when it seemed impossible for me. I'd always been a big fan of trading books that featured interviews with the best traders and really dove deep into what they thought it took to become a winning and consistent trader. I really liked the diversity of views, strategies, and styles in those books. At the same time, I thought some of the interview books were quite weak. I could sometimes tell that the interviewer wasn't really a trader, so he or she didn't direct the questioning in a way that made sense to me. I wanted to create a book in which traders were interviewed by someone who was also a living, breathing trader.

The result of all of that was this book. By interviewing successful traders and learning from them, I discovered all kinds of traps that I was falling into due to the rise of High Frequency Trading and the new era of electronic markets. I discovered that I had to dramatically change the strategies I used. If I wanted to succeed, I had to focus more on the basic fundamentals of good day trading, key risk management rules, and technical changes. I implemented several changes, and a few months after I started these interviews and thought about the advice I received, I achieved profitability — finally, consistent profitability. I actually struggled to write this book, because once I'd done the interviews, I already knew what changes I had to make and could refresh my memory by listening to the audio files anytime. So why even put in the time and effort to produce a book? I knew it wasn't likely to be a good source of income (especially compared to the significant number of hours I had to put into it). But ultimately I decided to write it because I just wanted to do something nice and give back to other people.

For most of my life, I was not a charitable guy. I was always too busy with my own projects and goals. This time, I thought, why not do something nice and help struggling or new traders who might be making the same mistakes I or my profiled traders had made? Supposedly, you're only truly happy when you help other people. Giving is said to be one of the major ways people can be happy. I wanted to find out if this was true.

This book is the result of my blood, sweat, and tears, as well as of these traders. I hope you find the information contained in it as helpful as I have found it.

Best,
Fernando Oliveira
March 09, 2014

Chapter 1

The Fundamentals of High Frequency Trading

High frequency trading (HFT) is a term that's being used these days to describe all kinds of different styles and strategies. It can mean anything from basic stock market trading using an algorithm (algo) to the use of news algos that parse news and buy or sell futures, stocks, or bonds. In this chapter I'm going to go through some of the main elements about HFTs and why it's important to understand them if you want to be successful at day trading these days.

According to the *Financial Times Lexicon*, HFT is:

"High-frequency trading (HFT) is high-volume trading used by proprietary traders and a new breed of electronic trading outfits (typically privately held). It relies on synthesizing information faster than other traders using sophisticated trading algorithms and powerful computers, often co-located near the electronic matching systems within securities exchanges. By co-locating their trading systems close to the exchanges' matching 'engines', these firms can speed up their orders to the exchanges ever so slightly (the time savings are in the milliseconds) and thus provide a competitive advantage over other traders whose systems are not as fast.

In addition, the HFT firms' orders are designed to be not only faster but also potentially more nimble by strategically and swiftly placing buy and sell orders (and, in many cases, quickly canceling them). In this way, HFT firms can detect or anticipate changes in the depth and direction of order flow from institutional and retail investors.

For example, the HFT traders can position themselves to profit from momentary order imbalances and fleeting intra-day price trends by placing aggressive buy and sell orders (thus putting them first in line to gain by either first buying low and selling slightly higher in less than second or by first selling high and then buying moments later at a slightly lower price)."

According to Nasdaq.com, HFT:

"Refers to computerized trading using proprietary algorithms. There are two types high frequency trading. Execution trading is when an order (often a large order) is executed via a computerized algorithm. The program is designed to get the best possible price. It may split the order into smaller pieces and execute at different times. The second type of high frequency trading is not executing a set order but looking for small trading opportunities in the market. It is estimated that 50 percent of stock trading volume in the U.S. is currently being driven by computer-backed high frequency trading. Also known as algo or algorithmic trading."

In addition to high frequency trading (the above definitions), HTF is commonly used to mean high frequency trades and high frequency traders. Back in the old days (90s and early 2000s), the HFTs were the day traders. They would try to manually make markets in stocks with sufficiently large spreads (buy at the bid and sell at the offer). They would read the news then try to reprice a stock. They would also try to read the supply and demand by looking at things like the Level 2(L2) window, arbitrage securities, and profit from mispricings. All of these activities have been taken over by HFTs these days simply because computers are more efficient at this job than any human could ever be. They can make all the calculations and predictions, create/submit/cancel orders, before a human can even finish looking at the screen.

Some of the main strategies by HFT firms are statistical arbitrage (exploiting deviations from statistical relationships between different securities), market making, news trading (trading after using an algorithm to "read" the news and make a quick assumption of how much an asset should change its value based on that news), and latency arbitrage (arbitraging differences between the faster direct data feed that they pay for and the slower SIP feed that everyone else gets).

HFT firms frequently "collocate" their computers by placing them inside the exchanges. This guarantees them a fill before everybody else given that their latency will be the smallest among all the market participants in a specific financial instrument. This compounds their speed advantage over other participants even further.

In addition to colocation, HFT firms also get special benefits from exchanges and ECNs. According to the book *Dark Pools*[2] and the *Wall Street Journal*, firms with special connections get special order types that are not available to regular market participants.

This enables them to get an advantage that they would otherwise not have, especially in terms of avoiding adverse selection.[3] *Adverse*

---

[2] Scott Patterson 2012.

[3] For Superfast Stock Traders, a Way to Jump Ahead in Line – WSJ -

selection is an important concept to learn in order to understand these modern markets, but instead of using sophisticated language to explain the term, I'll give you an example.

Let's say you want to buy a stock that's currently trading at $15 with a spread of 6 cents (meaning a bid at $14.97 and the ask at $15.03). You send a limit buy for $14.98. Frequently (as in virtually every time), the HFT who's making markets in that stock will immediately join you at $14.98 or "penny jump" your order at $14.99. You might think, this is fine; maybe we'll both get filled, and I'll save some money by not having to hit the ask. You then proceed to see a lot of trades going off at $14.9901 — so called **subpenny trades** — which according to rule 612 from Reg NMS are fully legal when they happen off-exchange. These are liquidity taking orders that are intercepted by some HFT firms and don't interact with your limit order because they paid for the order flow privilege. You think, this is strange. How come I'm not getting these fills? I just want to be long on some stock here. A few minutes later, you start to get frustrated, then all of a sudden, you get filled, but the problem is that the stock is now down to trading at $14.90 with a bid of $14.85 and $14.92 offered. Yes, you got your fill and a rebate, but the cost was that you got filled because the stock was going down so much that the HFTs stopped playing their games and your order got done.

In this case your order was suffering from adverse selection, meaning it was likely to get filled only when you were wrong (in the short-term), and it was unlikely to get filled when you were right (in the short-term). This creates a huge problem for you because you get stuck with 100 percent of the losers of your trade setup, but you miss out some winners because you never get filled.

Scott Patterson and Jenny Stratsburg – September 19, 2012.

What are some of the games that HFTs might play against your order? First, there's payment for order flow. HFT firms pay for retail brokerage houses' order flow and trade against them. That's where most of the subpenny trades come from. The retail traders and investors are usually the most uninformed participants in the markets, meaning that they're the least likely to be right about the short-term direction of a security. When they take that order flow all to themselves (and provide a negligible "price improvement" in return) your order gets exposed to order flows that are more toxic. They're more likely to know more about short-term price direction than you. The flow could be other market making HFTs (that can tell that the supply and demand has shifted before you can), news algos (that can read and trade on the news way before any human can even understand what's going on), professional traders, etc. The result of trying to save a few cents by not hitting the spread is something that might cost you way more than that in a particular trade.

An order to take liquidity might have been improved by a subpenny, but a resting and displayed order had its fill taken away by somebody else with a special advantage. The truth is that markets are rigged against players who are not engaged in the business of trying to get special advantages.

In addition to payment for order flow, there are also all kinds of special orders that firms can get these days. The *Wall Street Journal* exposed the hide-not-slide order in 2012. [4]

That special order type gives an HFT firm order priority over a regular order and enables them to be executed first. The nonprivileged order will only be filled later, which means its way more exposed to adverse selection than the order that's on top of the

---

[4] How 'Hide Not Slide' Orders Work – WSJ – Scott Patterson and Jenny Strasburg September 2012.

others. In market making, avoiding adverse selection is the name of the game, and being at the top of the queue is the best way to achieve that.

This might be only the tip of the iceberg however. It's Wall Street, after all. If the stuff that's being openly talked about looks unfair, imagine what's being done behind the scenes by people with questionable ethical standards.

Eric Hunsader, founder of Nanex Research, uncovered a scheme in which some HFT firms were being given the news before everybody else. (He's profiled in this book and explains more about it in his chapter) When I say they got the news before everybody else, I mean a matter of milliseconds before, but in today's electronic markets, that time frame can amount to millions of dollars in profits during a big event.

It's said that HFT market making is good for markets because it tightens up spreads. But that's only part of the story. While spreads have decreased from the early 2000s to today (mostly due to electronic trading), the actual displayed size of the bids and asks has also decreased. In the old days, you would see much thicker bids and offers, but these days a lot of stocks are 100 shares each side. When there are more than 100 shares, if you try to hit an entire level for all the liquidity available, frequently HFTs will cancel their orders, and you will get a partial fill (and even worse, your size will be displayed in the Level 2 window because your buy/sell order will become the ask/bid after you clean up that particular level. You just showed your hand to the HFTs, who now know your intention to buy/sell).

If you want to get in and out of size these days, it's harder than ever. There are all kinds of algos and computers programmed to try to detect big orders that are being worked in a specific security. As soon as a "whale" is detected, they'll immediately try to make that big buyer or seller pay or lose more than would otherwise be the case.

This chapter is not meant to be a complete guide to HFTs and how they affect the markets. Such topics are beyond the scope of this book. If you want to know more about it, I would encourage you to read the books *Dark Pools*, by Scott Patterson, and *Broken Markets*, by Sal Arnuk and Joe Salluzi. You can also find more materials about it on the website and Twitter feed of Nanex Research (nanex.net and @nanexllc). I'm more interested in knowing the necessary adjustments you have to make if you want to succeed at day trading in an HFT world. In the following interviews, I asked traders how to do that and what they think are the keys to making a living off day and swing trading.

The traders I selected had to meet a certain criteria to make sure I was sourcing advice from folks who knew what they were doing rather than trying to sell something. They had to up $150,000 per year *minimum* in the period leading up to the interview and they had to be experienced, meaning, they were around for many years and had seen the markets change. There are two interviews that are exceptions for the income criteria (The Former Winner and The Market Structure Expert). The reason why they were included will become clear once you read their chapters.

Keep in mind that during these interviews, I had to be careful as to not get the trader defensive by specifically asking about their main money making strategies right away, as a result I had to have a more indirect/patient interview style (with longer interviews) and try to learn from their little snippets of info or when the trader volunteered strategic information. At the end of each chapter, I list the lessons I learned from each trader. Now, the interviews.

Chapter 2

Flemming Kozok - The Big Bet Sniper

I came across the following trader (twitter @flemmingkozok) while in a trading chat room. Everybody was talking about FNMA and FMCC, two Over the Counter (OTC) stocks that had been hot lately and had just had a large crash and rebound. People were pleased that they made a few thousand dollars in the stock. Some even made $10,000. Flemming, on the other hand, said he made more than $100,000. Even though it sounded like a lot, it was very doable given that the stocks were extremely liquid and put in some huge moves.

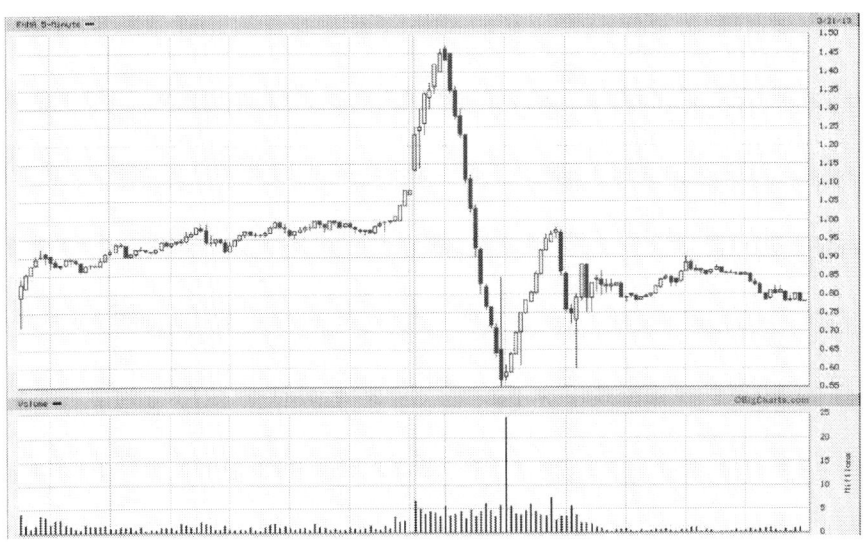

FNMA 5min chart. Source: BigCharts.com

After that day, I realized I had to push my comfort zone more if I wanted to make big money in the markets. I decided that when the right setups came along, I would go for it more aggressively. What was amazing was that those two stocks came back and made an even more impressive run, going from $0.50 in March all the way up to $5 in May.

It was the same sort of setup, a parabolic bubble, fueled by retail traders and "investors." It was doomed to failure. Such a greater-fool speculation is self-reinforcing on the way up and down. It's only a matter of whether you can stand the losses that happen when you short the move too early. In addition, you can play the bounce that inevitably comes when the stocks overshoot on their way down as well.

©1999-2014 StockCharts.com All Rights Reserved.
Chart courtesy of StockCharts.com

I decided to play the move in May with a bigger position than normal, and I ended up making about $7,000, mostly on the short side but some on the rebound as well. That was my best day ever at that time and I was quite pleased. Flemming then posted screenshots of his platform, and the results were staggering. He had just made almost $800,000 in a single day! It sounds huge but these stocks were so liquid, and the moves so gigantic, that he even said he left a lot of money on the table. After that, I decided that I wanted to learn as much as I could from him, and I contacted him for an interview.

I'm glad I did as he has a very interesting perspective on what it takes to get good at trading. Contrary to what some people might think, he's not a big swinging-dick-style trader who makes huge bets every day and has large swings. He has a patient style and only bets big when the right setups come along. "I'm more patient than ever", he says. He's similar to a sniper who takes his time, waits for the right opportunity — the perfect headshot — and then pulls the trigger.

He's based in Copenhagen, Denmark, is thirty-five years old, started day trading with $4,100 in 2000, has executed more than 350,000 trades, and has made nearly $4.5 million after trading costs and fees.

This interview was conducted in August of 2013

When did you become a trader, and why did you want to?

Being from Copenhagen, I started trading Danish stocks many years ago. I immediately felt that it was an interesting line of work, and I also felt a natural ability to assess how certain stocks would behave in the market. From the very beginning, I felt that it was only going to be a matter of time before I made a lot of money, even if I made nearly nothing in the beginning. I started in 1997 but only started to day trade US stocks in 2000. I became attracted to the US market because of the large number and high variety of stocks. I have always been drawn to stocks with the highest possible volatility, as those stocks are the ones that can deliver the fast money. But, of course, they're the most risky as well. So basically my job is to manage risk while I seek risk.

Did you start out well, or did it take some time to make money?

When I switched to day trading US stocks, I was very profitable right away. Prior to making the jump, I spent many months analyzing how to approach day trading. My strategies actually worked from the very beginning. The fantastic thing for me is that to this day the main principles of the approaches I used in 2000 are the same. As such, I have never needed to alter them fundamentally. My main line of thought is the same but, of course, I have refined them due to changes in the marketplace. But yes, I was profitable right away.

Starting in 1997, how did you do?

I made money but gave it back. That was not day trading. At the age of fifteen and sixteen, I was just finding out what this trading thing was all about, so it went slower. I started with $1,100 and probably made around $130,000 in a period of three or four years, and then I lost everything. That's when I realized that I needed to take what I had left, which was around $4,100, or 32,500 DKK, and move into day trading with a different strategy. So overall, I didn't make money. It was slower and harder than day trading.

Do you think it was important to have lost everything?

Yes, absolutely. I lost everything and I was indebted. You learn in a very intensive way when you lose everything, but you don't have to do that in order to learn. In 2000, I almost did it again. I didn't lose it all but it felt that way. I'd made 6.4 million DKK in the first four months of day trading, and then I lost 4.3 million DKK in five weeks. It really felt like I was losing everything once more. Those two losing periods are important to me to this day, as they added some really substantial fundamental knowledge of how to do things and how *not* to do things.

Those two times that you lost a lot, was it that you just bet too big in a single trade?

The first time around, it was a trading combination that I don't really remember the specifics of. I do know I was using lots of margin. Now, in general, I seek not to use margin and recommend others not using it. The second time was a mistake of breaking the rules of the strategy. I tried to convert into swing trading, but I'm not a swing trader. I wanted to try to do it because I could see some big opportunities in it. I also used margin, so I lost most of what I'd made. I had made about $800,000 then lost around $550,000.

Do you have an educational background, a college degree?

I have a master's degree from college, but it's never helped me in stock trading. Stock trading to me is a game of psychology; it's not a game of who can crunch numbers. I let other people, like analysts, crunch numbers. For trading purposes, I have no interest in reading reports and that kind of thing. The result of the number crunching is what you see in the ticker tape — price action. The price action is the key, not reading reports.

What are some of the great trades that you had early on in your career?

I must admit that I remember the bad trades better. They were short sales where I mistimed entries; I was convinced that things were going to break down. So the combination of mistiming and holding stubbornly to positions resulted in large losses, and eventually I got margin called. Having executed so many trades in my life, I must admit I don't really remember the specifics of many of the good ones. I do remember having done some short sales as well as great bottom plays on the long side. Being primarily a short seller, I'm very happy about catching a good long, especially if I let my profit run more than I'm used to. I have never been really good about letting my profits run.

There are many categories of good trades. An amusing category of a good trade is the ones that you enter and flip three, five, seven seconds later. You make $500, $1,000 — it's not a lot of money, but when you consider that the operation only took a few seconds, it's actually a very good trade. I remember not so long ago I traded 100,000 shares and made $7,000 in eleven seconds. Flipping a position that was this big so fast is uncommon, but I managed to do it in a matter of seconds, getting hit on the bid and the ask. That was a very good trade because of the beauty of the trade, the way it was executed.

In the early 2000s a lot of traders were using the strategy of buying the bid and selling the ask, scalping-style market making. Was that a big part of your approach?

I have many different approaches. One of them is market making. I have done lots of that. It has become harder to do that over the years because of the market changes and higher costs related to trading. I have had to shift focus to other areas.

So over the years your market making has become less important and the other strategies more important?

Absolutely. I have always sought to have multiple strategies and approaches to different types of stocks. I have always been afraid that some areas would stop working, so I would have the other areas to rely on. I have about twelve different types of trading that I do, different kinds of setups and other strategies.

A lot of traders say that the US markets are difficult because of the computers and lack of volatility. You live in Europe. Why don't you trade the European markets, which seem to be moving more?

I'm not all that fond of the European stocks. You don't have any market in the world where you have such a huge volume of stocks and different markets as in the United States. Also you have extreme volatility in many different stocks in different exchanges. Stocks also trade in a technically different manner on different exchanges, which is both fun and interesting. You also find different ways to approach them. I don't see that happening in Europe. I also like the consolidated tape in the United States. If you look at the Danish market, you don't see a lot of games being played in the way they are in the United States. You have people trying to manipulate stocks in the United States because of the different kinds of routes you can use. You don't see much of that happen in a less fragmented market like in Denmark. Those are the kinds of games that I like to observe.

I first came across your results in March of 2013 when FNMA and FMCC had a big day and you made more than $100,000 that day. Then in May, you made $800,000 in an even bigger volume day. How do you go from making small trades to all of a sudden making a huge bet like that?

It's a good question. In March, I was actually feeling more insecure, even though I felt it was the right thing to do. The thing was, I had seen those kinds of setups in those stocks in 2009, but just not that extreme. I'd also seen those kinds of setups in other OTC stocks multiple times in the past. I felt very safe in doing what I did. I even felt safer in May with the bigger bets than in March with the smaller ones. It was all the result of having observed similar setups many times before. There were many traps along the way in those plays, but I didn't have any significant unrealized loss on them, so I was able to think straight when I had to. When the time came, I knew that this was it and it could be a big trade. I wasn't questioning that there was going to be a big move at all.

These other stocks that you saw similar patterns in, do you have an archive of charts saved somewhere, or is it all in your head?

The archive is in my head only.

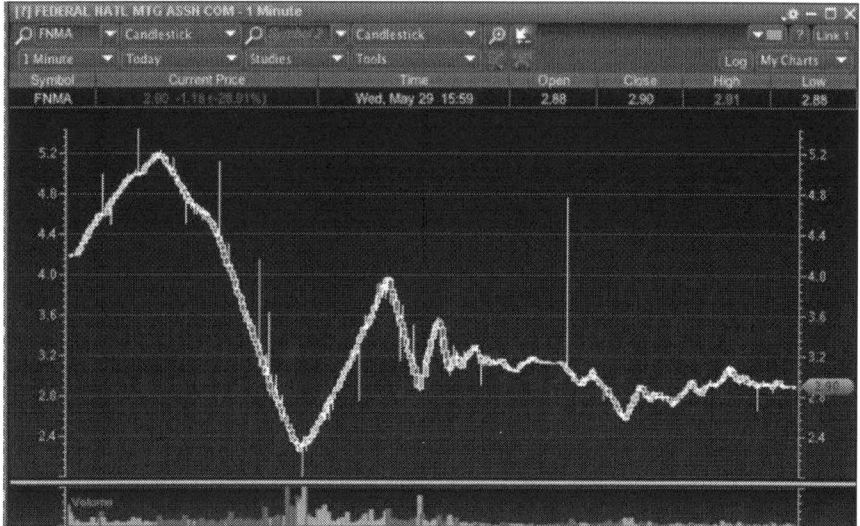

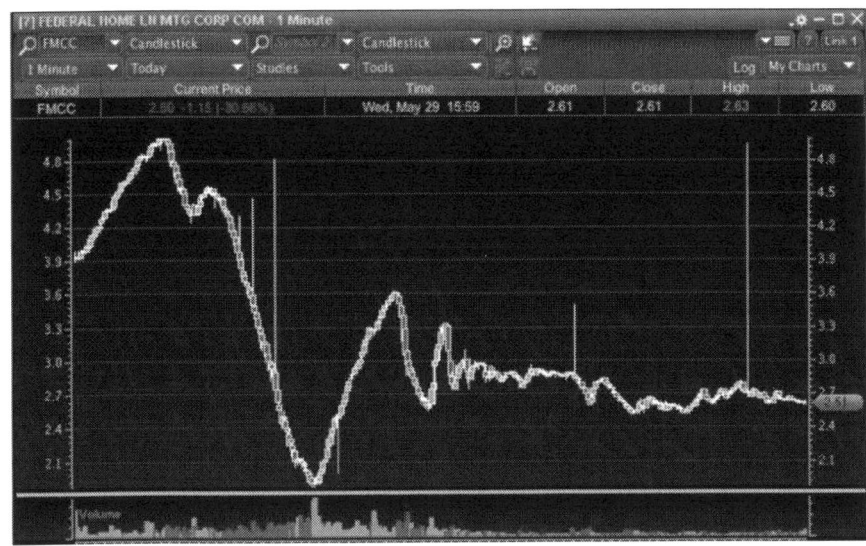

FNMA FMCC 1 min chart. Source: Etrade Pro

You made more money on the way down or on the way up from the rebound?

I think it was fifty/fifty. I was short pretty heavily in FMCC because it was hard to get borrows on FNMA. Both FNMA and FMCC couldn't bounce after the first attempt, so I thought, this is going to flush down strongly. I held it for quite a while. I didn't really care about how much I was making, as I was focused on covering and catching the bounce on the long side. I ended up catching the very bottom, focusing only on FMCC due to a slight laggard delay relative to FNMA. I did well that day because I was mentally strong and able to think straight when I had to. Problem is, you can look at a great setup, but if you time it wrong one, two, three times, and you're down $10,000 to $20,000, you have a bad beginning in a nice setup, and then you always get weaker the more you try. That day I was strong because I had a good start. I made something like $150,000 on the first drop, so I thought, this is the point you have to get in the long side. I bought something like 400,000 shares averaged slightly below $2.

You mentioned catching the bottom in those stocks, I was trading those stocks that day…

You traded them?

Yes, I made some money but not $800,000, not even close. I noticed that ARCA and NITE would flip sides and then the stock would change directions from downtrend to uptrend or vice versa. Did you get in before the flip or after?

Did you look at the bounce in FNMA/FMCC in March?

Yes.

Which one did you trade?

I believe I traded FMCC.

FMCC had trades at $1.88 and $1.89, that was the bottom. I had an average of $1.92 on 400,000 shares. The thing was FMCC trailed FNMA.

I remember that.

That's what I used to guide me. When FNMA confirmed the bottom, there were still huge ask orders in FMCC that needed to be taken off. I always get in gradually, never all at once, so I started buying 25,000 to 50,000 shares at a time. Opening the position, I wasn't nervous at all, but managed to get a bit nervous as FMCC was still heavy on ask, having problems getting released from its low. But at that point, FNMA confirmed the move once more as it started getting released. That's when it was OK to add to the position, even if I was already loaded. I knew that everyone else thought that when ARCA switched sides it would be the time to buy, it would confirm the bottom. At this point in time I was loaded and wanted the stock to move, so now I bought more using ARCA so it would switch, knowing more people would start to jump in the trade. I bought all the way up to $2 using ARCA. I hope you understand what I'm saying here.

Yes. You took the displayed liquidity from ARCA, and when it crossed, everybody started to jump in because it was a sign of rebound.

Yes, because for whatever reason, ARCA wasn't being used by other traders, so I was the one who made the decision to use it aggressively. Even if I didn't really need to add to the position, it was important to send that signal to get others to pull the trigger.

You said you have problems letting winners run. That day you just knew it was going to move, so you just held for the whole thing?

I didn't hold for the whole move. It went all the way to $3.5. I started selling at $2.8, scaling out because it had some bumps along the way. I probably sold my last shares at $3.10 or $3.2, but I don't really remember. I held them percentage wise much further than what I would typically do. It's always been my problem that I have to do lots of trades, because I don't let my winners run. If you can let them run, you can do many fewer good trades. I let these run much more than I normally do, but in hindsight I could have let them run much more, I left a very significant amount of money on the table.

I noticed that in those stocks, that day was great, and the next day was good, but then it started to get choppy and the range got smaller. Did you still make money in them for a while?

I continued as a long as there was liquidity. I only focused on those for a while. I made nearly $100,000 the next day, then nearly $50,000 on the third day. Then it decreased to $40,000, $20,000, $10,000, etc. I was active in them for a while, but level of activity will always correlate with level of liquidity.

What is the feeling of making almost $800,000 in a day?

Most people think that I was screaming to the sky, being really happy and all, but the thing is, I never really react that way to the money I make. I have always had an extremely humble attitude toward the market, and I'm very fearful about it. When I make money — and it doesn't matter how much money — I only really feel one thing, and that is *relief*. I never feel too much happiness about making money. I'm much more grateful than happy. When I made $795,000 in three and a half hours, I felt a huge relief. When I lose money, even smaller amounts, I suffer a lot. There's a very significant mental imbalance there. The negative emotion related to losing is much more profound than the positive emotion related to making money. I've always been aware that I felt that way, so I try to handle that mental imbalance.

If you don't handle it, you will suffer so much in trading that you will go crazy at some point.

So you don't over celebrate, because otherwise you get attached too much, and that is going to hurt down the line?

That's not the way to put it actually. I never celebrate, but not for that reason. You don't celebrate for things that are just necessary. Making money is something that is necessary. You have to do it. It's not like I over accomplished in any way. For me, it's a necessary step toward the overall objective. The other thing is that I'm very fearful about the market. I'm humble, so I don't dare to be too happy. I know that the market is a black hole that can take everything away from you, and you don't even get an "I'm sorry" or anything. Just stay humble no matter how much you make.

Take money out of your trading systems and only leave what is needed to execute your strategies. Always take some off the table.

Did you trade AAMRQ two weeks back?

It was a very classic setup for me, and I would have traded it, but I was on vacation. When I got back I looked at, and I was like, damn — I would have definitely traded it.

How important is tape reading for your style?

It's very important. I'm very much focused on that and price action, getting a very good sense of what is happening with the stock. There are no two stocks that are equal, which is fascinating. I always viewed stocks like a living organism, which has a heart and rhythm. You need to be able to feel that heartbeat. What is the state of this organism? That's why L2, tape reading, and all of that are the most important tools to get you close to that heartbeat, the state of it. You can look at a chart, but it doesn't get as close as tape reading.

Is that just for OTC stocks, or is it for NASDAQ and NYSE too?

It's for everything.

Do you trade mostly on the OTC or a lot of NASDAQ and NYSE as well?

Sometimes, for some reason, you have some crazy times in the OTCs. You have liquidity flowing into many different kinds of stocks. When you have significant volatility in the OTCs I choose to trade it. I like the price action, the way the pendulum swings. They're dangerous. You have to be right, but to me it's always been fairly easy to pick the bottoms and tops because of the way the Level 2 acts. But when you don't have liquidity, I tend to avoid OTCs.

Would you say that you got good by watching markets a lot and remembering situations?

Yes, absolutely. When you trade so many years, and you've seen so many setups, it's like having a small library in your head. The good thing is that when you sit down and look at action in a stock, you don't necessarily feel as if you analyze it. Everything is very mechanical. That's when you've reached the next level of learning. Everything becomes automated, and you don't feel like you're struggling with analysis. Your analysis is very relaxed. It's all the result of having the library and so many experiences, observations, etc. The library increases the ability to identify the ideal setups — the low risk, high probability setups. Those that are golden.

Did you have a mentor, or did you learn everything by yourself?

I never had a mentor. I never read books about it. I always thought that I could do this by myself. When I found a system in the Danish stocks, I went with that system. Then I had theories on how I could I improve — various ideas. The same goes for the way I day trade US markets.

I didn't want to mess with my pretty clear picture of the markets by taking on indicators and analysis from others. I still want to continue to refine what I feel is *my* truth about the markets. How *I* can make money. I've always been afraid of taking on many indicators. At some point, when you respect the indicators too much, you'll have too much contradictory information. Then you'll be paralyzed by your analysis and you won't be able to act. I've only read books like *Reminiscences of a Stock Operator* and Jack Schwager's interviews with top traders.

A lot of traders say the markets are difficult now, but in 2013 you had your best year ever. What do you attribute that to?

To a great extent this is due to the success in those two particular stocks. If you take those two stocks out and just look at all other stocks combined, I made about $400,000. In total around $1.5 million, so yeah, this year has been good, and I say that there are two elements to it. For one I'm very relaxed. I'm more relaxed than ever. I'm more patient than ever. This year I've made fewer mistakes than ever before. At the same time, I'm not as trigger-happy. I'm sitting on my hands in a way that I've never done before. For instance, if I see a stock that just keeps rising, and I know that I want to short it, I'm better than ever now at just waiting for the right moment. If I miss out on the really big spike, I don't really care. I'll wait, and I'll hit it in the sideways action instead of hitting it in the high-risk parabolic move. That's when you have those days where you can lose a lot, if you time the parabolic wrong, you can get forced out at really bad prices.

I'm more patient than ever, and that means I don't take many losses. When you don't take many losses, you will be surprised at your results. It doesn't really feel like you have to have that many good trades before you make a lot of money. I've always taken lots of losses, and then you have to make up for those losses. At the end of the year you can look back and say, "Hey, I made a lot this year." But then you look at how much you've lost along the way. If you could cut just half of what you lost, then you could make extreme amounts of money. That's my focus right now—be more patient, take fewer losses.

Would you say that your approach right now is to do fewer but bigger trades when the right setups come along?

Yeah, I think you're right about that. It needs to feel safe to increase size. I'm trying to cut down on the number of trades, to be better at timing things, more patient. Then hit it with large size.

What are your thoughts on HFTs. Do they hurt you?

They definitely have cut some areas of activity. I only trade stocks that have thick layers and thin spreads, like 1-cent spreads. You see that in low priced stocks, like $3 to $7 a share typically. In a higher priced stock, you would see that in Gold ETFs, but I like trading $5 stocks, in which there's huge liquidity, thick layers. The thing with these HFTs is that they're faster than you. Let's say you need to make 1 cent to cover your costs of entry and exit. You'll probably lose at least 1 more cent from the HFTs, as they're faster than you. You used to have to make 2 cents to profit. Now you have to make at least 3 cents. You have to be even more secure. When you enter the trade, you need to have the right timing, because you need to make 1 or 2 cents more per trade. That's why I've cut lots of that scalping activity. The risk/reward is not good anymore.

In those thick (big volume), low-priced stocks, do you wait for the right daily chart setup and news, and then you jump in?

Actually, I don't care about news. I would like to know what is moving a stock so I can know the context, but the interpretation of the news I don't care about, because the whole market is the result of accumulated interpretations. No matter what my opinion is, I just need to look at what the market feels about the news. When I look at these stocks, I look at the correlation to the Dow Jones, S&P 500, or gold. Then I look at the L2. If that looks good, I'll trade combined with a short-term bias of the S&P 500 or gold. When it aligns, then you have a good setup. I also never show my real size when sending orders.

Do you use stuff like hidden orders or icebergs?

I don't do hidden; I use iceberg. When I sell a stock, I will never, ever show my real size.

Are some ECNs better than others?

I usually do ARCA. The fees aren't cheap, but relative to others it's fair enough. You get a rebate if you're hit. ARCA seems to be working very well for me. I use Interactive Brokers (IB) along with some other brokers. At IB I also use their SMART router for some orders.

You mentioned that you have many different strategies. Do you have one for trend following, one for reversals, etc.? Do you have many different sorts of biases in these strategies?

Trend following is actually one that I do very seldom. Generally, I'm a pessimist. If a stock has a nice trend upward, I can't put my money on a bet that it will continue higher. The same applies to something that has been beaten down. I would wait for a contrarian move rather than try to participate in the trend. I don't do trend following, even though I feel it's potentially very profitable. I do shakes and bounces, mainly in momentum stocks.

Sometimes I play some momentum stocks that are in an intermediate top intraday. They form a base, and because they're like this living organism, they can't simply stay in the same level for the rest of the day. They give a cue that they'll go up or down, and you have to follow that cue. Sometimes I play breakouts. If I feel that the support is there and buy orders are imminent, I just remove everything in the book, assuming there's not too much out there and there will be some follow-through. I can easily be the one guy who takes the step and removes everything, and then others can follow. You need to be able to time it well, because if you buy everything and there's no follow-through, you'll have a problem.

In general, I like overextended stocks in both ways. I like sideways action too. If there's a fairly tight range for a number of days, I try to get a feeling on the stock, because I know that at some point it has to make a directional move. You need patience with that. Sometimes it takes weeks or even months. I'm often the one who starts removing either support or resistance in a stock that has traded sideways for a while. At that point, I can be quite aggressive. I like playing lagging stocks too. You just need to be familiar with a lot of stocks and be able to sniff out what is going on.

I also do "magnet play" to round numbers as well as breakouts through such levels. It's a very basic psychological human thing. People love round numbers. I love that they love them, because if you have the right timing, you can play the breaks and typically get some follow-through, and you can dump everything at 10, 20, or 40 cents higher or whatever.

These breakouts to round numbers, do you have a software that alerts you it's about to happen, or is it just in the stocks you follow?

Just in the stocks I follow.

How many stocks do you follow?

Typically, in my system it will be two hundred at a time, and that changes on a daily basis. The stocks that are no longer interesting are removed. Early on it was four hundred, but I changed to two hundred. In addition to that, I do some scanning for volatility and momentum. If you find a stock that has momentum, there are some reliable setups that you can trade there. When that momentum disappears, it's not necessarily thrown out. It can be sideways for weeks, and there are some setups on sideways action as well. That's why I like to have many different ways to profit. Many traders would say they're momentum traders, and they just stick with that. I used to do that but no longer. I also like blue sky breakouts.

What do you mean by blue sky?

Blue sky is like when a stock reaches its highest level ever, or a level it hasn't seen in a long, long while. This means that everybody is watching closely, especially the shorts. If you have a stock that's close to the blue sky breakout, then you have some real potential. If it's rejected because of the resistance of the former high, then you can play it short instead.

I also like red to green, green to red moves. If a momentum stock has been red all day but has been slowly rising and going toward the green, you can buy and ride them a bit. You also have that reverse setup on the short side with green to red moves. A stock turning red is a cue for many people to sell it, and if you call such a move early, it may make for a good short. Again, this is for stocks with momentum, otherwise you don't have as many eyes following these signals.

I also have the preplay approach. Sometimes you look at stocks and you feel that something is brewing there, especially in the smaller stocks. It's not a scanner. I have always been good at sniffing out when there's something about to happen. You need to look for slow accumulation in some stocks, and you have to be part of that accumulation just before it makes a good move.

The preplay stuff, is that for subpenny or one-penny stocks that start to go to two, three, and four?

Yeah, some are 2 to 3 cent stocks. Some are 10 cents, but I'm not so interested in them anymore.

Usually OTC stocks?

Mostly, but sometimes AMEX, NYSE, and NASDAQ too.

How important is the daily chart for your approach?

The daily is something that I use for context. When I get a stock I think is interesting, I take a look at the daily, then I get the overall feel for where the stock is.

Do you avoid stocks like AAPL, AMZN because of the spread?

Yeah, I don't like to trade those. Ever since I started, in '97, it was natural to me to avoid the largest stocks. It wasn't really all that interesting to me. I always focused on small and medium size stocks.

Would you say that your approach is about finding key points and predicting human psychology there?

Human psychology is deeply embedded in everything that happens, so yeah, it's a major part of activity.

It's not everything that you do? It's just one part of the puzzle?

Yes, the beauty surrounding chart reading is that history has a nice way of repeating itself. This is due to human psychology, but there's also the L2, the manipulation there. You can't look at the chart and say, it's overextended, oversold, so it should bounce. It's more complicated than that. It's the game of manipulation, with many factors that all come together, but to a large extent it has to do with what people believe right now. So you're trying to predict how that will change in seconds, minutes, hours, etc.

In terms of discipline, were you always disciplined from the start, or did you have to build that up?

I was almost always very disciplined. When I was not, that's when I lost the most, and I knew that was the reason. One thing I always have been extremely disciplined in was taking my losses. I'm blessed with having no problems taking a loss. Most people have a hard time with that. For some reason I always knew that if I was to survive in trading, I needed to take my losses. I could also see that I was mentally able to do it as well. It's absolutely necessary. I view that as the single most important thing. My rule has always been, seek protection before you seek profit.

A recent example of protecting against losses is a fat finger error I did, selling short a 650,000 FNMA shares at $2.48. For some reason I mistakenly hit the "submit order" button instead of the "cancel order" button. The order was absorbed right away, meaning that the stock had underlying strength. Even if it hurt, within just fifteen seconds I was covering the whole position, taking all the shares I could get, resulting in a $6,000 loss. Five minutes later, the stock was 8 cents higher than my cover, which would have meant an additional $11,600 loss had I not covered right away. Most people would hesitate to take an immediate loss of $6,000 based on a fat finger mistake, but my conclusion was clear, and when the conclusion is clear, you don't have an argument for hesitation.

Which software do you use for your trading?

I use three different brokers, but I only use one information system.

So you have one just for the charts and other data and the others for entering orders?

Yeah, the one with the charts and data can also take orders, but the others are only for orders and trading.

Which one is it?

It's integrated in one of the trading platforms offered by a small New York broker called Track Data Securities. Not many are acquainted with them. I like their system and their AIQ charts. They have lots of indicators, but I never use them, as I have my own way of doing chart reading, without the use of indicators.

You mentioned that you went on vacation after your big win, how important for you is to take breaks, vacations, and things like that?

Actually, I have never been good at vacationing and taking breaks. Because of my discipline, I always felt I should never allow myself too much freedom, because of some goals that I want to achieve. About six years ago, I started to allow myself to travel more. I usually travel two to three months every year. Sometimes I trade and travel as well. Now I'm thirty-five and have made nearly $4.5 million. As I've gotten older and felt privileged to have made quite a bit of money, I've allowed myself the privilege of traveling more.

When you travel and trade with a laptop, what kinds of adjustments do you make?

The screen real estate shrinks a fair amount, so I set up the software in a different way, but the main problem is being in sketchy places without a backup Internet connection. If the connection is lost, you don't want to get caught in a big position. In these situations, I'm cautious about size, and I take trades that I don't have to hold the whole day or for the next day. I prefer to do trades that I hold for seconds, maybe minutes. I will take positions that I have to hold for hours if they're potentially very profitable, but I prefer not to.

When you're trading in your house, what kind of computer do you have?

In recent years, the computer chips have become so super powerful that even a laptop will have sufficient processing power. I like the freedom of a laptop. I have also two external monitors.

I don't have a huge setup. My strategy doesn't demand six or eight screens. I have always tried to keep things as simple as I can without compromising the efficiency of my strategy. I just have one high resolution laptop and two large external screens. Typically, I don't need more than that. In that setup I can see what I need, which is, eight L2 windows and four order books — like ARCA, NSDQ, and so forth — to see the extra depth of those books. I don't need ten or twenty charts.

So even though you're following two hundred stocks, you only have a handful that you're paying attention to on a given day?

The thing is, I can see the L1, volume, price change, etc. Just by switching pages I can see forty stocks at a time. I don't look at the two hundred all the time, just the ones that qualify. The most important thing is for them to qualify to be in the 8 L2 windows. The four most important ones I'll put in the windows with the extra-depth books.

When you're flipping pages and looking at forty stocks at a time, you're looking to see big moves, big volumes, that kind of thing?

The main thing is the price change and the volume. I usually can sense when the volume is higher than what it usually is. I also build in some scans in all the two hundred stocks I follow, so I know if there's something unusual going on. I also do some market-wide scans.

The money you take out from trading, do you just keep it in the bank, or do you buy stocks, bonds, etc.?

I don't run risk with what I take out. I always viewed the market as a dangerous place to be. So with my trading capital in a dangerous place, I need to know that the rest is at zero to little risk. I don't own one single stock, not even bonds. I only have cash and a couple of real estate properties. I need the feeling that this is secure in order to be able to fully focus on trading in the risk zone.

When you're going to make a trade, how do you decide how much to bet? Do you use a mathematical algorithm, or is it just a feeling?

It's just a feeling. It depends on liquidity. You need to know when you're pushing the limit with regard to your exit. Sometimes you can easily buy a lot of stock, but it's not the right thing to do. The stock has to be liquid enough to absorb your exit. It's always a matter of liquidity.

When FNMA and FMCC were trading hot, you could easily buy 200,000. I bought about 600,000 shares in March and sold it way too early. The stock easily would absorb that. Buying 600,000 right now would be suicidal.

What kind of advice do you give to traders that are starting out or are trying to get better right now?

First, focus on protecting yourself before seeking profit. It's a typical mistake not to do that. People come to the market wanting to make money fast, so they focus on the opportunities, and then they get killed because they are wrong and don't know how to exit. They need defined exits and clear stop-loss strategies. They need to learn that opportunities will always come. They need to focus on living to fight another day.

Also, a new trader needs to focus in developing a tight relationship with the market in the particular stocks that they want to trade. You want to feel the heartbeat of the stock so you're much more likely to be able to assess what's going on. You need to dive into the tape, L2, understand the mechanics behind it. It's a process, a journey.

They need to watch the markets to develop an instinct, a feeling of how things will move?

Yes.

Do you do any backtesting at all?

Everything I do is inherently a backtest in the sense that I always evaluate what I do. When I tweak, modify something or do something new, I move slowly. I try to feel how it works on a smaller scale. It's not simulated trading; it's with real money. I never had a system that I only tested on a theoretical basis. Everything was trial and error with real money. You will always get a better feel with real money, because that's when it hurts. You get a sense of what you're doing because you know it hurts. It's practice, not theory.

It's backtested, but it's in your head?

Everything is in my head.

Would you say that your secret is your observational skill combined with your discipline to take losses?

Absolutely. It's all about instincts, charts, and a history of observations. Between chart reading and instinct, I would say 60 to 70 percent is instinct. It has always been like that. The beautiful thing is that technology gives us great tools. For instance, the order book is a tool, the chart is a tool, and so forth, and the tools can help confirm the hypothesis that your instinct provides. It's a very nice combination.

Does it concern you that HFTs are becoming more present in the markets and some opportunities are being closed by these computers?

Yes and no. It's always a concern if your profits get squeezed in some areas of activity, but in many stocks you don't have that many HFTs, or they don't affect you that much. Lots of traders got hurt because they got squeezed out of the particular stock group they traded. I always traded a wide variety of stocks and strategies.

Some traders talk about these thick stocks as a way of getting away from the HFTs.

Yes, but I also trade stocks that are slightly illiquid, not too illiquid, usually above $10. You can swing plays in them and hold for a few days. You'll capture the order flow movement that the HFTs can't control.

What kind of Internet speed do you have in your country?

I think it goes as high as 50 to 100MB. I have 20MB, but it seems to have a similar response delay as that of 5MB.

Now that you're trading less, doing bigger positions, and having more patience, do you think the tendency for you is to become a swing trader at some point?

I have been thinking about it. After thirteen years, I'm considering setups in which I can extend my time horizon. I tried to do that in 2000 and I failed, losing more than ever before. Now I'm considering it again, but I move slowly with it because of my past experience. In an ideal world, I would convert to swing trading at this point in time.

Lessons from Chapter 2

1. Experience is king. Flemming was able to make huge bets in FNMA and FMCC because he had seen those patterns before. He had stored in his head the way those moves play out when he watched them in other stocks. If you're starting out, realize how important it is to accumulate information about charts, situations, patterns, etc. Don't try to go for a big trade if you're not feeling confident about it.

In chapter 11, in the section titled "How to Best Accumulate Market Knowledge — aka How to become a Student of Price Action and Market Situations", I describe my favorite way to speed up the information accumulation process and develop a mental library of market situations.

2. Have the courage to bet big. If you've seen the situation before and you know what the course of action is, don't be too afraid of making a big bet. The thing to keep in mind is that in an HFT world there are fewer opportunities to make consistent money every day, but there are still plenty of opportunities to make big money every once in a while, when the right setup comes along. Days like the flash crash, Knight Capital, some Fed announcements, FNMA, and FMCC are days on which, if you have courage, you can make your entire year.

3. In ideal setups, it's very important to be mentally strong. Flemming says he was more secure in May making bigger bets than in March with smaller bets while trading FMCC. It's very important not to ruin a good setup by weakening yourself psychologically by accumulating losses immediately prior to the big play. You have to be patient, even risk being a little late. If the setup is good and the move will be big, there's plenty of time to get in. What you can't afford is to be upset by losses then play a fifth of your normal size when the move finally occurs.

4. Don't be afraid of being the one who takes the first action. Flemming mentions being the one who took the ARCA displayed liquidity on FMCC. That made the L2 look bullish to everybody watching the stock and sent the signal to other people that the stock would bounce. He also talks about playing round-number breakouts in listed stocks and being the one who makes the first move and takes out the ask, as well as often being the first to remove support

or resistance orders after periods of sideways action. If you trust the situation, don't be afraid of being the one who makes the first move.

5. Seek protection before profit. He says his ability to take losses is his most important trait. While it's great to have the courage to go for it and take chances, you always have to keep in mind that even the best setups may fail.

6. Addition by the lack of subtraction. Decrease the amount of losses you have. Flemming talks about how your year-end results can be improved significantly by simply focusing on cutting down the amount of losses you have. This will also improve your mental clarity, given that losses can be debilitating. How exactly can you decrease the amount of losses you have if you don't know if a trade will work out or not? That's when lesson seven comes in.

7. Focus on the best setups—ideally, what Flemming calls "low risk, high probability" setups. By only taking what you would consider the best setups, you can be sure that your ratio of dollar return to time invested in trading will be very high. If you're new and don't have a lot of trading experience, it can be detrimental to only take great setups, because then you don't accumulate market knowledge and learn from different situations. If that's your case, you're probably better off only **playing with very small size in many different situations**. Save the bigger bets for situations in which you're familiar and have seen the results before. If you're already experienced, consider improving your results by playing less frequently but playing bigger when you do. The good news is that this style leaves you with more free time to travel and enjoy the money you make.

8. Develop a tight relationship with the market. Get to the heart and rhythm of the stock. Flemming talks about stocks being like

living organisms that have heartbeats. Your job is to use tools, like the chart, L2, order books, tape, etc. to get a read on those heatbeats so you can make a tradable call. You can develop this relationship by watching stocks very closely. They have to be stocks that are "alive," meaning they're momentum stocks, stocks with news, etc. If you watch some illiquid HFT driven stocks, you're just seeing the result of random action, and you won't learn much.

9. Avoid HFT games by playing lower-priced stocks with thick layers (big volume). Numerous NASDAQ and NYSE low-priced stocks have a lot of volume with plenty of liquidity on both sides of the L2. From time to time, they're also in play, so they can put nice moves. The spread is less of a factor in these stocks so the "HFT tax" is smaller as a percentage of the move that you are trying to capture.

10. Watch out for limiting beliefs. If you think markets are terrible and there are no opportunities, you might end up missing some huge days that become available every once in a while. It's true that HFTs have decreased the consistency of day trading but if you're always on the watch out for those special days — and don't worry, they'll come — you can capitalize on them big time. Flemming had his best year ever by May, being up more than $1 million at that point, even though markets were supposed to be "horrible."

11. Your instincts drive a hypothesis that you can confirm using trading tools. When you accumulate a lot of price action knowledge, you'll develop a feeling when things are about to happen. You can't merely trust the feelings blindly, but you can construct a hypothesis that you seek to confirm via tools such as the L2, order book, ticker tape, etc.

12. The power of ARCA. In listed stocks, ARCA balances out with good execution, rebates, and solid liquidity. ARCA also allows

you to place iceberg orders[5], which are important when using limit orders. Never show your hand if you have significant size.

13. Order books as an additional tool for developing a read in a stock. Most people have the L2 in their platforms, but not all have depth of the book from sources like ARCA or NSDQ, because they come with a cost, and many believe that L2 is sufficient. In the L2 you only see the best price from any given ECN or exchange. By diving deeper into the depth of the book, you can get a sense of the overall supply and demand of that exchange or ECN. This can provide you with additional information that might tell you if a stock has true support, or if a stock will break out or fail to break out. Because there are fewer people looking at that data, there's more room for you to have an edge there.

14. The power of focusing in one stock only. When FNMA/FMCC are in play, Flemming doesn't trade anything else, he focuses 100 percent on those stocks. That's what enables him not to miss critical turns and to make huge bets. If you try to watch other stocks, you might make an additional $500 to $1,000 in them but miss a $10,000 profit in the stock in play.

15. Price action is more important than crunching numbers and reading reports. The market price already expresses the collective opinion of people that are processing the fundamental data. If you pay attention to price action, you don't necessarily have to know the data behind it.

---

[5] Iceberg orders are orders where you only show part of the size that you intend to get done. For example, you might be trying to sell 30,000 shares but only display 100. You are only showing the tip of the iceberg to other participants.

16. "It needs to feel safe to increase size". When pushing yourself to bet bigger, remember that it needs to be a solid setup with plenty of liquidity otherwise you might find yourself caught with a big position and not knowing how to get out.

The decision to go bigger should be based on technical and logical factors not on gambling urges or the fact that your results have been hot lately.

Chapter 3

Dennis Dick — The Base Hit Trader

I first heard about Dennis Dick (Twitter @TripleDTrader) when I contacted Don Bright (one of the founders of Bright Trading, LLC, a professional stock trading firm) to ask him for an interview with one of his top traders. He sent me Dennis e-mail address, along with his SEC testimony for the Commission's Concept Release on Equity Market Structure, which I immediately read.[6]

What struck me about that testimony is how well he explained issues like informed order flow, internalization, and how subpenny trades lead to situations where limit orders sitting on the order books tend to be filled when they're wrong (in the short-term) and not filled when they're right. This was exactly the experience I had while doing day trading on my own, but I was simply not aware of what was going on. That testimony opened my eyes and made me realize that things were not as simple as the older trading books could lead one to think. (Most of the older books say people who blame the markets for losses are just making excuses. It might be true in a lot of situations but in an HFT world, it's less true than you would expect).

---

[6] http://tinyurl.com/o652gh6

What also caught my attention about him was that he's the exact opposite of the big-ego Wall Street trader, I found him quite friendly and humble about trading and his experiences. Of course, everybody has a little bit of an ego, but Dennis is the type of guy you would want to hang out for a beer after a long trading day.

He exemplifies a principle that I heard a long time ago, with which I agree wholeheartedly: "If you can't explain to a ten-year-old, then you don't understand." He's not the type of guy who will get all fancy with indicators or algorithms. He tries to make trading as simple as possible, probably because it leads to lower stress and it fits his easygoing nature. (This might be true for his hedging tactics that you will read about in the interview.)

He's the type of trader who rarely goes for big gains. This limits his losses dramatically and makes his results "shockingly consistent" on a week to week basis, as he says. For those who are familiar with the book *Moneyball*, by Michael Lewis, Dennis would be like the hitter Jason Giambi, a player that is very consistent at getting singles and that is known for his plate discipline and high on-base percentage. Sure, he might not get big scores all the time, but he'll grind out his profit in a low-stress fashion.

He also hosts a free Benzinga Internet radio show called "Premarket Prep" along with his friend Joel Elconin. Every morning before the market opens, they go through the major news pieces of the day, stocks that are moving, key support and resistance levels, market structure lessons, trading tips etc.

This interview was conducted in August of 2012 and updated in November of 2013

What initially made you want to become a trader?

I started trading back in university. My dad and uncle had some money invested in some stocks, and I was helping to manage their money a little bit. This was from 1996 to 1998, in the bull market. I think by pure luck I did well, because everything went up back then, but looking back now, I see that I probably didn't know what I was doing. In those markets, everything seemed to be rising no matter what you bought. I can remember buying Amazon at $100 and selling at $130 a week later, it was just a crazy tech bubble back then. I was pretty much hooked on trading at that point. I graduated in 1999 and knew that I wanted to trade. I had a friend that was trading with Bright Trading in Detroit. I went over there and checked it out, met the trading supervisor, Joel Elconin, and opened my account the next week. The first few months, I struggled, but that was part of the learning curve. After a while, I started to become consistent.

What do you think was the difference that enabled you to get better?

I think it was just learning the basics, learning what works and what doesn't work. I started in May of 1999, and in the first few months I was kind of all over the place. I actually remember that in my first week I got lucky and made money. But in the second week I got killed. I had seventeen or eighteen losing trades in a row, and I was thinking, man, I suck at this. But I was trading small. I was only trading 100 share lots, so when I lost on that many trades in a row, I was only losing $150 or $200. I wasn't really getting slaughtered and that's what Bright had taught me — start with 100 shares, learn how to trade, and slowly bring in size when you start to become consistent. The key factor that made me turn the corner was discipline. Learning to cut your losers and hold on to your winners a little bit longer.

But was your overall edge something they provided you or something you learned on your own?

A lot of stuff came from myself. We did a lot of filter trading back then, where we would have filters searching through the market for certain criteria. I started doing a lot of market making too, basically trading to scalp the spread. We traded in 1/16 fractions back then. I remember trading Lucent Technologies. I would be sitting on the bid and sitting on the offer trying to make the spread. As opposed to making market calls, we were just making markets, trying to capture the bid-ask spread. Obviously, that game doesn't work well anymore, but back then it worked for a number of years. I can remember trading Lucent almost exclusively in the year 2000. The stock was bouncing around, and I was just capturing the spread.

You didn't have much of a directional bias?

We listened to Ben Lichtenstein on Traders Audio and we would get a feel for the market. You would see the S&P 500 start to take off, and back then we were pretty quick. If the market started to take off, we would start grabbing stocks in the S&P 500. So you would grab GE, Lucent, IBM, and they would start to take off too. There was a lag of a few seconds back then between the equities and the futures, and it was just enough time to profit. It wasn't instant execution on the NYSE. You had to send your order to the specialist on the floor and the order execution time was as much as eight seconds. If you went to Instinet or another ECN you could get an instant execution, but at that time, even the market makers had around fifteen seconds to respond to your order.

You have a CFA charter, right?

Yes, I do. I got it in 2002.

Did it help?

With overall market structure understanding, yes, I would say so. But do you need a CFA charter to be successful in trading? I don't think so. It doesn't hurt. I think it gives me a good understanding of the overall picture, like who's on the other side of my trades. A CFA charterholder can paint the big picture of how everything works — institutions with a longer-term horizon seeking liquidity, with short-term traders providing that liquidity. I think it's an asset, but I don't think it's a necessity.

So you were trading that market making strategy for a number of years. When did you notice that things started to change and some inefficiencies started to go away?

I can take you back to the root of when everything started to change, which would be in 2001 with decimalization. That's what changed everything, because with fractions, market makers would make $1/16^{th}$ of a point. Then, all of a sudden the spreads tightened up, which put a lot of human market makers out of business, and that's what led to the rise of the machines. There were some HFTs before that; however, that was when the pendulum swung, so to speak, where the machines started to dominate the humans. It didn't start immediately, but if you wanted to pinpoint where it started, it was with decimalization.

So the market maker's edge started to dry up after that?

Yes, because a computer is much more efficient at market making, as they can adjust quotes faster and get to the top of the order queue. Before Reg NMS you would have computers that would step in front of your order not by a penny but sometimes by a subpenny. Eventually the SEC, under Reg NMS, enacted rule 612, which banned subpenny trading on the exchanges, but these days we still see subpenny trades away from the exchanges. Once the spreads tightened up, the computers were probably more efficient at doing it, but we still did well. We would still make markets. The market makers on the floor probably suffered more once we got to decimals, (because of this battle to be at the top of the order queue), and computers can be very efficient at doing this.

Did you use the opening trading strategy that Bright is known for?

Yes, and I still do some of that. In 2000, 2001, and 2002 it worked very well. The basic strategy is just to provide liquidity into an opening imbalance of a NYSE stock during the opening print. You would be trading on the same side as the specialist, now they're called designated market makers—DMMs. You would basically provide liquidity to a stock that was opening bellow fair value. A simple way to calculate that would be if the market was going to open down 1 percent[7], a stock that has a beta of 1 would typically open down 1 percent, all other things being equal, meaning there's no news on that stock. If the stock were to open down 1.5 percent, we would possibly buy it, and vice versa. If the stock was opening down only 0.25 percent, we would short it. It worked quite well for a number of years, but I think over the last few years the strategy has got crowded. There are too many participants playing that strategy, and all of a sudden, when they need to hit the exits, the liquidity isn't there for them.

I noticed that sometimes with this strategy when you get filled, you don't want that fill, as the stock just keeps going in the wrong direction.

It's a crowded issue, for sure. I think Bright was one of the first firms to focus on this strategy, but now it's being done by a number of

---

[7] This can be inferred by looking at the S&P500 futures.

firms. HFTs do this strategy as well. When you get everybody on one side of the trade like that, it can lead to shakeouts. I did a video on IBM yesterday, and it's on YouTube[8]. It talked about the shakeout that IBM had yesterday at the open. When you get too many short-term traders on the same side of the trade, they start to look for liquidity and bids. If the bids aren't there, then they start to hit whatever bids they can find, and that can start a shakeout. This gets a lot of traders scared. Eventually, they sell their stock and the stock just continues to go down.

You never really want to be on the same side as all the short-term traders if you can avoid it, because it usually goes the other way. That's probably what a lot of my trading is based on, identifying which side what I call "the trading herd" is on, and try to go the opposite way.

Is the opening strategy still profitable?

I would say it cycles. I've been saying this for a number of years. It will be good for a while, then everybody catches on and thinks it's working again. Then everybody goes back to trying it, and the strategy gets crowded and stops working. As it stops working, and people stop doing the strategy, then it gets less crowded and starts working again. It keeps going from working to not working. In the last couple months, it hasn't been working well. If you look over the last number of years, it has cycled a lot. Because of this tendency to cycle, I never stop doing the strategy, but when it's not working, I decrease my size so I don't lose very much. That's a way of monitoring it. If I were to do well with it again, then I would increase

---

[8] "IBM Shake-out" by premarketinfo.
http://tinyurl.com/p39bbop

my size. Instead of stopping the strategy, I would rather change my size.

It seems that Don Bright doesn't use stop losses in the opening strategy but just profit-taking exits. Is that something you do?

Don automates in and automates out. I automate in on this strategy because it would be cumbersome or impossible to send hundreds of OPG orders manually. I know a lot of people (like Don) automate out too. I don't. I manually trade out of my opening positions. These days we have so much more information than we used to. We have the continuous book price that tells us where the stock is about to open, so we can tell which stocks we're going to get filled on. If I'm going to get filled in all the longs, I would quickly hedge it with SPY or something. I do a lot of hedging tactics off the open to eliminate market risk. The whole point to the strategy is to capture the trading anomaly of a stock opening too high or too low relative to its fair value. If I get filled on a bunch of longs, and the market starts to tank, I'm going to lose on all of those positions. But if I hedge out the market risk, I can still make money on those positions, even if the market tanks. This allows me to stay in the trade longer.

Right off the bat, there's often a shakeout, because the trade is crowded. If you can hold through the initial shakeout, the stocks will often come back to their fair value. That's where hedging helps me. It can keep me in the trade. You would probably be better if you walked away from your computer for thirty minutes once you're hedged, and then you wouldn't have to have the stress of holding through the opening shakeout. I never do that, but I wish I could. It's also loser management. When you get filled on twenty or thirty stocks off the open, there are going to be winners and losers. The key is to work out of those losers as best you can and try to let the winners run.

Cutting down size a little bit?

Yes, maybe selling half or maybe hedge with something. That's kind of what this job is, to minimize damage as much as possible. If you have a bunch of bad trades it can ruin your week or your month. That's what I've been good at, minimizing damage so I don't have the losers that can destroy my week or my month.

Is that how you deal with your other strategies as well?

Yes. In thirteen years of trading, I've probably been through hundreds of strategies. It's funny, a strategy that hasn't worked in years can all of a sudden start working again. So I try to monitor them. But it's all feel for me too. I watch the technical aspect very closely and would consider myself to be a technical trader, but there are intangibles as well. On my online radio show, "Premarket Prep," I talk about technical issues all the time; however, I do trade a lot on feel. I can feel whether the market's been really holding up well or it's starting to turn, and that's a hard thing to teach. You need a lot of screen time. Sitting there and being able to feel the market, feel the turns, and being able to feel that the trading herd is short is a huge asset. For example, a few days ago when we had a vicious short squeeze in the market, we had a gap up the next day. I could feel that the trading herd was really caught short. It was predictable that it was probably going to continue to rally, at least until we had some macro or fundamental news knock the market back down.

Do you think intuition can be an edge because it sometimes can involve inputs that can't be computerized and backtested so easily, so it's not as easily exploited?

I would say that backtesting is good to find an idea that has worked in the past. I don't do a lot of backtesting with my overall strategies. I just play around. I'm always researching and developing new strategies. I always have a strategy that seems to work, and that's where I make my money, but I'm always playing around and doing things differently. I'll try some new strategies with small size to see if they work. If I find something that clicks, I start to increase my size. I'm not a big fan of backtesting, but I'm a big fan of research and development. I think you have to always be researching new strategies, especially in these markets, because there's always new stuff that seems to start to work.

The key to being successful in an HFT world is to stay ahead of the bots. The machines are just doing what they're programmed to do. When there's some type of new strategy, it takes some time for them to find out. Then they have to give it out to their programmer, and then they have to build it, replicate it, and backtest it. This takes time — sometimes a couple of weeks or even longer. You could be exploiting this strategy for a few weeks with no HFT competing with you until they can deploy the whole thing and be ready to go. Now they're much quicker at this then they used to be. Years ago, a good strategy would last six months to a year. Now it seems that a good strategy lasts only a few weeks, because the HFTs will figure out that its working and exploit it. So you have to be doing even more research to stay profitable.

After decimalization and before Reg NMS, what were your main strategies?

I don't want to get too specific, but I can give you an overall idea. There was the opening strategy that we talked about before, we were doing…

Pair trading?

Yes, we were doing some of that. I would do different arbitrage type strategies. For example, I used to do share-class arbitrage in Viacom.

I would arb the Viacom A class shares versus the B class shares. I did that in 2003 and 2004 almost exclusively. Those two stocks would just track each other very closely, because it was the same company. I would just try to scalp a few cents by being on the bid and being on the offer. I think at one point, I was doing 7 to 8 percent of the volume on the class A stock, which was the illiquid one. The B shares were much more liquid. If the B shares were rising, I would just try to get long the A shares or vice versa. I could make markets on the A shares and then quickly hedge with the B shares. But these days the HFTs are all over this strategy. They've written programs to do exactly what I was doing. You don't stand a chance in trying to do that now, at least manually.

You would frequently hedge out your exposure?

Yes, you always put the hard side on first. That's something that goes back to the basics of trading. Put the hard side on, and then take the easy side. The B shares had a 1 cent spread, while the A shares would have a 10 cent spread. I would just pick up the A then hedge out and make 6 to 7 cents all day. If I had to carry it overnight, it didn't matter, because it was the same company, so company-specific risk was out the door. There were a few others stocks with dual classes as well, some more illiquid ones, but that was the main one that I focused on.

Then Reg NMS hit. How did that immediately impact you?

I don't think it affected the market until a couple years later. I think what started to happen, especially in the last two or three years when things got more difficult, was that most retail orders that used to interact with our orders were now entirely intercepted (100 percent) by the internalizers. If I'm getting too deep here let me know, but they're called OTC market makers and they basically intercept any retail order flow so we don't get to interact with retail flow anymore. By retail flow, I mean, for example, the TD Ameritrade traders, the guys sitting in their basements, etc.

For the most part, retail flow is more uninformed with less market knowledge. Now, there are good retail traders too, don't get me wrong, but with all things being equal, the average retail trader won't be as good as the average proprietary trader, because most of these people have day jobs. They're kind of doing this on the side. Their order flow is attractive to trade against. What we see is that the retail brokerages sell their order flow, it's called payment for order flow, to OTC market makers, where they have the first chance of trading against those orders. What happens on the exchanges is that when you place your limit order, it often doesn't get filled. You'll see these subpenny prints going off in front of your order. You'll have trouble getting filled on the bid or the offer because the order of the person who was trying to hit your bid was intercepted and traded against off exchange.

I read your report to the SEC and thought it was very interesting. Do you think that with this subpennying going all around, sometimes it's just better to use a market order and take liquidity?

I would never advise using market orders. I hate using market orders, because it's just a blank check. It's such a fast trading world right now, and I believe that some HFT participants can see your market order coming down the pipe, especially if your order is pinging multiple destinations. If they're on the offer, they'll move the offer back as far as they can to extract as much value from that order as they possibly can. I would rather use a marketable limit order. For example, if the offer was at $94.50 and I really wanted to own a stock, I would maybe put a $94.55 limit or something like that. I'd probably get filled at the $94.50 offer, but if the price changes rapidly, I'm not going to get filled at something crazy like $95. I hate using flat out market orders, because the market moves so quickly right now that you can get some really bad fills. I don't like using standing limit orders either, so I usually just take liquidity. Most of the time, I just take the offer or hit the bid. If you're trading illiquid stocks, that doesn't work as well. You don't want to be paying big spreads, but if you're trading stocks like GE or stocks that are relatively thick, I don't mind paying a 1 cent spread to get into the trade.

You see subpenny prints because the internalizers provide subpenny price improvement to the retail orders that they're intercepting. It's their way of justifying the practice. If you ask me, that subpenny price improvement does not justify taking an execution away from a displayed liquidity provider.

What about pricing your limit order aggressively in illiquid stocks but inside the spread?

Sometimes I do that too. It all depends on what stock you're talking about. If you're talking about a stock that has a 25 cent spread, let's say it's bid at $24.25 and the ask is at $24.50. If I bid $24.26, there's an HFT that will automatically step ahead of me at $24.27. If I go $24.28, he will go $24.29. If I go $24.40 he might not go there. So, if I didn't want to pay the offer, I might go $24.40 and see what happens. That is an aggressively priced limit order and can sometimes be a better alternative to lifting the offer.

If you wanted to sell, could you fool these guys by bidding up and getting them in front of you then hitting them with your sale?

Be careful with stuff like that, because it can be considered by the SEC as gaming or spoofing the quote. A rule of thumb is, if you're bidding for something, you actually want to be a buyer of that stock.

The SEC is cracking down on anything like that right now. If you're intentionally trying to drive up the bid, trying to get a higher bid just so you can hit it, the SEC will likely have a problem with that. You never want to do anything gray or illegal.

Let's move on to more recent events. How did you do during the flash crash?

It was my best day of the year.

Did you buy during the panic?

Yes, but you know what? It was still hard to buy during the panic, because there were bots that were automatically stepping in front of my order even during the flash crash. I can remember trading stocks where there were no bids. It was a crazy experience. There was literally a vacuum in some stocks. For example, Accenture was bid at $0.01 and offered at $33. If you watch the trades, it was like one trade at 1 cent, then one at $33, and on and on, due to market orders. I wasn't participating on that one. I knew that if you were buying something that low, those buys were going to get busted and the trades wouldn't stand. But I was trading some other stocks, even some preferred stocks. I was making two or three points in some trades, because there was nobody providing liquidity. I put out some low bids, and some of that stuff I was still getting subpennied on, but sometimes I did get filled. I did very well that day just by being a human trader, because the HFTs weren't participating as much. I just provided liquidity and really got paid for it.

Weren't you afraid though of accumulating some kind of inventory and facing an '87-type situation where it just goes from -10 percent to -15 percent to -20 percent?

Well, I wasn't putting myself in a situation where my margin would lead to trouble. At Bright Trading, if your account goes red, you're done. I was also hedging with other stocks, doing pair trades on similar stocks in the sector. I wrote an article on ZeroHedge in January of 2010 in which I was predicting that this could happen, so I was somewhat prepared for it. That's probably why this was one of my best trading days. However, I wasn't just randomly buying everything. I was buying something that was getting killed 10 to 20 percent down, but then I would sell short something similar to hedge, so if the market continued to crash, hopefully my hedge would work out and I would be OK.

So it was similar to the old days with the Viacom market making?

Yes, but not on pure plays like that. That was a pure share-class arb. Here it was more like stat arb through pair trading, a calculated risk.

Did you also do well in 2008?

That was my best trading year ever. That was an unbelievable year. In 2007, it was really starting to get good, but 2008 just blew away every one of my other years. We were just doing a bit of market making, providing liquidity. I can remember on the opening strategy and other strategies, everything was working back then. You essentially had institutions throwing out all their stocks, not caring about anything, they just wanted to liquidate. If you ask any trader, 2008 had to be one of their best years, because every strategy that I had was working.

Do you think that short-term trading is naturally long volatility? It sort of wants the bad times to come?

I think short-term traders do better when bad times come for sure. Do we want bad times to come? No. I'm a trader, but I'm also an investor in the market. I have an investment account, managing my own and my wife's money. I obviously don't want to see my investment account be cut in half from a crash or something. But traders definitely do better whenever there's economic uncertainty, because that's when irrational decisions are made by money managers and big money. Like in 2008, institutions were throwing out the baby with the bath water. We would basically find a good stock that was being thrown out and buy it. From a pair trading perspective, you can buy something and short a similar asset, and by the afternoon, or sometimes even within minutes, the price would converge. So yes, short-term traders definitely do better in crisis situations. I think a human trader is really equipped to do well, because there are so many human traders that aren't even in the game anymore. We live in such an automated HFT world, and when those HFTs say, "We don't want to participate," there's way less competition. Back in 2000 and 2001, I was competing with a lot of day traders, short-term market makers, specialists. Now I just compete with HFTs and a few other day traders. Probably 70 to 80 percent of the time, I'm competing with HFTs. If you eliminate four-fifths of your competition during a market impacting event, you're going to do better.

So essentially, during the opening, you had these big funds, hedge funds, and institutions creating distortions due to human emotions and people like you repricing the assets and profiting from it?

This is exactly what happened. You can vilify HFTs, and I sometimes do that myself, but not all HFT is bad. I criticize the predatory aspect of it, like when programs are written to step in front of your order or take advantage of your order. A lot of HFT is just statistical arbitrage where they're taking advantage of inefficiencies like that

Viacom class arb that I used to do. There's nothing wrong with that. It keeps the prices in line. You also need market making type participants, and I think that's the problem now, because most of the market makers are HFTs and they don't have any affirmative obligations. When things get tough, they'll press their stop button, and all of a sudden, you'll have a liquidity vacuum where there's really no liquidity available. Any trader sending a market order at that time is going to get a really bad fill.

How much do you think HFTs make from subpennying as a percentage of their revenue?

For the OTC guys—the internalizers—it's a big chunk. It's their bread and butter, but they have a lot of different strategies. Not all HFTs are internalizing orders. I would say there's probably only a handful that are participating in that game. They're basically your big OTC guys like the Knights, Citadels, and UBSs of the world that have that order flow relationship with retail brokerages and have the ability to trade directly against that flow. Those guys make a lot of money by stepping in front of everybody else's limit orders. They're just capturing the spread, but at the expense of whoever's limit order is not getting executed.

But there are a lot of good HFT strategies out there too. The stat arb guys make a lot of their money by keeping prices in line, not engaging in sketchy practices. I think predatory market making has an unfair advantage over other participants, and that practice should be eliminated. I want a level playing field for everyone.

Besides subpennying do you think they should change other things as well?

I think the structure has become very complicated. If you look back ten years at NYSE stocks, 90 to 95 percent of the volume used to be executed on the NYSE. Now you have thirteen different exchanges, thirty or forty dark pools, and a hundred internalizing broker dealers/HFTs. You have so many different places where your order can get executed. The market is very fragmented, and this fragmentation can lead to confusion, which can lead to problems. I think the market has become way too complicated in this way. I want to see it simplified. I want to see fewer exchanges, fewer dark pools, and more orders in the lit market where there's pretrade transparency (where you can actually see the quote), as opposed to dark trading where many participants are just free riding off the public quotation. I would like to see the market structure get simpler somehow. I don't think it's going to, but in a perfect world, my wish list would include less fragmentation, elimination of subpenny trades, and more transparency in the overall market. I don't like firms getting a sneak peek at orders and then cherry picking which orders they're going to trade against.

Do you think there's an edge in watching subpenny trades in the Level 2?

Yes, and this is something I wrote an article about for *CFA* magazine recently[9]. Tape reading is more important than it ever was before, especially if you're trading illiquid stocks. You can see when the internalizers are subpennying the offer, stepping in front of the offer. Sometimes it's just market making. On a stock like GE, for example, they're just trying to capture the spread, so I don't think it means anything there. But if you get into the small or mid-caps, it can definitely give you an idea of the direction the stock will go. If the internalizers are willing to step in front of that offer, that means the smart money is placing its bets that the stock will go down, so you might want to aggressively sell it or hit the bid knowing that

---

[9] http://tinyurl.com/paxt6xu

information. I believe tape reading is very important, and the subpenny trades provide valuable information for traders.

Other than that, did your tape-reading skill come from just watching it a lot and getting a feel for things?

Yes, especially if you're trading illiquid stocks. I don't trade as many of those as I used to, but if you're trading them, you can really get a feel from the tape. You can get a feel when these HFTs have caught everybody short and they're going to try to pop the stock. You can almost read it on the tape through the size, subpenny printing, etc. If there's an internalizer that's willing to step in front of the bid all day long, that makes me confident that the stock might be going up. It's not a perfect science, but if it goes up 55 to 60 percent of the time, there will be an edge there. I believe there's an edge in figuring out what the smart money is doing.

Do you pay attention to rebates? Do you try to minimize your costs routing orders?

Not as much. Some of the guys at Bright really do. I know Don is a big proponent of really managing those expenses. I used to be a scalper, but now I've lengthened my time horizon, which is important in this HFT world. Scalping strategies have been taken away from us by the HFTs, but they haven't taken away the longer-term stuff. If you can make smart market calls and hold on for a little bit longer, you can do well. In the past, I used to hold some positions for just seconds. Now, I hold positions for minutes, sometimes hours. Rebates were important to me when I was a scalper, but now they're not as important, because I hold longer. Some days I used to trade 500,000 shares, now I trade a lot less volume. So I don't mind paying the take fee (up to 3/10ths of a cent), because I'm making more on my average trade. If I was doing scalping type strategies, I would be more concerned about take fees and rebates. I'm conscious of them though. If I see BX and ARCA offered, I would take BX because I would be paid to take liquidity as opposed to paying for it on ARCA, but I wouldn't say that I'm concerned about it.

Is that lengthening of the time horizon something you see in your profitable trader friends?

Yes, I think so. I used to hang out with a lot of Bright traders, and the ones that remained profitable all lengthened their time horizons. I think we all used to be scalpers for the most part, but now we've had to become what I call intraday traders, where we are making a call on a stock. Before, we were just making markets. Now we just think, wow, this is setting up nice, I'm going to get long some stock here. Then we hold it for a while. You also have to be conscious that there's going to be a shakeout. If an HFT thinks you're long, they'll try to shake you out of your position, so it's critical to position yourself well enough that you'll not get shaken out. You need to be able to take a little bit of heat. Years ago, I never had to take heat, but now the market is a lot choppier. That has a lot to do with decimalization as well. When you had fractions, there were only sixteen pricing increments per handle. Now there are a hundred, so you're never going to be perfect. Sometimes you can scale in a little bit instead of getting in all at once. That can help.

These shakeouts that you mentioned, do you think it increases the value of having a time stop — holding XYZ based on time instead of a hard price point?

Time stops are scary because what if the market goes into a downturn? I like to watch relative strength. I like to see that if the market is selling off, my stock is not selling off as much as the market. If the market is going up and my stock is not going up, that's a pretty good tell that there's some extra selling pressure in the stock that day. I don't use time stops very much. I try to gauge relative strength. I used to use hard stops too, but I'm probably looser with them than I used to be. Sometimes it helps to be a bit smaller so that you don't get shaken out. That's the key in trading — don't be so big that you can't make rational decisions on the position. You want to be small enough that you can hold on when you're taking heat, but big enough that it's worth it too. You have to find the sweet spot.

You think momentum is one of the edges that have survived in the markets over the years?

Actually, I think there are a lot more momentum plays than there used to be. Contrarian strategies used to work better, where you would fade the moves. A stock would be going up so you would sell it, or if it was going down you would buy it. That's what market making kind of is, to a certain extent. I think momentum strategies work better now. When these HFTs get a trend going, they keep pushing that trend higher because they can catch a lot of contrarian traders. Let's say a stock is falling hard, there's always that buy-the-dip crowd that's naturally attracted to the cheaper price. HFTs know this and can sense that the stock is still heavy with short-term traders. They'll try to take the stock down further, to shake out those traders, before allowing the issue to reverse. So yes, I think momentum strategies are probably more effective than they were three or four years ago.

Do you think the key to those plays is news interpretation? Knowing which piece of news will affect a lot, affect a little, etc.?

I do watch the news very closely. I got Benzinga Pro. I think I pay $99 a month or something, but it's solid.

If the news source lags a bit, is that a big deal?

If I get the news a few seconds after it breaks, I'm fine with that. I'm not going to beat the HFTs in the speed game anyway. If I was getting the news five minutes after it breaks, then that information would be kind of useless. But a delay of a few seconds is no big deal. If a trader didn't want to pay for news, there are a lot of free sources too. You can just Google the stocks you're trading, go to stock twits, or Twitter. Social media is a great asset to use.

Can't you just use a Bloomberg terminal to get ahead of everyone?

If you're a news trader, sure you can get a terminal and spend like $2,000 a month, but I just don't need the news that quickly. If Benzinga Pro gives it to me a few seconds after it happens, that's fine for me. If you're an HFT firm, those seconds matter. To a human trader, they're much less important than they were years ago.

Have you ever provided training for traders?

Yes, I do a lot of webinars[10]. A few times a year I do some lectures, usually about something to do with high frequency trading. This is where your book is interesting to me, learning to be profitable in an HFT world. I have a number of PowerPoint presentations that I've made about this stuff. Everybody complains that the market is rigged. Sure it is! I'm not going to lie to you, it's rigged, but you can still beat these bots. There are still successful traders out there that are doing very well. They're finding their edges, understanding who they're competing with, and adjusting their strategies accordingly.

The advantage of the human is that they can think rationally, whereas the computer will just do what it's programmed to do. Take the flash crash for instance. I can rationally think that PG was just

---

[10] An interesting webinar he made about trading in an HFT world is this one:
http://tinyurl.com/lww4tj3

trading at $62 and now is trading at $45. This is irrational and makes no sense. I can rationally think the Accenture is not worth 1 cent a share when it was trading at $40 five minutes earlier. That's a nice thing that we have. We can be rational, whereas a computer cannot. The programmer behind the computer can be rational, but we're going to be quicker because we can think and execute. The programmer needs to think, program, and then execute. We skip a step there. So if you can stay one step ahead of the computer like that, you can still be profitable even though the game is rigged against you.

In the case of PG, what would you have done if the stock didn't come back? Would you have held longer?

No, like I said, I was doing a lot of hedging. I don't even think I was buying PG. I was buying a lot of different stocks, so I can't recall which ones exactly. I was buying a lot of them on the way back up. I don't think I even took any heat, but I was hedging with a lot of other stuff. PG you can hedge with so many things. You can short Colgate, JNJ. They have very similar business models. It's not a perfect hedge, but it's going to have a relationship there for sure. The correlation between a JNJ and a PG over time is very high. Like KO and PEP, they tend to be very correlated over a long period of time.

You prefer to look at correlation instead of cointegration?

What do you mean by cointegration?

It's a statistical tool that tells you if two or more time series share the same stochastic drift.

I like to keep my trading very simple. I don't have to get into the fancy quant stuff. I just need to understand the basic relationships. I do a lot of crutch trading. For example, KO has some bad news come out. I'll short PEP or something like that. Sometimes those relationships don't hold as well as they used to, but in a market impact event, that stuff tends to hold very well. If PG drops 25 percent and I'm buying it, I can easily hedge with something else.

So you do a lot of sympathy plays?

Yes, but not as much as I used to. But off the open a lot of this stuff still works. During the regular trading session, it gets a little bit tricky, because there are a lot of other factors involved. In the first five minutes, sympathy plays can work—not always, but sometimes they work for sure. There are hundreds and hundreds of ways to make money in these markets. You only need a few of those that work for you.

How much confidence do you have in your ability to keep making money in the next five to ten years?

I'm thirteen years into my trading career, and I've never had a down year. In May 1999, when I started, I was down until about August, but I think I ended the year up about $8,000 or so. I haven't had a down month since the year 2000 or something like that. I have down days and down weeks, but I haven't had a down month in a long time. So I'm still fairly confident in my trading ability because I'm very consistent. You just have to keep adapting to the new environment. If I started losing money on a consistent basis, maybe I would have to reevaluate, but as long as I can grind out my decent living, I still think this is one of the best jobs in the world.

Do you think this consistency is the result of being good at pattern recognition in the price action?

I think the number one factor that contributes to my consistency is discipline. I'm very disciplined in my overall trading. I'm never letting positions get out of hand. That's the one thing that traders do all too often, especially novice traders. They cut their winners too soon, and they let their losers get out of hand. You also have to be able to make adjustments. You can't keep tight stops or you get stopped out of everything in this market. You have to reduce your size a little bit and adjust your time horizon. I think these adjustments keep me profitable. I'm always adjusting my strategies to make them more effective — things like scaling back on strategies that aren't working, moving to strategies that are working, cycling them through. I think all of those things are factors that contribute to success. I'm not going to say that I'm the best trader in the world, but I grind out a good living.

Do you keep very detailed records of everything that you're doing in your trading?

I've never been a good secretary, but it would probably be an asset if I could do that. I've been doing this for thirteen years and have done 50,000 or a 100,000 trades a year for so long that it's probably second nature to me now. But for anybody just starting out, yes they should keep good records. I used to have a list back in the day for NYSE stocks with the specialists. In the list I would keep track of the specialists that I felt were screwing me. I would see which stocks were in their posts, and I wouldn't trade any of their stocks. I would put in the list, "This specialist is an asshole." That sort of thing. And a couple of other traders in our office would do the same thing.

So your adjustments come from looking at the P&L rather than record keeping?

It's more on feel than anything. It's mental. I have a lot of records in my head. When a strategy is not working, I change it. OPGs[11] have

---

[11] This another name for the NYSE opening strategy.

not been working well for the last two weeks, so I've scaled back significantly in this strategy. I'm still doing some, but I scaled back. If it starts working again, I'll increase the size. By scaling back I ensure that I'm not losing as much money when the strategy is not working. This is probably why I have losing weeks but not months. Continuously making these adjustments keeps me profitable.

What kind of equipment do you use for trading? Do you have the latest processors and hardware?

I just bought a Mac because everybody is saying you have to have a Mac, but I haven't integrated it yet. I'm always pretty up to date. I upgrade my computer usually every other year, so right now I'm using a core i7 from HP, but I'm going to switch it over to the Mac in the next week or two. But yeah, don't try to trade with a really cheap computer. If this is going to be your career, buy something near top of the line. But keep it within reason.

The thing is, because I've lengthened my time horizon and am not competing in milliseconds, I don't have to spend thousands and thousands of dollars on a super machine. It just needs to be fast enough to get the job done.

What is your best advice for average traders that are having to deal with these markets over the last few years?

My best advice is to understand your competition. If you think you can come into this game and immediately make money without understanding how the microstructure works, I believe you're already at a disadvantage. You need to become educated about it. Then you have to adjust your trading tactics to suit the environment. What I say to new traders, and the information that I would pass on to even seasoned traders, is that there are three or four main things I've done to stay profitable in my career:

1. Lengthen your time horizon. I don't want to compete in a scalping trading world. Unless you want to spend millions of dollars developing these HFT collocated systems, it's very hard to compete with them on time, so lengthen your time horizon a bit. I'm not talking about becoming a long-term Warren Buffett type investor, but it's better to think about trading in terms of minutes as opposed to seconds.

2. Never show your hand. If you tip off the HFTs that you want to buy the stock, they'll try to take the price higher on you and vice versa. I don't like putting limit orders out there, unless I'm fairly confident I'm going to be executed. In liquid stocks like GE, it's a little bit different, but if you're trading stuff like small or mid-caps, you don't want to show your hand in any of that stuff, because they'll try to make you pay.

3. Take liquidity as opposed to providing liquidity, for the reasons I mentioned earlier.

4. Try to learn how to read the tape. Take your time if you're learning. Trade small size off the bat, but understand and learn how to read the consolidated tape, because there's some great information in there.

Have you found yourself reading more about rules, regulations, and micro structural issues?

Yes. I knew nothing about rules and regulations five years ago. I knew what I could and couldn't do, and that was about it. Now I'm more active within the CFA Institute, and I'm a member of their Capital Markets Policy Council, so I'm digging deeper into market structure. I don't think any trader has to dive down as deep as I have in the microstructure of the markets, but I find it interesting.

A great book I just read is Scott Patterson's *Dark Pools*. He did a great job of outlining the history of the markets and the microstructure. This book is a good overview. Keeping up with the market structure is also still essential. For example, the NYSE just got their dark pool approved yesterday and that affects me. My limit order that is sent there is now going to be executed even less, so I'm going to use fewer limit orders. It's important to understand where your orders are going and how they're getting executed. I'm a big fan of direct routing as well. If the stock is offered on NSDQ, I'm going to route to NSDQ. I don't want to route to ARCA first and ping that exchange, which would tip off some HFT, allowing them to see my order coming up the pipeline. They can then grab the offer before I can. By understanding microstructure a little bit better, order execution quality gets better as well.

Do you think the trend of lengthening the time horizon is going to continue for five or ten years? Are we all going to become swing traders?

I don't know, maybe. The trend is definitely going that way. If I look back to 1999, I was the scalper. I was the HFT in 1999, scalping the spread. Scalping basically died for me (and for all manual traders) in 2007/2008, so I adjusted by lengthening my time horizon to minutes or hours. Maybe eventually we won't want to deal with the daily intraday fluctuations at all, and we'll move entirely into swing trading, where we're holding stuff for days. I think there's good value in swing trading. I argue sometimes that the inefficiencies that HFTs eliminate in the short-term can actually lead to inefficiencies in the longer-term. HFTs are just leaning on orders, stepping in front of orders, momentum buying, etc. When some institutions are buying, they'll press the stock higher, trying to extract as much money as they can from the order. Because they pressed the stock even higher than it would have naturally gone, there's an opportunity there. A trader with a longer time horizon might say, "Look, this stock is irrationally getting bought here, and once the short-term traders stop pressing it higher, it's going to come back down." So maybe he takes a short position as a swing trade.

Do you think it happened in NFLX yesterday?

I don't trade a lot of NASDAQ. I've always been a bigger fan of NYSE issues. But I do think that happens. As momentum traders jump in, the HFTs take it even higher. I'm not saying you should fade every move up. These moves can continue for quite some time, but I do think there are some opportunities there, especially if you can be quick to identify the turn when it happens.

Do you think the HFTs can just tell when these trends are going to take place?

I believe they're very quick at identifying new trends. They can smell the orders. These computers are smart man. The predatory HFTs can sense there's some institution buying, and they'll make them pay. They have a lot of access to information that we don't have. It's not all HFTs; it's the more connected ones.

Do you avoid mid-day trading?

Yes. If I look back to 1999/2000, I would never take time off during lunch hour. But now during the hours of 11 to 2 EST, I do very little trading. I find it very choppy and unpredictable. You have HFTs trading against HFTs, and when you step into their shark pool, they see your order and try to attack you, especially if you're trading illiquid stocks. I do the majority of my trading at the open and at the close. Those are the best times to interact with non-HFTs. I find that when I trade from 11 to 2, I just trade a lot, pay a lot of commissions, but don't make a lot of money.

What do you do with the money you don't use for trading? Do you buy stocks, bonds, real estate?

That is the big question everybody asks. "What do you do with the money when you don't trust the stock market because of flash crash issues?" You can't stick it in T-Bills when you get less than 1 percent. I do have my own stock portfolio. I like dividend stocks. I like to get paid to be in stocks. I do some covered call writing. I'll buy higher yielding stocks and write calls on them to enhance the yield.

November 2013 Update

Do you think today is one of those days when guys who've been trading for a long time know they shouldn't be doing much? The market barely moved.

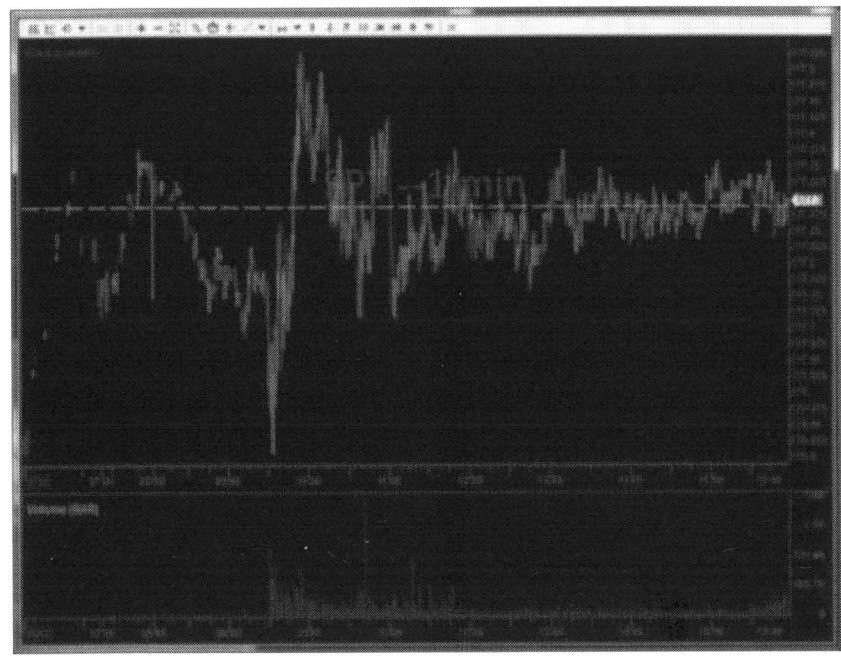

SPY 1 min chart. Source: DASTrader. Veteran's Day Holiday 2013.

The issue is that we're coming off earnings season, so there's no catalyst here. Another issue is that in the first ten to fifteen minutes, there's no liquidity at all, because there's too much risk to the HFTs. As real participants start to place orders and HFTs start to do the same, they start to lean on each other, and that thickens the market up. I know Joe Saluzzi calls it "the HFT vice grip," and that is a pretty good name for it. Because what happens is that the market thickens up so much that stocks hardly move. The HFTs are just scalping for their pennies or rebates.

Is the liquidity a bit like a self-fulfilling prophecy? Is it that if there's some, then there's more, and soon a lot, while if there's just a little, then there's nothing.

Yes, that's exactly it. It's what I like to call dependent liquidity. That's what the majority of HFT liquidity is. I'm not saying it's bad or good, I'm just telling you, that's how it is. The HFT liquidity is dependent on other participants being there. If there's nobody bidding, like in the flash crash, everybody cancels. Once there's one bid, then others start to join. You can see that as a trader when you put an order out there, and all of a sudden, two or three orders show up ahead of you. Those are mostly HFT orders piggybacking on you. It might have started as a 100 to 200 shares, but because they're all leaning on each other, all of a sudden there could be thousands of shares at the NBBO. If the original order cancels, then they all cancel. It's like a lean party.

How would you rate this year in terms of profitability compared to other years?

I'm actually a little bit ahead of last year in my own trading, but the thing is I'm always moving around strategies. Good strategies don't seem to last that long these days, when people (or the machines) figure out these edges you have to move on. I'm trading quite a bit in options lately too. I've always traded them, but I'm starting to focus on them more. I feel that there's more opportunity there. You see some overextended moves in small caps a lot of the time, and buying some OTM[12] options can be like lottery tickets. They sometimes pay out.

You're using the options for the leverage or for the staying power that they give you?

Leverage is the number one reason, because I can buy a hundred contracts in something for a dime and it gives me a ridiculous amount of exposure to something. I will often play the weeklys too. I played JCP a few times this year. When it starts to consolidate and you think it's going to have another down leg, instead of shorting

---

[12] OTM – Out of the Money.

the stock, your risk/reward might be better if you buy some OTM options. Sometimes you can get those options pretty cheap. I don't do a lot of spreads and stuff. I like to keep it simple. Nine out of ten of my options probably lose money, but that 10th one can be very lucrative.

Did you catch a lot of the down move on JCP?

Not really. I just caught a couple of smaller moves there. I'm usually in the options of smaller caps, like some of the biotechs. I was in QTWW and caught a nice trade in that one. I had the $5 calls and it ended up going to $7.

Chart courtesy of StockCharts.com

That goes to show you, many years ago I was a scalper, but now I'm trading in a much different time horizon. I'm looking at options, and exploiting different edges. I always traded options, but I'm still in the R&D stage of my option strategies, I wouldn't say they're my bread and butter yet.

The support and resistance numbers from Premarketinfo, how do you use them? Is that something that you should use to fade those illiquid extremes off the open?

It depends. Joel Elconin is the one that puts those numbers together. He has been doing that since the '90s. It's kind of old school but still works. It's not a simple method where you use the numbers and you're going to make money, but they're another tool. I will be aware that if a stock has bottomed three to four days in the last six days in a certain area, there's probably some institution that's accumulating the stock there, or there's some other reason, because stocks don't normally do that. I become aware of areas like triple tops, triple bottoms, etc. The numbers that Joel puts out are based on things like that. He will put a one-star rating if it's a one-time high or low, but if it has four to five stars, that means it probably has multiple highs or lows in that area. It's a quick way for me to know the important levels instead of having to look over the chart. If I'm long the stock, and it reaches a key resistance level, I probably will sell it or possibly reverse it and short the stock. There are a number of ways to use those numbers, but it's just another tool in the toolbox.

Are you still trading that opening strategy this year?

It has been tough, but like I said, all strategies cycle. It's been very tough in the last few months. I still play around with it a bit. The reason it's been tougher is that the liquidity is so low in the first few minutes of trading. So what happens is, you get short that opening print in XYZ, 50 cents above its fair value, but there's nothing behind you. A lot of other traders are probably short as well. It might be overvalued relative to fair value, but it doesn't matter. Because the trade is so crowded, they'll be scrambling to get out, and all of a sudden, it will move up another 50 cents. You can get some really exaggerated moves, because there's not enough liquidity in the first few minutes. The original strategy, the way Bright used to teach us, of just getting in when the stock was away from its fair value is not working the way it used to. You have to adjust. For example, instead of shorting that opening print, wait a few minutes, and short the stock when the OPG traders are scrambling and covering to get out. Maybe you can short the stock up another 50 cents.

What you used to see was that the trade would just work. You would put it on in the opening print, and it would go back to fair value. Now you have to think it through. Now the play is to sometimes fade the opening strategy until it gets to a point where it might reverse. All of these strategies still have relevance. It's just a matter of using them differently.

You mentioned that you were trading 150,000 shares a day. Isn't there an advantage there to move from per-share commissions to per-trade commissions in a retail firm?

No, because you lose the access to serious capital. It's not an issue of how many positions they'll let you put on but rather how many orders you can put out at the same time. The biggest advantage of prop is always the capital. I can send a lot of orders without having to think that maybe they won't let me send that many orders due to lack of margin. The prop firms can negotiate commissions too. If you're doing a lot of volume, they're going to give you a good rate. If you'd interviewed me three years ago, you'd have found me doing something like 300,000 shares a day. One year ago, I was something like 100,000 to 150,000 a day. Now it's more like 50,000. In a day like today, I did about 20,000. Obviously, I'll trade more when there's more action, but over the years, my volume has come down.

Would you say that the number of trades is also coming down?

Yes. That's mainly due to the transition from being a scalper to holding the trades for longer periods of time. We have to extend our time frame, because we're paying an HFT toll. They have monopolized the spread. In order to remain profitable, you have to make a little bit more in the trade to absorb the extra cost of paying the spread. Scalping is pretty much dead to human traders. I used to sit and scalp all day between the bid and the ask, and that's how I did the 300,000 shares a day. Now I'm holding trades sometimes for hours, maybe overnight, or even for days. So my volume tends to come down a lot. You might be trading the same size, but you're not in and out as much.

Profitability is still not that bad in these markets. We still have Bright traders doing well. I've still had no down months this year. It's not as awesome as it was in 2008, 2009, but that has to do more with volatility than with HFTs. The good traders have adjusted to this environment and they're still making money in it.

What would you say was your best trade and worst trade of the year?

I'm always hitting for singles. I'm never in big and cleaning up on something. It's hard for me to remember.

You're always in for small and medium sized bets?

Yes, I'm always going for base hits. In a typical day, I probably trade thirty stocks, make money on twenty, and lose on ten, or something along those lines. Usually I'm in 500 to 1,000 shares in a lot of different stocks, making $100 to $200 here and there. Very rarely I will make like $5,000 in one trade. I never had a day that I lost more than $5,000. Sometimes I'll play the big movers too and make like $1 to $2 per share in something. In AAPL I had one trade where I made $8 a share.

What was your best day ever?

It was in 2008. I made $110,000. It was in October. Every single name out there was getting dumped off the open, and it felt like capitulation. They were just throwing everything out the window.

You played the bounce off the washout?

It was actually a lot of preferred stocks that were crashing. Everything was getting thrown out. I got in stuff like Citigroup, HSBC, and JP Morgan preferreds. Some of these preferred stocks closed the day before at $10 to $11 and they were opening at $5 to $6, down 50 percent on the opening print! We were like, "This is ridiculous." I was buying these preferred stocks and hedging by shorting the common stock. If the company went under, I was going to be OK, because both would go to $0. I remember some of these preferreds were yielding like 40 percent, and they were still paying. It was crazy.

Would you say you use a lot of hedging and swinging for base hits in order to avoid the stress and the worse decision making that comes from big losses and big volatility?

I would say that for sure. The reason I've been successful pretty much every month since 1999 is because I'm very risk averse. I'm always entering a trade and thinking how much money I can lose and not how much money I can make. I'm entering low-risk trades as much as I can. When the trade starts to go against me, I'm looking at how I can get out, how I can minimize that loss. I'm not thinking, oh it's going to come back. I'm never in the "hope trade." I'm out before I'm even hoping. I never add to a losing position. It's a cardinal sin for me. I probably never will. I'm always playing defensive. That's why I'm always looking at base hits. My losses are small and my gains are relatively small as well. Consistency is the key for me. There are guys that do it completely differently. Some guys in the firm will make $30,000, then lose $30,000 the next day, make $20,000, then lose $10,000. Maybe at the end of the week they're up like $5,000 but they had a lot of stress the whole time. Meanwhile, if I can grind out $1,000 a day, that's pretty good.[13]

I believe I noticed that you follow this style more than other traders I've spoken to.

Yes, there are some wild traders out there, but there are guys like me as well. That's how HFTs make money every day too. They're very risk averse. They're very good at getting out of the way when there's danger. They're very good at managing adverse selection risk. I always felt that I was pretty good at that too, but I'm not as quick as an HFT, because I'm still a human being.

Did you trade the TWTR IPO?

I was out of the office, so no.

Would you have traded it?

Probably, but just to play around with it — maybe 100 to 200 shares. You can lose too much too quickly in these types of situations. It's like going to a casino really, it goes against all my trading fundamentals. I wouldn't trade it with size, because you can't really control the risk.

You mentioned tape reading in our first interview. A lot of traders I spoke with don't really do it very much. Why are you able to read the tape?

---

[13] This would add up to something like $200,000-$250,000 a year, not bad in an environment of low volatility and HFT dominated markets.

The one thing with tape reading is that now it's different than the way it used to be. There's so much fluff now, stuff that isn't really happening. The tape used to have a lot of information. Back in 1999, when I started, the majority of the information that I gathered from the tape was incredible. It's not like that anymore. You can still get a lot of information from it, but you have to know what you're looking for. Nine-tenths of the trades that are going by on the tape are just short-term HFT rebate trades and stuff like that. You have to be able to read the real liquidity off the tape and the quote window — find out the real buyers and sellers. Once you figure that out, then it becomes like old school trading. You have to be able to filter through what is real and what isn't.

You have to get a sense of a big buyer or big seller?

Yes, we still do that. In the old days it was all about that. Leaning on the big bids and big offers, that's how you eliminated your risk. There are still institutions out there, and they're the real market movers. When you identify an institution that wants to get the hell out, it's a trading opportunity for sure. The HFTs are doing that. They sense real buying or selling pressure and they trade ahead of that. An opportunistic human trader can do that too.

With regards to small and mid-cap stocks that have wider spreads, I've been playing around with hidden orders, and it's really amazing how much better the fills are when you use the native 100 percent hidden orders. Sometimes they'll play games and fill you for ten shares or one share, but these HFTs must hate hidden orders, because it prevents a lot of their games.

That's why everybody has gone to hidden orders now, and this is a concern for the overall market. Off exchange volume is 35 to 40 percent, and hidden exchange volume is 5 to 10 percent. The market is going dark, and that's because there are so many games being played against displayed orders. You sit an order out there and everybody leans on it. They're using your order as insurance. When you hide your order, now they don't know it's there, and you won't have as many people leaning on it. It's tricky, because sometimes you want to have your bid out there, so that if there's somebody that wants out, your order might get hit. But you have to use both hidden and lit orders. That's what I do. I would say 30 to 40 percent of the orders I place are hidden. Sometimes I do a combo too. I put a lit order out there and put a hidden order in front of that. If someone tries to lean on my order, I'll be ahead of them with my hidden order. Being able to use both of them is essential to traders these days.

Are you optimistic that some of the HFT games are going to get shutdown?

Some games are being shut down, but there are always new games being played too. HFTs are here to stay. If someone thinks that the regulators are going to make the environment profitable to human scalpers again, then that's just wishful thinking. It's just not going to happen. Traders have to learn to trade in this environment that we have. It's not going back to the way it was. It's all about making the adjustments. The biggest adjustment for me was to rarely use limit orders. They're too toxic. I prefer to just pay the spread. I play less in the small and mid-caps because of that. The spreads are wide and too costly to pay, but it's too hard to get filled on your limit order. Hidden orders help a bit, but it's still difficult to get filled without paying the spread.

Do you think that with your style, you sacrifice some profits in order to lower your P&L volatility?

I believe my P&L volatility has always been low. Obviously every trader will have a bad day or a bad trade, but I'm shockingly consistent. Over the course of years, I always seem to be able to grind it out. My week to week profits are very consistent. I'm a steady climber. I'm usually making money by getting base hits, and I'm probably profitable four out of five days. Before 2009/2010, I was probably profitable forty-seven or forty-eight out of fifty days. I still have an occasional bad day, but it's never terrible. I don't blow out my weekly profits because I'm so risk averse. I think what keeps me successful is that I have so many tools in my toolbox, whether it's reading the tape, trading levels, technical analysis, etc., and I'm always using them in different ways. I rely a lot on my feel for the situation. When I don't trade for a couple of days, I usually lose that feel a bit, because I haven't been watching the trade action. It takes me a couple of days to get that feel back. When I'm in the zone, I can feel the reverses. I can feel that the S&P 500 futures are due for a spin. I can feel that we're getting toppy for the day. I even use social media to get a sense of things. All of those tools help to keep the volatility of my P&L low.

When you do trade mid-day, do you wait for breaking news or big setups?

In a day like today, where we were stuck in a two-point range for three hours, the best thing you can do is to sit on your hands, because nothing is going on. For the most part, when there's nothing moving, you shouldn't try to make something happen. I used to do that. I would get bored and try to make something happen when the setup wasn't there. It's all about knowing when to swing your bat. There are only so many balls out there for you to swing at. From 10:30 to 2:00, sometimes it's just a grind—HFTs grinding it out with other HFTs. You jump into that and it's like jumping into a swimming pool full of piranhas. They'll eat you alive. You've got to know when to trade and when not to trade. I like to trade when other participants are trading, not just HFTs, and that's why most of my trading happens at the open. The majority of my money is made in the first thirty minutes of trading.

What percent of your trades do you initiate outside of the opening period?

Probably at least 50 percent of my volume is in the first twenty minutes. About 25 percent is in the last twenty minutes, and 25 percent in the other time periods. I'm very aggressive at the open, aggressive at the close, and just picking and choosing in the middle of the day.

Mid-day it pays to wait for stuff like news?

Yes, I like to play the laggards instead of the leaders though. It's hard to control the risk in the leader, but it's not so hard in the laggard. For example, if there's bad news in an airline stock, I'm looking at the other airline stocks and shorting them. It's amazing how quickly a sector turns. The other day the market whacked the TLT[14], then all of a sudden, they started hitting all of the utilities, the preferred stocks, etc. They hit anything with yield in it, because all of that stuff is correlated. I thought, with TLT down $2, anything that has yield is probably going to be weak. Some of the utilities opened flat and then tanked. Knowing and being able to see those relationships creates opportunities for me.

In the middle of the day, if there's news in something, I might get in the laggards and play with them.

How do you prepare for a new trading day?

---

[14] The TLT is the 30-year Treasury Bond ETF.

It starts with the after-hours of the previous day. For example, somebody is selling eBay tonight. There's no news in the stock, but somebody is whacking it down just while we're talking. They hit it at $52.75, $52.50, $52.25, and it's the same guy. I can just tell by the way it's trading. I'm already writing on my sheet for tomorrow, "Somebody was selling eBay after hours." Maybe there's going to be news that breaks overnight, maybe not, but my point is, someone wanted out of that stock. I'm going to put eBay on my ideas list for tomorrow as a potential short, especially if it doesn't open down much.

Do you come to the open with a full list of stocks you're going to watch, the levels and so forth?

Yes, I'm very prepared ahead of time. The market closes at four, but then you have the after-hours session for four hours, then you have the premarket session for five and a half hours, and then the open the next day. Between today's close and tomorrow's open there are two full trading sessions. There's so much information in these sessions. I'm logging highs and lows from them. I want to know where the stock has been. If something trades like 200 shares away from the close by $1, that's nothing, but if it's trading thousands of shares then it's important to log the levels that it's trading at, because those levels might come into play in the regular session as well.

Would you say that a lot of the moves premarket or after-hours are an overreaction a lot of the time?

I'd say overreactions happen all the time because the liquidity is so low. If somebody just wants out, they'll have to pay to get out. I've seen stocks like PG go down $4 a share on a headline outside regular trading hours, which is a bit crazy, because it's a thick low-beta stock. Once the real liquidity comes back in during the regular session these moves tend to reverse. Knowing the average range, the beta, etc., helps too. I won't bet the farm on it in these overextended plays, because the liquidity is so low, but I will nibble in them.

Do you think that at some point we're going to have a volatility expansion and an opportunity like 2008/2009 to short stuff and not have to cover one hour later when the dip gets bought?

Sure, it always ends badly, but maybe we're going to ES 2000 first. But at some point it's going to reverse. I often play these sell-offs through options. If I feel like there's a vicious washout coming because we're drifting down and some people are caught long, I'll often look at the weekly options. Maybe we're trading on a Thursday and I sense that things are heavy — I'll buy some cheap OTM puts.

Do you hold the weekly option no matter what?

No, if I feel like it's not working out and things are grinding back up, I work out of them. I don't want my puts to expire worthless. But it depends on the price as well. If I bought the put at a nickel and it's down to 1 or 2 cents, then I might just ride it to zero, but if I bought it at a dime and I can salvage 7 or 8 cents out of it, I'll close it out. This is just one way to get cheap exposure to a sudden move. A lot of times it won't work, but when it does you can make a lot of money.

I've had options that I bought for like $300 and banked $3,000.

Do you get concerned that these weekly options get manipulated at expiration?

They are, for sure. You have to be aware. If you're at a big level, the options will tend to pin at the major strike price. For example, if JCP is at $8 and there's a lot of open interest at $8, the best way for the option writers to make money is to get the stock to close at $8 or very close to that. Maybe you can even short at $8.10 to capitalize on that. There's also a natural drift to the major strike, because the option holders are hedging themselves using the common stock. For example, if JCP is at $7.95 and you're holding the $8 puts, you'll need to sell the puts or buy the stock to lock in the profit. A person holding the puts may buy the stock at $7.95 to lock in the gains. If the open interest is quite high, the players hedging themselves will put buying pressure on the stock driving it closer to $8. You have to be aware of that so you don't get caught off guard.

Lessons from Chapter 3

1. Adjustments. A key factor that enables Dennis to stay successful is making adjustments to his trading. It's easy to get attached to a certain style of trading or certain technique, but in these ever changing markets, without adjustments you'll perish. This is where being humble and respecting your P&L statement comes in. When things aren't working, you have to change, try different things, do a lot of research and development as he calls it (on small size). One thing that can help in these adjustment-making processes is to be connected with other good traders. I didn't ask him in the interview, but I suspect a key factor that helped him become a better trader and adjust is the fact that he stays in touch with other successful traders in his prop firm and via Skype.

2. The importance of simplicity and base hit trading. I believe having a simple trading method can help in many ways, but the main one is that it enables you to act without hesitation and stress.

Being a prop trader, Dennis must have seen hundreds of traders show up and disappear over the years, many of them with all kinds of fancy mathematics, indicators, and wild position sizes, but a lot of day trading is having mental control and not feeling like you're in a battle every day. I believe this is why he engages in SPY hedging or pair trading type hedging in his positions, as well as why he goes for base hits instead of home runs. Even though these types of hedges are likely to cost money in the long-term, (since you're taking a secondary position without an edge but paying the bid-ask spread plus commissions), it's likely to make you money indirectly by lowering your P&L volatility, which will lead to several benefits:

A. You won't have stop trading early that day as often because you feel that you're getting too emotional and making poor decisions.

B. Your mental clarity will enable you to make better decisions later on in the day.

C. If you're a prop trader, you might be able to get better deals with your prop firm because they can see you're a low volatility trader that's not smashing keyboards all the time.

D. It makes the overall experience of working as a trader more enjoyable.

The same can be said about trading for base hits instead of home runs. As he says, "That's kind of what this job is—to minimize damage as much as possible."

People like Warren Buffett don't need to decrease their P&L volatility, because if he gets emotional or angry he might quit that day but no harm will be done, because he probably wouldn't close a deal or buy a stock that day anyway. But for a short-term trader it's crucial to be relaxed and in a good place mentally as you have to make dozens of decisions every day. **It's important to protect your "mental capital" as much as your trading capital.**

This idea was hard for me to understand in the beginning, because I come from a blackjack and poker background where you're supposed to take pretty much any edge and avoid any negative expectation move. But in day trading, if you do that and create excessive P&L volatility, your mental game is likely to suffer, and this will cost you other edges later on in the day. In blackjack, the strategy is already set in stone, and you don't have to think very much. It's not as important to be on top of your game mentally, you just have to have good memory to remember the basic strategy. But in trading, there's a lot of discretion involved, so it's more crucial to be able to think clearly.

Trading offers opportunities for hedges and ways to minimize volatility (such as scaling in or out of a position, using small and medium position sizes). These tools are useful even though they might seem to have a financial cost in the surface.

Low stress "base hit" style trading can be extremely beneficial for traders that struggle with discipline and suffer from extreme emotional swings as a result of losses. Try it out and see if your results improve.

3. Avoid being shaken out by sizing your positions correctly and using wider mental stops. Intraday noise can be quite high in an HFT world. There are all kinds of moves and fakeouts that happen during the day. Having tight stops or a position that's too big can be your worst nightmare, as you get taken out and then the stock reverses and does what you just thought it would. This is a mistake that's very easy to make, especially when you're confident in your position. You have to expect to be "tested" by the price action at some point. If you go with a stop that's too big or too tight, you might end up closing the position at the worst moment.

4. Don't use market orders or passive limit orders. HFTs can game these orders. The market orders can be gamed by well-connected HFTs that can see the order coming and leave you with a worse fill. Passive limit orders will be gamed through subpenny trades. These orders tend to get filled when you're wrong and not filled when you're right.

5. Screen time is crucial. Dennis doesn't do much backtesting or uses indicators. He just developed a sense for price action by watching it a lot for more than a decade. This is something that I'm finding in my trading as well. Over the past year, by watching markets and stocks trade intraday constantly, I'm finding myself developing a feeling that something is about to happen. It's not always correct, but when I miss these trades, more often than not I regret it, as it would have been a winner.

My own personal theory on why instinctive trades can sometimes provide an edge is that some situations are harder to code and therefore less exploited by HFTs and arbitrageurs. As a result there's more money to be made for people who can see what's about to happen. Our unconscious mind can be a great backtester if we feed it correctly.

Not everybody has the luxury of having many years' worth of market data in their heads like Dennis, so for those that are starting out or looking to improve, it's important to record your observations and lessons about price action, tape reading, etc. In chapter 11, I detail how I personally write market notes using the popular software Evernote. Research indicates that the act of writing something increases the retention rate of the brain significantly, so it's definitely a good habit to have as a trader.

6. The importance of tape reading. Dennis lists this as one of the top things a trader has to do to adjust to current markets. By

watching subpenny trades in the tape, HFTs trying to display fake size in the L2, and a number of other variables, you can start to develop a sixth sense for what's about to happen, and this can be an edge. The main idea is to look through the noise so you can detect a big buyer or seller. This enables you to trade ahead of the big player and profit like in the old days.

7. Hidden orders are an important tool for your toolbox. In larger-spread stocks, you can improve your order execution and decrease your costs by using native hidden orders. The thing about hidden orders is that they will only be executed for the order flow of that particular ECN and they can be traded through. Ex: You put a hidden order on BATS for $20.22 when the market has a bid of $20.20 from ARCA. If someone tries to sell at ARCA, he will get filled at $20.20 even though you are offering a better price. This is because your order is resting at BATS. In this case, you would be better of cancelling and sending a hidden order to ARCA, that way you get filled in all the order flow to ARCA.

Ask your broker if they offer native hidden orders, and if they're not, consider switching to another broker. In Chapter 11, I recommend a retail broker that allows the use of native hidden orders.

8. Capitulation can be enormously profitable. Dennis had his best day in 2008, banking $100,000 when preferred bank stocks that were still paying were being thrown out at ridiculous prices. By accumulating market experience you'll be able to identify when moves are just too large and unjustified, which can lead to great trades. Even in this situation, Dennis stuck to his risk averse style and hedged by shorting the common stock of the banks.

9. Sometimes the best risk/reward trade is in the options. When you think a stock is about to make a significant move, it might pay

to take a look at the options. Depending on what you expect the stock to do, you might get more bang for the buck by buying out of the money calls or puts. Notice that Dennis doesn't get fancy with complex option spreads. He just uses for them directionally, mainly for the leverage they provide.

10. Strategies get crowded. At that point, doing the opposite is what works. The opening strategy lost a lot of its profitability as a result of lots of traders and HFTs exploiting it. This created a crowded trade, which the liquidity off the open can't absorb. The way to adapt to this is to not participate in the opening print but wait for the shakeout of the opening players and then take the other side. This applies not just to the opening strategy but to other strategies where there are too many short-term players compared to the liquidity available. You can observe this in momentum trades as well, when they reverse you will see the "trading herd" trying to get out and a large move in the other direction. Try to always be aware if the trade you are in is crowded or not.

11. Play the laggards instead of the leaders. In news plays, even if you miss the initial move in the stock with the breaking news, you can still profit by going into the laggards, sympathy plays, etc. Try to think of the ramifications of the news and how it will impact other stocks. The example Dennis gave of the TLT and utilities trade is a great one.

12. Last but not least, discipline. Dennis says he always remained fairly disciplined in his trading and has no issues taking losses. Given that taking losses (By being disciplined) is such an important factor in short-term trading success, how do you improve your discipline and make it easier?" I wrote a quick, practical course on how to boost your discipline in Chapter 11 titled "The Boost Your Discipline Mini-Course". You might find the advice different from

what you are used to reading. It is based on recent findings and studies in the field of neuroscience and psychology. It isn't the bumper sticker trading advice you probably have already read a million times.

Chapter 4

Jeffrey Goldman — Market Maker Turned Prop Firm Trader and Manager

Jeffrey Goldman (twitter @jeffg44) is a veteran former market maker who manages the prop trading firm JC Trading Group. Over the years, he has seen literally hundreds of traders in his firm, some successfully becoming full-time traders, many others losing part or all of their trading stakes. He's the voice of experience, having watched markets and traders for a really long time, which allowed him to develop a strong opinion of what it takes to succeed. In the pharmaceutical industry, there are all kinds of large empirical tests that can help shape someone's views of what works and what doesn't. Think of him as someone who has overseen a large empirical study of traders by managing his prop firm and seeing pretty much everything under the sun.

Even though he manages JC Trading Group, make no mistake, he's still a trader at heart and trades quite actively. "It's in my blood," he said in the pre-interview.

This interview was conducted in August of 2012 and updated in November of 2013

Why did you decide to get involved in the markets and become a market maker?

My first job after I graduated from Michigan State University was at the Chicago Mercantile Exchange. It's always been my passion, always being my interest to trade.

Were you a market maker?

I started at the CME doing research and running trades. I did that for a couple of years. I became a market maker in 1992 for a firm called Olde Discount, making markets in NYSE listed stocks.

Were the profits you made just for the firm, or were some of those profits for yourself?

Olde was one of the first firms that internalized the order flow of their customers. I would take the opposite position, like all the market makers did. If a client sold a stock, I would buy it from them instead of the trade going to the exchange, and if a client bought a stock, I would sell it to them either by shorting it or selling from my inventory. I was definitely trading for the firm, and I got paid out a percentage of the profits.

How did you deal with having to make markets when there was a lot of volatility and news?

As a market maker, you had your book to trade against. You always have buyers and sellers lined up. For example, if a stock was trading at $10 and you had many buyers at $9 7/8, you could buy all the stock you wanted at $10, because you always knew you could sell at $9 7/8. You actually wanted volatility as a market maker, because you wanted the price of the stock to go through your book. For example, let's say I had sellers in my book of 25,000 shares at each level between $15 and $15.50, and the stock was at $14 ⅞ x $15. Once the stock went through the $15 offers, I would automatically buy the 25,000 shares. Once it went through the next offer at $15 ⅛, I would buy another 25,000 shares from our clients. So as the stock was going higher I would get longer and longer! My job was to manage that position and determine when to sell the position to another market maker or to the NYSE.

For some stocks, you didn't mind that it just sat there if you had a lot of customer order flow, but for the most part you wanted the stock to move. As a market maker there's a lot less trading and more just managing your inventory. Sometimes the position was just given to you instead of you going out and taking a position because you felt that you had an opinion on the stock's movement.

So you were able to make steady and frequent profits by just trading around the book?

Correct. I traded a lot of K-Mart, because the company I worked for had their employee stock option plan. I probably traded one million shares of it every day, and it rarely moved. I would buy and sell stock all day long. I would buy on the bid from the firm's clients then sell to other clients on the offer, thus capturing the spread of 12.5 cents every trade. It was easy money. I wasn't really doing anything unless my position got too big either long or short. And when that happened, I could usually liquidate my position in the middle of the spread on Instinet and still make 6 cents.

Did you do any directional trading for your own account?

Well, you would add value if you could position yourself correctly. For example, if you thought a stock was going to go higher or you anticipated the firm's clients wanting to buy a stock, you could go long the stock by going to the exchange or other market makers and buying some. Once the stock went higher, you could sell your inventory to clients who wanted to buy the stock, or sell it back to the street. So anticipating demand and supply for a stock definitely helped with your profitability.

You stayed as a market maker for how long?

I worked as a market maker at Olde from 1992 to 1998. Then I worked as a market maker with Knight Trading in Chicago from 1998 to 2001.

Do you think that by watching the markets for so long were you able to develop a sense for price action?

That is definitely the case. Watching stocks over and over again act the same way definitely helped me transition from a market maker to a prop trader. I left the market making industry because I knew computers were going to take over my job. Eventually they did and these days there are just a few market making firms, and most are automated. Guys who were able to watch the markets and learn from them have become better proprietary traders than the guys that didn't.

I also think my years at the CME helped. When you're down on the floor and by the pits, you're literally in the middle of the market. You get a great feel for the ebb and flow of markets just based on the excitement and noise level of the pits.

Did you decide to leave Knight Trading because of the decimalization rules?

You're 100 percent right. When the exchanges went to pennies, there was no longer an advantage for me to be a market maker. The spreads are your margins. So basically our margins went from 12.5 cents to 6.25 cents, then down to 1 cent. At Knight, we took the opposite side from pretty much all the major online brokers, so when there was news in a stock we would get bombarded by orders. For example, if there was negative news on a stock, we would get inundated with sell orders that we would be forced to buy. So basically we were forced to buy stock while it was going straight down. As a market maker, we took the good with the bad and accepted these situations. But when spreads went to a penny, the bad was much worse than the good. Fortunately, I was able to make the transition to prop trading, but yeah, when they changed the rules I left, and the writing was on the wall for all market makers at that point.

Couldn't you back out from orders or drop down your bids?

Some market making firms would do that but not Knight. They had agreements with customers that they would fill up to 5,000 at the best bid/offer, even if they were displaying just 100 shares in the quote. If the stock went nonfirm you could pull your quotes, but that was a last resort and didn't happen often. There was one time I had to buy 20,000 shares of Celera Genomics on a 100 share bid. The stock was $200 and extremely volatile. The stock was even halted for some of the executions, but for some reason our system was still filling sell orders. The stock opened down $20 after the halt, and I lost $400,000. We wouldn't cancel any of the trades. Once we reported a trade to a firm, we didn't cancel that order, so it was a real loss.

When you started trading prop, were you directional right away or did you trade scalping strategies?

When I became a prop trader, I was mostly directional and also looked for inefficiencies of the NYSE specialists that I could take advantage of. One of the easiest ways I would make money was when specialists went wide. For example, if a stock was trading at

$28.00 x $28.01, and all of a sudden it went to $28.00 x $29.00. The specialist would go wide because there was news out or the specialist received a big block of stock to buy or sell. In my example, you could just throw orders out to short all the way up to $29. When the block would print, you would be short at that high price, and 95 percent of the time the stock came back down. It was the easiest money you could possibly make. These days the specialists just don't do that anymore. Most big orders are thrown into a time slicer or worked more efficiently by a trader.

That was like the opening imbalance trading?

It was the same philosophy of the specialist opening the stock too high or too low because he took some of that side as well and wanted to make money on it. It was similar, but it was a lot easier because in the opening strategies you had to put hundreds of orders out. You didn't know which ones were going to get done. In this strategy, you knew he was going to put a print up. If he didn't put up a print far enough away from the last sale, you wouldn't get filled and you didn't lose anything.

Did you use momentum strategies as well?

I mostly trade breakouts and breakdowns. I was always the type of trader that would buy new highs and short new lows as opposed to what most traders do.

I noticed a lot that at those key levels the HFTs tend to widen out their spreads.

I mean, they could, but I'm a big believer that at the end of the day a stock will go from whatever it is now to whatever it's going to go. There might be a lot of noise. That's what you're seeing in these markets lately. That's what's getting a lot of traders in trouble. It's definitely real now. It's coming from the HFT guys trying to make fractions of a penny. So you see a lot of movement in the quotes of the stocks and movement in a 2, 5, or 10 cent range. Like I said, I'm still a big believer in the idea that at the end of the day a stock is still going to where it's going to go. I try not to get caught up in all the noise.

For example, if a stock makes a new high, it made a new high for a reason. A stock that made new 52-week highs usually goes on to make higher highs. It's just the way it's. In that first breakout, there might some games being played, and that's all I think they are. But at the end of the day a stock is going to go where it's going to go, and I try to capitalize on it.

Did Reg NMS have an impact in your trading or did it take some time?

It definitely took some time, like any other rule or change. I can remember back when I was a market maker and they passed what they called the Manning rule, which limited how we would interact with our book. Basically if we had buyers in our book at $10 and the stock was $10.00 x $10.01, we had to cross the two orders for our clients. Before Manning, we could buy the stock for our own account at $10. Everybody said, "Market making is dead. No one will ever make a penny again." That turned out to be wrong. When stocks went from 1/8ths to 1/16ths, everybody said the same thing. When Reg NMS came along, you had to change the way you traded. That's why you're seeing a lot of traders struggling now. They're not changing with the times.

What is the biggest difference that you notice in these new markets?

I notice that it's a lot harder to trade off the Level 2 window now. You have to concentrate a little more on charts and where the stock is eventually going to as opposed to looking at the Level 2 and time and sales. You have to take a longer-term perspective of where the stock is going to go.

Is that something that you notice in other traders in your firm as well? I mean the successful ones?

Absolutely. Traders have to adapt. In my opinion you have to move to a longer time frame, and when do to that you inherently are taking on more risk. That's one area that some traders just didn't get. If you were trading in a small time frame and trying to make a penny or two, that was great, because you were only going to lose about that much as well. Once you start expanding your time frame, you have to make a little bit more money per trade, and you're also in a position where you can lose more per trade. The prop traders that didn't adapt and transition well to that didn't make it.

The noise that you referred to, do you think the HFTs do stuff like triggering stop points and then they bring the stock back just to create more activity and profits for them?

I hear that a lot, but I don't think that takes place that much. I don't think there's enough money in it for these computers to try to fake out the retail trader or the prop trader. I'm always in the conspiracy theory camps, but I don't think that's one of them. I believe what you're seeing is the noise generated by the algos and the HFTs trying to make their fractions of a penny.

You mentioned there's less of an edge in the Level 2. Do you think there can be an edge in watching subpenny trades in the tape?

Depends on your style. Some guys are doing a lot of rebate trading right now. For those guys, yes, but for the typical trader that's trying to make more than a fraction of a penny I don't think that makes that much difference. Personally, I look less and less at the tape than I ever have before. I very rarely look at time and sales or Level 2. I used to, but I don't use them much anymore.

Do you try to take advantage of rebates when routing your orders?

Nine times out of ten I take liquidity. I rarely add liquidity, I might if I have a winning position and I'm scaling out of it with limits. I never use a passive limit order to get into a trade. I'm not the type of trader that will pick a point to get into a trade. If I want to get into a stock and it's at $20 I won't say, "Well, I like it here, but for some reason I feel like I should be in at $19.90, so I'm going to put a limit there." I don't trade that way. If I feel like a stock is going to make a move, I just go ahead and initiate a position in it. Some guys can trade that way, but I just don't.

Do you think these limit orders are a trap because of subpenny trades?

I know some traders that do use them successfully. They pick their points well. Let's say a stock is trading from $19.80 to $20 and the trader identified some kind of range or channel. That's their edge. Guys who can trade like that should use limit orders. Will they get pennied sometimes? Yes. But if you pick your spot in that range well enough, you're going to get it done. That's not how I trade though. I would never knock someone who can trade based on support and resistance like that. I just don't trade that way. I buy when resistance is being taken out and short when support is being taken out.

Did you trade in the flash crash?

I was on vacation, believe it or not. I was in Vegas and had my partner called me saying that the market was crashing. I wish I was trading that day.

Do you think that day showed a lot of the weakness in the market?

I really do feel that way. The HFTs are now the new market makers and liquidity providers. There are no old style market makers anymore. When you look in the Level 2, you're not seeing Merrill Lynch, Goldman Sachs, UBS, etc. You just don't see market makers anymore. All you see are ECNs, and for the most part they're HFTs orders. When the market decides to go down like it did in the flash crash, and everybody pulls their bids, you see a vacuum like the one you saw that day. I do think that's a problem, and I think it can happen again. The HFTs are out to make a fraction of a penny. They're not going to stand in the way of a market that's free falling. That's just not their game.

In the old days when you were making markets, were prices more stable because you had to put real quotes out?

Yes, absolutely. You had to quote a real, two-sided market. There were actually rules with regards to how close you had to be depending on how much volume you did in the stock. You couldn't just go really wide without facing a fine. Also, your retail book became part of the inside market, which doesn't happen anymore, because they're just not displaying anymore. Now they're mostly sent to dark pools and are not displayed. Again, that's one reason I've moved away from trading based on the Level 2.

A lot of traders say their passive limit orders only get filled when they're wrong. What do you think about that?

I do think it happens a lot. The traders that complain about that are the ones who have strategies where limit orders are important. They might be rebate traders or a trader that's waiting for a stock to come down to where his limit order is resting. That doesn't really affect me, because I don't trade that way. The one type of trader that is effected by this is the type of trader that tries to play market maker in thinly traded stocks. They look for stocks that might have a wide spread like 50 cents and improve the bid for a couple cents with a buy ticket. Once they get hit, they'll offer the stock out higher and improve the offer. HFTs are really hurting these guys because you have the subpenny trades as well as the computers that will go 1 penny in front of you. I do know of a few traders in Europe who took advantage of that. They figured out the algorithm to fool these penny jumping programs and made a lot of money. They actually got in trouble for that. For me this is not a problem, because if I want to buy a stock I just go ahead and buy it.

So you just use marketable limit orders most of the time?

Yes, I will never do a market order. I just use marketable limit orders. If a stock is 19.99 x 20.00, I will buy it at 20.01 or something like that. I don't use market orders, because there will be a few times where you'll get really bad fills on that.

Do you route directly to the exchange displaying size?

I will usually use a smart order route that will route the order automatically to the exchange or ECN with the most liquidity and the lowest cost.

How did you do during the 2008 crisis?

I did very well. That was my best year as a prop trader. If you were able to capture the trend you did very well. That was a really big year both ways for traders. Either you got washed out or you made a lot of money. Either you couldn't identify and/or fought the trend or you went with the trend and made a lot of money.

Do you think that was because day trading is inherently long volatility?

It was because the market trended hard, it was a huge downtrend. I was extremely bearish. I put my money where my mouth was and I made a lot of money. Then it looked like the markets were going to bounce. I waited for it to settle down and I got long and made money on the upside after. It was extremely trendy as opposed to being choppy. It was a good market for somebody like myself who plays breakouts and breakdowns.

Did you catch the trend in a day trading time frame, or did you do a lot of swing trading as well?

It was all day trading.

So flat every night?

Yes.

Are you always flat every night?

Yes. I like to control the risk, and I can do that when the markets are open. I've found that when I see a trader take a position home, he's usually down on it. He's usually taking it home because he doesn't want to take the loss. And 90 percent of the time it's just as bad the next day if not worse. It becomes like that saying where a trade becomes an investment. If you make that conscious decision to never ever take a position home you'll never fall into that trap.

What are the main characteristics of the traders that do well in your firm?

The ones that do well manage their losses well. That is the most important thing you can do. When a trade is not going well, you get out. For me, a good trader will always get in a stock with some sort of target on the positive side and on the negative side. That's where a lot of traders fail. It's very easy to get into a stock, but it's very difficult to get out of a stock. Traders are so fixated on the perfect setup that they don't take into consideration their exit strategy.

Another example of managing losses is the ratio of a good day to that of a bad day. What I see so often is that a trader will make $300 one day, then $500 the next day, then $400, and then he'll lose $6,000 the next. They'll make a lot of small gains doing the right things, and then they'll have one big trade where they just lose everything. The best thing you can do is take the losing trade. Every trading psychology book talks about discipline, and that can't be overstated enough. You have to avoid that career ending trade. You can be right on a thousand trades, and in one trade you can wipe out everything because you hang on to a position. If your losing days are several times the size of your winning days, the math is just not going to work for you.

Have you found a way to predict if a guy will do well or not?

Yes. Like I just discussed, if a guy has bad days that are so much worse than his good days, he probably won't make it. If a good day for you is $500, a bad day shouldn't be $2,000. If you see that happening a lot, then the writing is on the wall for that trader. It's a sign that the trader doesn't manage losses well. Consistency is the name of the game. Another bad sign for a trader is that he always holds a losing position until the last possible second of the trading day, and that's when he gets out. It's good that he's getting out and is not taking it overnight. But it shows that he didn't have an exit strategy and his only strategy was to wait until the last possible second.

What kind of computer do you use to trade?

I just have a midrange DELL computer. In this day and age I don't think you need a super computer. The biggest thing is your bandwidth. You need high bandwidth like DSL or cable modem. Also you need a good graphic card and extra memory. You can get a really good computer for $1,000 these days.

What is the speed of that Internet?

I have DSL, it's 14MB down and 3MB up.

What do you use for news source?

I use Briefing.com.

Do you like to trade news events?

No.

What is the best advice you can give to the average trader?

Don't get caught in the noise. Always have a plan when you get into a trade. Know where you're going to get out. Especially on the losing side of the trade.

Do you try to stay on top of rules and regulations in these ever changing markets?

Yes. I definitely try read about the new rules and things like that. I follow it more as a general interest rather than something that will impact my trading.

Do you avoid mid-day trading?

No. Mid-day is usually a little quieter, but I don't avoid it.

Lots of traders say that it's difficult, that the bots are all over the place and it's choppy.

I agree that it's not as profitable. If a trader says he only trades from 9:30 to 11 EST and then from 2:00 to 4:00 EST, I won't knock him for it, because I do feel mid-day is more difficult to trade. But I still find profits in there. In trading there's only one right way to trade and that's the profitable way. My way of trading might be different from your way of trading.

You manage a group of traders for a proprietary trading firm. For those that don't know, what is prop trading?

Proprietary trading is where you're trading the firm's capital, not your own. You're then paid out a percentage of your profits. This is different from a retail account where you're trading your own money.

Why would someone trade with a prop firm?

The three main reasons are the ability to utilize a professional trading platform, professional pricing, and professional leverage[15]. Using a professional platform allows you to have direct access to the exchanges, ECNs, and dark pools. Your orders are sent directly to the destination without first going to a middleman like a retail account does. Orders and trade reports are sent and received in milliseconds.

Next is professional pricing. Most prop firms have very low clearing rates and are on a per-share basis (as opposed to per-ticket pricing). This allows a trader more flexibility to scale in and out of

---

[15] You can also avoid the PDT rule by trading through a prop firm. You do need a "Series 56" or "Series 7" license to be able to trade, also, as professionals, prop traders are subject to professional data fees.

positions. It also allows a trader to trade strategies that rely on ECN rebates.

Last is professional leverage. Trading through a prop firm, a trader has access to the firm's capital. Usually a trader is assigned a certain amount of the firms overall capital to trade. For example, a trader might be given the ability to have $1,000,000 of positions on at any given time. It also allows a trader to trade strategies such as opening and closing imbalances that require hundreds of opening orders, but only few get executed. Those can't be done in a retail account.

What are the drawbacks?

Prop trading isn't for everyone. It's geared toward the person that wants to be a full-time trader. Also, traders are attracted by the leverage aspect of prop trading. However, there's an old saying that leverage is a double-edged sword. A profitable, well-disciplined trader might benefit from increased leverage. But an undisciplined trader will just see his trading career end quicker with increased leverage. A prop trading firm needs to be responsible in allocating the buying power, and a trader needs to be responsible to use it in a reasonable manner.

November 2013 update

How would you rate this year's profitability compared to previous years?

2013 was a very profitable year, especially the second half of the year. We had some very profitable traders, some of them weren't making money, but now they're making it.

Would you say that was because of the Fed starting to scare the market a little bit and creating volatility as a result?

No, I would say there's a little bit more volatility, more volume, more predictable moves, more follow-through in some of the moves. We had a lot of guys trading Facebook. That was a nice move. If you aren't that type of guy who's fighting every trend, which a lot of guys do, you could make a lot of money on FB. Looking back now on the FB chart, that was a great stock to trade. It went down then sideways, and then it had a really great up move. We don't have a lot of guys who trade the high flyers like GOOG and NFLX, but we did have some guys making money on that. TSLA too. A lot of money was made on that stock, the long side and the short side. Again, looking back you can see that those were some really good-looking charts. There were some predictable moves with follow-through.

What are your thoughts on futures trading and why it's not offered in prop firms?

It's so hard to trade futures. In my opinion, there are only five or maybe six futures contracts you can trade. There are so many people trading them that they become so efficient. You can't find an edge trading futures in my opinion.

Which are these six contracts?

You can trade the NASDAQ, ES, gold, oil, maybe the bonds.

Maybe the Russell 2000?

Yeah, they move a little bit. The thing is, the edge is just not there. It's like Forex. Everybody just trades the EURUSD or the USDJPY and that's it, that's like 90 percent of all trading, it's hard to profit because of that. That's just one of the reasons it's hard to trade Forex, a lot of the time everybody is underfunded to begin with. One whipsaw and they're completely out of money.

In the first interview we didn't really go deeper into your strategy of buying breakouts and shorting breakdowns. Would you say that in this style, reading the daily charts is one of the biggest components of the strategy?

Yes, not necessarily reading the chart but knowing where the key levels are, like today's highs and lows and yesterday's highs and lows.

If you buy every breakout and short every breakdown, that's probably not going to work. Do you filter out by instinct or a criteria?

I will usually just trade the active stocks of the day, the news stocks. I'll also trade some of the recent momentum stocks, like the TSLAs or the FBs of the world. You always want to be trading stocks that are moving for a reason, you want stocks with volume. Those are the stocks that usually have follow-through. I think that's something some traders fail at. They'll find a stock they like and they'll always trade that stock. The issue is that in a particular day, that stock might not have any catalyst or reason to move. You'll just have some random buying and selling. The real stocks are the stocks that are moving for a reason and everybody is trading them. That's where you want to be. I would say it really pays off just to trade the most active stocks of the day, some people just keep going back to the stocks that they're comfortable with. Lately that has not been paying off.

Isn't TSLA a little tricky to play the breakouts and breakdowns? I noticed that a lot of times it just runs one way and then it reverses

all the way back. It just shakes everybody out before making the move.

I definitely agree with you. Of all the momentum stocks, TSLA is a little trickier. That's sort of because of the new trading world we live in. There's a lot of noise out there, depending on the price of the stock. In a cheaper stock there's a lot of noise in the 5 to 10 cent range. In the more expensive stocks like TSLA, maybe that noise is 50 cents to $1. You have to just ignore the noise — the HFTs and the back and forth battle between them. At the end of the day a stock will go where it's going to go. The better traders are the ones who can see that and capitalize on it, but I'd agree that TSLA does whip around a little bit.

When a stock like TSLA is up like $7, it's usually going to go to $9. I don't know it for a fact, but the chances are that it will keep going. You can wait for that pullback and get in.

Did you play that back on MSFT? It had a nice multiyear breakout.

I played MSFT a little bit, but that stock doesn't move enough for me.

When you play your strategy, how do you decide for how much you'll let your profits run?

I always put stops in. Usually it will be in a relationship to where I got in. When you're doing breakouts and breakdowns you have to assess how much that stock is likely to move. If I'm playing a breakdown of $30.25 and I think the stock will go to $29.50, that's a 75 cent profit potential. I can then tell myself, "OK, maybe I can give myself a 25 cent stop on this one." That's a three to one ratio. I get out of my trades when they're not working. I'd rather get out at $30.40 or $30.45 and get back in when it goes back to $30.25. If I'm right, I only have to be right once, but I can be wrong three times.

Are the profit taking exits based on support and resistance levels or just a feel thing?

It really is just a feel. When you're playing breakouts or breakdowns, there usually won't be a current-day or previous-day high or low anywhere, because it's a new level that's being reached. A lot of times it's just a feel. I'll also protect my profits by lowering my stop. The best trades are the ones that become profitable really fast. Then you move your stop, so even if you get hit, you're still in the money. It depends on the stock, on what the Average True Range of that stock is that day. That really determines how far the moves can go. If there's news in a stock, you can just never know how far they can go. In the last couple weeks we have seen some stocks double, some cut in half. There was that NQ, don't know if you watched that.

Yes.

I mean that thing is just crazy, who knows where these moves stop. I shorted it. It was a perfect example of a breakdown.

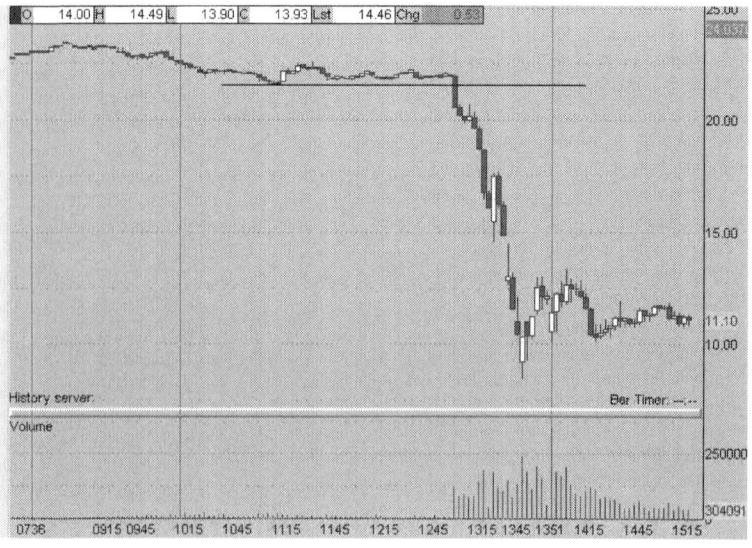

NQ Mobile 3m chart. Source: MBTrading Desktop Pro

So you play these 2 to 3 day breakdowns and breakouts. How about 52 week or all-time highs?

I usually only will play them if there's news out.

Would you recommend this strategy for people who have issues letting profits run?

I wouldn't say I do or don't recommend it. I would say it's definitely a strategy that has to fit the person's personality. Some people see breakouts and they immediately want to short it. Some people want to buy them. Both can make money.

Would you say that in your criteria, there's a lot of feel to it and it's not scientific with a lot of scans, filters, and things like that?

I keep an eye on fifteen to twenty stocks in a given day. I do use trade-ideas[16] to find intraday highs and lows. I also use our Fusion software, which has a scrolling list of stocks making highs and lows, so I keep that up as well. I will also watch big cap stocks that trade a lot of volume. I'll keep the one-to-two-day highs and lows on watch.

If you keep that type of watch list and you keep seeing the same stocks all day long making new highs/lows, you know there's something there. You look to see if there's a logical place to get in, like yesterday's high/low or today's high/low. You assess and take action if there's a play there.

Is it fair to say that you don't really care about what the news is, that you just want to know that there's some kind of news behind a play?

---

[16] Trade-ideas is a paid service.

Exactly. I don't really try to interpret news. I let the market do it for me. I have a friend that makes maybe one or two trades a day. He's not very active. He holds core positions for quite a while and trades around them. After an earnings report comes out, sometimes he asks, "Hey, what did you think of that earnings report?" I say. "I don't know. Who cares what I think? I care about what the market thinks." The market will tell you what it thinks. I don't try to interpret news, economic numbers, or earnings.

Lots of times traders will try to interpret news or numbers. I find that more often in traders that are failing. Once you interpret something and you have that in your head, that's bullish or bearish. And if the market does the opposite, you'll fight it more, because in your head, you're right and the market is wrong. That doesn't usually end well.

Do you trade more NYSE or NASDAQ stocks?

It's probably equal. I don't differentiate one way or the other.

Did you trade the Twitter IPO?

I did, not successfully.

Yeah, most people that I know lost money that day.

I kept buying the new highs of the day. I mean, you couldn't short it.

Actually, I got a borrow of the stock.

Did you?

Yes, but it was really expensive — 40 cents a share.

The way I was playing was, I had my finger on the button to buy at $50. There were about 250,000 shares for sale there. I thought if it broke $50, it would rip to at least $50.30. It broke out, but it stopped at $50.09 and quickly tanked back to $49.40. I played it small though just for fun, just to say I was a part of it. I lost like $600 in the stock for the day. It was a day that I had a lot of good things going on. I was up a lot of money. I just wanted to play around a little bit.

So you wanted to buy a big level break and quickly scalp out a profit? Is this one of the ways that you play breakouts?

Yes. For example, GOOG. When it broke $1,000, it went to $1,000.60. I don't know if anything printed in that 60-cent move. I don't do it often, but when you see something like that, a big number, a big offer, or big bid for a breakdown, you can profit like that. GOOG was a perfect example. I think there were at least 150,000 shares on the offer there. You could see them slowly going, and then all of a sudden they were all gone. If you were quick enough, it was easy money.

You have the finger on the button. You have to have direct market access with lots of different routes, preferably a smart router that will go to all the ECNs and dark pools. You have to be fast. You have to see them start to go, take it, and see where the bid pops to, then get out. It's that quick of a play. We used to do it all the time back in the day. The thing is, everybody is looking at the same thing, so you have to be faster than others. That GOOG breakout was very predictable. The TWTR one wasn't, and there was no money to be made buying the $50 break. There were definitely lots of people taking profits on the stock at that point.

What would you say was your best trade this year?

I don't think I can pinpoint one particular trade. I can say that playing the gold ETFs and stocks was more profitable for me than any other instrument or any other stock. Whether it was the GLD, the GDX, which are the miners or the DUST/NUGT, which are the triple ETF of the miners, that's where I think I made most of my money. If you look at the charts of the miners, there are a lot of breakouts and breakdowns. I like to trade the miners, because they trade off something. Some people say the price of gold moves the miners. Some say it's the miners who move the price of gold. One way or the other, if you see something moving, the other ones will move too. I like them because there are just more signals and signs of where the market is going based on something else.

What was your worst trade?

I would say it has been the last month of this upmove in stocks. We are pretty much at all-time highs in the S&P 500, Dow, and ten-year highs on the NASDAQ. In the last month I started to short NASDAQ, using the QQQs. I would build a short position and then cover because it has been going up nonstop. That's probably the worst trade I made, shorting the QQQs and having to cover it. Thinking that maybe this bull market in the NASDAQ maybe has gotten a little tired. Definitely it has not been working out.

It's like the opposite of your normal strategy.

Yes, I just feel like the NASDAQ market is getting a little overbought here and losing some of its steam, and we are going to roll over a little bit.

When you get new traders in your office, what kind of advice do you give them?

Very easy to answer, because I give this all the time. I always tell them, "If a trade is not working out, get out of it, because you can always get back in." You can't fall in love with a position. You can be right in a thousand trades, but all it takes is for you to hang on to that one trade, feel like you're right and the market is wrong, and then it becomes your career-ending trade. I've seen way too many times where guys will be right many times in a row then get stubborn and lose everything. If a trade is not working out, get out. You can always get back in.

In my opinion, that is the most important rule. In my strategy of breakouts and breakdowns, if a stock breaks down and I shorted it, if it comes back up, the trade is not working. I'll find a spot and get out. In my opinion, traders just don't do that. They get into a position and they just stay in it. It goes 20 cents against them, then 40 cents, then they think they can't get out, because they're down 40 cents. Then it's 60 cents. Then it's $1. Then it's four o'clock and they think that it might come back tomorrow. Next day maybe it goes another 50 cents against them. Next thing you know, the next day they can't even trade, because they got this big loser sitting on their screen. It just never ends well. Maybe one time it does come back and they get negative reinforcement. They think it will always come back, but the next one it might not and it's all over.

My best advice is to get out. You can always get back in. Especially these days where clearing rates and commissions are so low. It's not like you're going to get eaten up in trading costs.

You have to balance that with not getting caught in the noise, right?

Right. That goes back to the other point. When you get into a trade, you have to know where you're going to get out. You need that pre-established exit. That exit should be at a place where that noise isn't going to affect you.

Do you use a number from the Average True Range (ATR) to stay away from the noise?

No, I guess you can say I pretty much just eyeball the chart. It really depends of the momentum of that day of the stock. I don't use the ATR, but I will go back and see how big a big bar is in that stock. If I see a stock that has a big bar of 70 cents, then I know that it can move 70 cents that day. I won't use ATR, but I'll eyeball a chart to see where that stock can move, what type of volatility I can expect.

Another thing I will do is, if it's a stock that just made a really long move, maybe one of these crazy Chinese stocks or biotechs that go from $2 to $22 in six months, I know that even though it's at $20, it can move $3 in a day, as opposed to a typical $20 stock that can move 40 to 50 cents in a day. I always like to look back to see where the stock came from. If a stock is breaking down after it just made a huge up move, there can be a lot of action there.

Lessons from Chapter 4

1. Avoid and respect the noise. As Jeff explains, there's a lot more movement in the 2, 5, and 10 cent range in cheap stocks and 50 cents to $1 in higher-priced ones. HFTs play all kinds of games with investors, traders, and other HFTs. I can't tell you how many times I paid too much attention to this intraday noise and ended up closing a position that would turned out to be a winner. It's very important to keep yourself out of this noise so you can actually have a shot of having your day trading strategy working out. Jeff's choice in dealing with this was to move away from staring at the Level 2 so he doesn't even see that noise anymore.

2. Extend your time frame. As he says, they used to play for 5 cents or something like that. Now you have to gun for at least 15 to 25 cents, possibly more. If you try to capture smaller profits,

particularly in illiquid stocks, then you're stepping in the HFT shark pool. They're better equipped and connected than you, so your chances of long-term success are very low.

3. Take liquidity. Jeff takes liquidity most of the time. He realizes that the game has changed the way orders are executed and that passive limit orders are being taken advantage of more.

4. Avoid taking positions home. In his experience, most traders taking positions overnight are simply stuck with a loser that they don't want to close out. It's easy to fool yourself into thinking it's overdone, but in his experience, it's just as bad if not worse on the next day.

5. Buy breakouts and short breakdowns. His bread and butter strategy is to bet on follow-through and continuation of a trend. The key to trading this style is to only get involved in stocks that are in play, have lots of volume, have news out, or are being traded actively due to momentum. You have to be able to assess how much the stock is likely to move after the breakout/breakdown, then you decide how large your stop will be to avoid the noise. A good reward to risk ratio is three to one. Ultimately, you have to be comfortable with the idea that stocks that are making new highs are likely to continue to make new highs and vice versa for lows. TSLA is a good example of a stock that tends to keep going when it has a breakout or breakdown.

6. Avoid holding losers until the last minute of the day. Jeff has seen hundreds of traders during his years managing his prop firm. He says that this behavior is a bad sign for the future of a trader.

7. Managing losses well is the number one characteristic of winning traders. Over the years he found that this was the number one factor in determining the future of a trader. You probably

already read about that in different trading books, but how can you actually develop your ability to take losses and make it easier? In chapter 11, I provide a different perspective with practical actions and exercises that you can do to improve in this area.

8. Your win/loss math has to make sense. If you tend to make $500 a day in your good days but then lose $5,000 in your bad days, you'll have a hard time having a career that lasts a long time.

9. Interpreting the news can be dangerous. When you read the news and develop an opinion about it, you'll find yourself fighting the market more often. You'll ignore price action signals telling you that you are wrong, because your ego will get attached to a particular view. This can lead to some big losses. I know I've been guilty of this several times in the past due to my background in macro trading, once you build up an opinion on what the data means, letting it go can be the hardest thing.

10. You can scalp big level breakouts and breakdowns for a quick profit. The GOOG $1,000 break was an example of a quick scalp profit off a level that everybody was watching. This made it likely that there would be some follow-through pop in the move. This kind of situation presents an opportunity for the trader to make good money very quickly if he has his finger in the button and can act faster than others. It's tricky to do this, because the HFTs will take out an entire level in milliseconds when they realize the level is going to be broken, but it's still possible to profit from this in select instances. This trading style is not perfect though, and in some situations, like in TWTR, you have to be ready to take a quick loss, because if the pop is not strong enough, a lot of traders and HFTs will be heading to the exit at the same time.

11. Always check the level from where the stock came from. A stock that has risen from $2 to $22 in one year will behave very differently than a stock that has been trading in a $20 to $24 range in the last year. The first has many people with large profits who will potentially sell once a stock breaks down, has bad news, etc. Also, potentially there will be more people shorted the first one (and people looking to initiate a short) then the second one. NQ provides a great example of that type of additional volatility.

This additional volatility has to be taken into account when deciding when to take profits and where to put your stops in.

12. Don't be afraid of getting out of a trade. You can always get back in. Jeff talks about how he can short a breakdown, take a loss if it rallies back up, but then reinitiate when it drops back down. His three to one reward to risk ratio assures him he can be wrong more than once and still profit from the trade. It's key for trading in general to look for situations where your payoff is several times your risk, this usually happen in major support/resistance levels, when a catalyst hits a security or when momentum shifts.

Chapter 5

Eric Scott Hunsader –
The Market Structure Expert

Eric (twitter @nanexllc) is not a trader. He makes that very clear. He is, however, one of the most informed and innovative market structure experts in the United States. Through his company, Nanex LLC, he monitors market data and shows the world disturbing occurrences that routinely happen in the US stock and futures markets.

After the rise in electronic trading and the HFTs, understanding market structure and how things work behind the scenes has become more important, which is why I decided to interview him for this book. A lot of the things he knows about HFTs and how they squeeze every dime out of orders would have helped me tremendously when I was starting out. In fact, to this day I have to keep reminding myself to cut back on scalping. I find that my toughest days in the markets are the days I'm taking HFTs head to head, trying to scalp stocks for a quick profit because I think its "obvious" that it's going higher or lower. The problem is that for a variety of reasons that he explains in the interview, it isn't so easy. If it were, the HFTs would have acted already.

Eric is known for his innovative charting methods that can explain price action in a way that aggregates all the information in one chart. If you browse around his website it's not hard to see why the US regulatory agencies like the SEC aren't aware of a lot that's going on in the markets. It takes quite a bit of brain power to figure out how to process the data and understand it. The SEC has too many lawyers using their brains figuring out how to watch porn and not get caught. Maybe they should consider significant personnel changes.

This interview was conducted in September 2012 and updated in November of 2013.

What made you interested in markets and market structure?

I started back in 1986. I was trading S&P 500 futures. I started collecting tick-by-tick data. I taught myself how to program, and I found that was what I really liked doing. I started processing, compressing, normalizing, and understanding market data ever since. I got involved in the market structure from monitoring of our feed and seeing the explosion in market information. Having just from lived through options going from a 100,000 updates per second to six million, with the projection going to the stratosphere, I saw the same thing happening in equities. It made me realize that there weren't going to be many people who'd be able to get real-time data. And that's when we began to investigate market structure.

Back in the '80s and '90s, where you up to date with all the rules and regulations, or is it something that only recently became more important?

We only tried to understand more of the rules and regulations side after the flash crash. We wanted to figure out how it related to the market data. Before data, we would look at regulations to see how it would affect the data that we would have to process.

So your company, Nanex, has been in business since the '80s and '90s?

No, I started this one only in 2000. There was a project at quote.com called qcharts, which was really the first source of streaming charts on the Internet. I realized the Internet was perfect for what I'd been doing. We were watching real-time streaming charts of S&P 500 futures back in the late '80s in a Motorola cell phone connected to a Compaq laptop. When the Internet came along, it was a no-brainer to get involved there. While at CQG, I started my own company. We wrote software to stream data on the Internet. It quickly got bought out, and then it became part of quote.com. I needed to find something to do for the rest of my life, so I came back to this field.

Were you monitoring the markets in the '87 crash?

Actually, yes. When the *Wall Street Journal* was doing the twenty-year anniversary of the crash, they were looking around for intraday data, and I still had it on floppy disk.

What was the main difference between the '87 crash and the flash crash?

Well, the '87 crash was in slow motion. The flash crash, I mean, if you went out for coffee you missed it. In the '87 crash, I remember the open. It was very jarring. It really made you want to buy it, because it was such a large drop, but then it just lasted the whole day. I remember that it wasn't until the end of the day that I looked at a daily chart and said, "Wow! That's a pretty good drop there."

In that crash, were there a lot of glitches in the system and things breaking down, or was it orderly selling?

Well, at the time I was only looking at futures, so I'm not sure what was going on in the stock side. I don't recall problems with the data in the futures side. It wasn't something that went really fast. When it opened down so much, it really kept a lot of people on the sidelines. It wasn't something that started rolling down and gathered steam. That might be why there didn't seem to be a frenzy of trading activity, unlike the flash crash. That one was a whole different league, because you had so many systems that were either broken or way behind. Like the Dow Jones calculating their DJIA, for instance. It was forty-five seconds behind the data that it was processing. You had all kinds of funky delays. Clearly the systems were overloaded. They hadn't been upgraded in a long time, and we broke into this new territory of higher volumes.

I believe I read that you said the hardware needs are going up a lot to meet the needs to process the data. What kind of equipment do you use to monitor the markets, and is that available to other folks?

Part of what I did was the NxCore product, which I started in 2000 with my company, Nanex. I wanted to solve the problem of having to deal with an aggregate of real time data and be able to process it without needing to have a large number of machines. A lot of firms will dedicate eight, twelve, or sixteen computers. Each one does a subset of symbols, but the way I structured it made it possible to process the data in any computer, really. It's hard to find a computer that doesn't have the specs that can process our feed. It doesn't take a whole lot of horsepower to monitor the markets. We use $500 Dell boxes, actually.

If a trader is at home looking at the Level 2 or Total View, is that a bit like looking at the past?

The biggest delays tend to be the speed of light. If a trader is using his eyes, that's going to take at least 50 to 100 milliseconds just to receive the data. Then you have brain absorption and being able to react. You're really losing 100 milliseconds just to go from screen to human. Getting the information to the machine itself at the speed of light has been the number one source of latency for a couple of years now. As a rule of thumb, 180 miles will cost you 1 millisecond. If you're in Chicago and you're getting the Total View data from NY, you're looking at least 15 to 20 milliseconds. That's how long it takes to send the information. A lot of times we see that the number of messages easily will exceed a 1,000 per second, which means each will last less than 1 millisecond. So yes, a lot of information that you see, especially in the active issues, doesn't exist. The orders don't exist anymore. You don't want to compete at that level. You want to compete at a higher time frame, knowing all the weakness of the algos, how they're all reacting to each other.

You want to play at least in the ten-second to one-minute range. My successful customers are not super short-term. I used to have some that were pretty successful arbitraging options, but when the market message rates climbed over a few million a second, it was impossible for them to compete anymore. They would need special feeds to do that, and you have to be an exchange member to get that top tier. Things have changed, and you can't really scalp off the screen, but there are successful traders that were able to extend their time frame a bit.

What is the main flaw of HFTs and algos?

They follow each other. Because they're based on speed, they really react a lot to current prices. They tend to be like lemmings and just follow along in a short-term trend. They tend to cause the market to move swiftly in one direction, then the move burns itself out and comes right back. You can see 1 to 2 percent moves that can start and stop in just two seconds.

Do you think these HFTs have special treatment, and if you take it away they all go bust, or would they make money even if stripped of special advantages that other people don't have?

I think the SEC should enforce Reg NMS, which is what it looks like they're doing now with this recent ruling against the NYSE.[17] But that's just the tip of the iceberg. They affirmed what the NBBO was and how it was supposed to be used and calculated and protected. If they go all the way to enforce that, which is likely because they wrote it out in the order against the NYSE, a lot of HFTs will be in a world of hurt. They'll no longer have that advantage, which is a significant one. The direct feed and colocation advantage is significant. In the end, there's only going to be one or two large HFT firms that are going to be making a market. There won't be room for somebody else to come in there and participate. A lot of what they're doing now are games. They're not really market making, they're working around this latency arbitrage between two data feeds. If the SEC goes down this path, that game will disappear.

When you look at your stock data from before the rise of HFTs, do you have evidence that intraday stock volatility is now higher than in the past?

Yes, actually we just did something that looked at the number of price ticks in SPY since 2004[18].We put the study up on our website. It's interesting, because right after Reg NMS came in, the number of price ticks in a day — and this takes into account the daily range and

17 NYSE Penalized by SEC for Giving Head Start on Trading Data - Joshua Gallu – Bloomberg September 2012.
18 http://www.nanex.net/aqck2/3563.html

things like the VIX — rose by at least twice, if not much higher. There are more different price ticks during the day than before Reg NMS, which started in 2007.

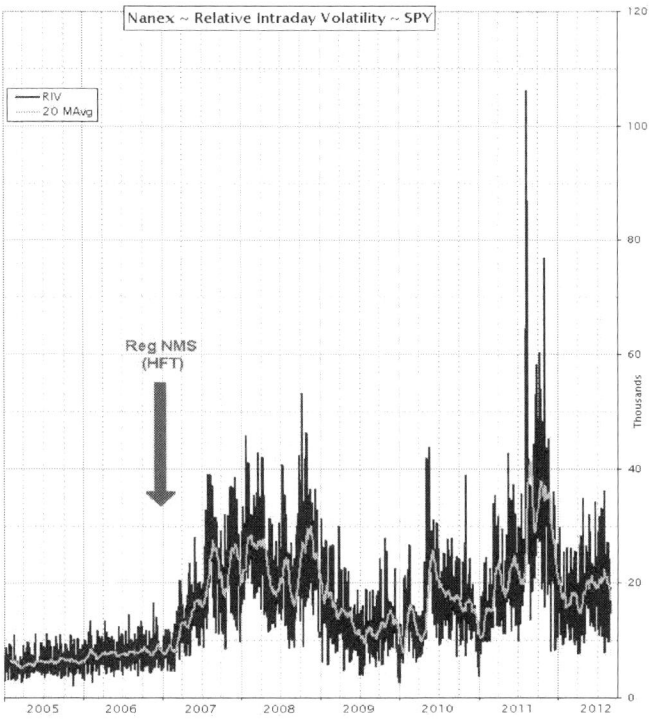

Source: Nanex LLC

It's quite noticeable in the chart that there was a fundamental shift and change. We see it in the data all the time, but it was really very hard to quantify until we came up with this method. The ticks will go up and down a lot more than they used to.

Doesn't that create an opportunity to fade the extremes of those moves?

Yes, it sure does. You would think that people who jump on activity would dampen it out and you wouldn't see this much. It could also be because there are so many ETFs out there that there's something else going on that prevents it from dampening. Or maybe there's just not enough profit in it. Hard to say.

Another thing that's interesting is that we looked at quote rates back in the 1999 bull market when tech stocks were going crazy. The NYSE had just upgraded in 1999 to be able to process 1,000 quotes per second. And this was for all stocks trading at the time. Now we're at 1.5 million quotes per second. This is the capacity difference between when we had a bull market in 1999 and now. Maybe we're in a bull market, but it's not close to what it was then.

Do you think market orders are a sucker play?

They definitely are, because market orders for more than 100 shares usually will get filled for the first 100 shares, where you're expecting it, but the rest of it won't. This is because the HFTs can see orders coming in the exchange, and they withdraw the orders. Or they'll just pull back before the router is able to spread it out. If you trying to do 1,000 shares and you have ten exchanges and each one has 100 shares, the order has to be split up to be able to go to each exchange. The router simply won't be fast enough to get it done.

They're able to see the orders in one of the exchanges and cancel their orders faster than that order router will be able to send them to other exchanges. This is why the first 100 shares will be filled but the rest will usually have inferior prices. There are strategies that they developed over the years. One is called Thor.[19] They try to time it so it won't show up in one exchange faster than it shows in the others.

---

[19] Thor is a smart router type algorithm that tries to make sure all the broken down orders from the larger order hit all the ECNs and exchanges at the same time.

What about limit orders? Is trying to post them and collect a rebate a sucker play too?

That's the other problem. They'll run right in front of you and wait you out. They jump in front of you, buy, and see if they can make the spread. If they can't, they'll dump the stock on you. Now, this is in an inactive stock, in an active stock you won't run into this problem. In NASDAQ stocks, I heard this time and time again from my customers and I've investigated several of these instances. These internalizer or wholesalers will buy and sell at subpenny prices. They can go 1/100th of a penny above you, and that's their total risk. They'll just dump it off on you if they can't make the spread.

What about using hidden orders to avoid that?

Oh, that's fine. If you put that in there and see no reaction then it really is truly hidden. If you put that in there and you see the market move, then it's not truly hidden.

Do you think some exchanges might be selling the hidden order books to HFTs?

According to Scott Patterson's book, *Dark Pools*, it could be true. There are all kinds of special order types that have been created to accommodate the HFTs.

Do you think stop books are also being sold?

There's no way for me to know. I can only say what I've heard. It could be that they just use the conventional wisdom that people tend to put stops around even numbers prior support or resistance.

Sometimes I use hidden orders and I get hit for one share many times in a row. They discover where I am. Do you think there's any reason an HFT firm should be allowed to use odd lots like that?

No, of course not. When there's a perception of unfairness or a two-tiered system, which Reg NMS says should be strongly discouraged, you end up losing a lot of participants. They don't want to play the game anymore. They feel like it doesn't matter if they're right on direction if they're going to get hurt in the entry or exit to the extent that makes them unprofitable. All you have left are these machines with special orders that are all going to react the same way when there's some unexpected news.

Do you think it's possible to look at subpenny trades and predict where order flow is?

Yes, you can tell what the retail is doing by looking at the subpenny trades in aggregate. Anything that's priced $1/100^{th}$ to $49/100^{th}$ is almost always a public retail trade sale. The $50/100^{th}$ to $99/100^{th}$ is a retail buy. If you can aggregate those, you can tell what retail is doing.

So you can get an advantage being on the same side as the internalizer?

You always want to be on the opposite side of the retail. Almost always, the retail is wrong.

When you personally invest your money, how do you work your orders?

I don't trade. I'm a very long-term trader. My last long-term trade was buying Apple in 2000. When I have positions and I worry about them, I can't get anything else done. I don't have the temperament to trade.

How do you see the market evolving over the next ten years?

Up until last Friday, I thought that the HFT issue would play itself out by having a lot of the retail traders just die off. After the SEC ruling last Friday, I'm very encouraged that we may have seen the worst of it. We might get to equality between HFTs and other traders. I just hope the SEC is not going to go back out what they've said in these orders against the NYSE.

What do you think is the best change they have to make right now?

They have to look at how order routing works. They have to ensure that the exchanges are using the consolidated quote to determine where to route the orders, not the direct feed like they're doing right now. Once they get past that hurdle, a lot of the latency arbitrage games will either completely disappear or greatly diminish.

Without this arbitrage, you don't think they have a lot of additional advantages to remain profitable?

No, it's all speed. A lot of what they're doing has nothing to do with economics. They're just trying to flush out or fool another algorithm into doing something stupid. So 99 percent of this type of code is antieconomic.

I've read about quote stuffing in your articles.[20]

That continues to happen, in spite of all. We used to think it might be stupidity or that they were unaware, but that time has long passed. The reason they do it is because the law of averages will tilt things in their favor. It allows them to see the Thor-like programs that are trying to time the orders that are trying to reach the exchanges. They want to tilt these orders and the order routers out of balance so the order router might misroute to one of the other

---

[20] Quote stuffing is essentially spamming an exchange or ECN with orders and canceling them immediately. Could be also constantly changing an existing order millions of times in a row.

exchanges. It's all about discovering which orders are real and which are not.

Do you think they're also trying to slow things down for other people?

Exchanges assign groups of stocks to different machines. Let's say stocks A through C are in one machine, and the network that carries that traffic into that machine gets stuffed. Basically, any stock in that group that has slightly higher quote rates will cause that machine to slow down in processing them. A Thor-like program is trying to time something so that order appears in all these exchanges at the same time. NYSE computers take a 100 microseconds from the time it receives an order to the time it displays an order. Let's say BATS computers takes 50 microseconds to do that, the Thor like program will time the order will wait 50 microseconds to send it to BATS. That means it will appear on the NYSE and BATS at the same time so nobody can detect orders on them.

But that only works in the ideal case. If you have a hundred quotes going through one of those stocks in that group during that time, now it's now longer 50 microseconds, it's 75 microseconds, and it's just enough that with the law of averages it will expose some orders every once and a while.

It doesn't work 100 percent of the time, but it works enough that it slightly tilts things in their favor, and because there's no cost to send that extra information there's no reason not to do it. You don't have to send thousands of quotes to cause it to happen. You only need to send a few more than whatever threshold exists. Back in July 2010, we were looking at NYSE system Open Book, and we noticed that whenever any stock had a message rate of more than a 1,000 in one second, it would immediately cause a delay of 16 to 20 milliseconds in the consolidated feed versus Open Book. If you take six random symbols and just put 5,000 quotes a seconds in those symbols, you effectively delay the entire NYSE consolidated quote update.

And you don't have to do it for a full second; you just have to do it for a few milliseconds. If you do it randomly like that, you cause these Thor-like programs to fail. It's kind of like an antistrategy to prevent people from executing large orders simultaneously in multiple exchanges.[21] Does that make sense?

Yes. The consolidated quote slows down, but the proprietary feeds work just fine?

Time is money. You can definitely slow down any feed, even a direct feed, whenever you want by simply putting a heavier load on them. The load doesn't have to be that high. Even NYSE's Open Book starts to have serious delays at 200,000 a second. You can do it for 15 milliseconds and knock out substantial information.

Do you think the exchanges have to update their hardware?

Yes. That's why we have these high quote rates. People are testing to see what the latencies are. You can tell when machines get upgraded or circuits get upgraded or get fixed by simply doing these tests at random times. A lot of what these guys do is that they build these tables. In a specific set of symbols, they know exactly what kind of quote rate translates to in terms of latency. A lot of the

---

21 This allows HFTs to cancel their orders from other exchanges when they see the executions going on in another exchange. When the Thor like program misfires as a result of all the quote spamming, the HFTs now see that there's some buying or selling interest going on and they can extract a few more cents out of that order. Without the data spamming the Thor program would execute in all the exchanges at the same time.

software engineering and expertise and brain power is going in this kind of activity.

I believe I've read that you think the BATS IPO was an act of revenge by the exchanges.

I just can't see how it couldn't have been. These were all ISO trades[22]. It wasn't one big one. It wasn't somebody selling. Who would have that stock to sell? Somebody who understands how markets work or an idiot? You put this all together and you see how the trades were executed. It just didn't hit all the bids on the way down. The algorithm would sell a bunch, and it would pause a little bit. Then it would wait for the bid to perk up a bit, and it wouldn't hit a single one. Then it would resume selling into it. It was something that was clearly meant to sell indiscriminately. You look at the people who would have the ability to sell. They used ISO orders, which means it was a broker/dealer, it rules out stupidity. To us it was pretty blatant. I guess it could have been some supreme stupidity, but I just doubt it.

---

[22] An ISO order is allowed to trade through better prices bid or offered somewhere else as a long as it respects the initial inside quote. After that, it can theoretically be executed at any price even if it doesn't make financial sense.

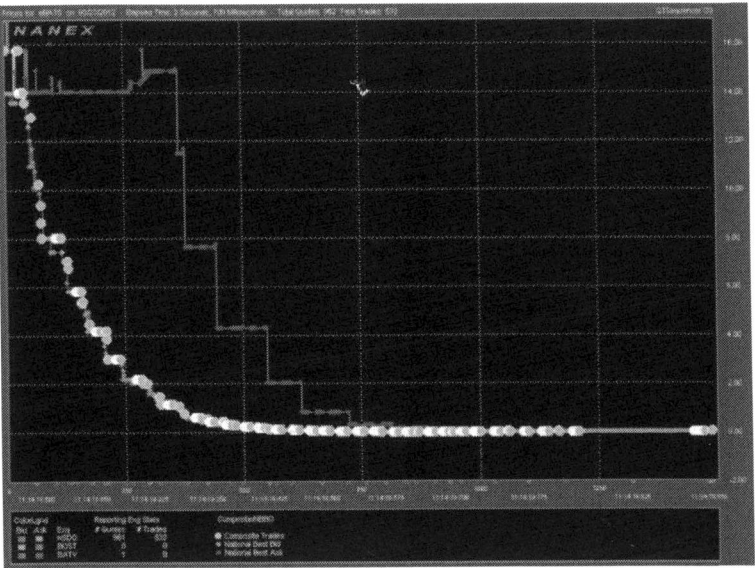

BATS IPO. Source: Nanex LLC

The NYSE and the NASDAQ had a lot to lose. They enjoy pretty nice listing fees, and BATS was coming along offering to list for free. So they were definitely big winners on that day when BATS's IPO failed. Unless someone confesses that they did it, we'll never know. Over the years we've seen people do this sort of thing. For example, I think it was in August of 2010 the AMEX just started trading NASDAQ stocks. In the first or second day, they open up a quote on CSCO. It was really wide. Somebody decided they wanted to pay more than 5 percent to the market price on AMEX. He sent an ISO order to AMEX, which caused it to execute on AMEX. That halted CSCO for five minutes. That sort of gave AMEX a black eye.

I heard later on from someone on the board of directors of one of these exchanges that the NYSE called up the guy who made the trade and asked if he wanted to bust the trade, and the guy said no.

Until I hear otherwise, I believe the BATS IPO was somebody intentionally trying to crater BATS stock on the open.

How long did the whole collapse last?

It was like a second and a half.

So there was no time for someone like a value investor to try to buy the stock?

The problem was that BATS couldn't get their quotes out. The only one quoting at the very beginning was NASDAQ. We don't know for sure, but if BATS had gotten a quote out there, it might have been different. But we can't be sure, because these were ISO orders, which means "do not route."

These ISO routes mean they're allowed to trade through better quotations somewhere else?

Yes, the trade-through exception applies to ISO orders.

So the guy knew it would only execute on NASDAQ?

Yes, whoever put it in did not want better prices. It was either supremely stupid or supremely wise. It wasn't a random fluke.

How many shares got sold on the way down?

It was a 100 shares each with 500 or so trades, so about fifty thousand. The total value was pretty high—something like half a million dollars.

Do you think IPOs in general are way glitchier and investors should avoid them?

Yeah, I'm really shocked at how they botched that stuff. NASDAQ was just asking for trouble when it used its order book for dual purpose. Before the open, the order book was used to compute an opening cross in a Dutch action. After the open it was supposed to be normal. What this means is that before the open NASDAQ would allow buy orders that were higher than sell orders. In a normal market those were going to cross and be executed. NASDAQ's problem in the FB IPO was that it couldn't clear out the book and it transitioned from before open to after open. It had these buy orders in for $70 or something for a couple hours — until something like 1:15 (EST). Its whole order book was crossed. That's what I think caused Knight and the rest of these guys, like the internalizers, to lose money. The software didn't properly handle it. Why NASDAQ did that was beyond me.

Do you think that because NASDAQ doesn't have a long history of handling auctions it suffered from inexperience, whereas NYSE would be unlikely to mess it up like that?

Yes, you're right. NYSE doesn't use the same order book for two different things. It doesn't do anything stupid like that.

So NASDAQ IPOs are a little riskier than NYSE IPOs?

The linkages between exchanges in an IPO always seem to have really wild quotes. One exchange can be way off from the others. I don't quite understand why. At the very beginning of the FB IPO, there were really wide bids and offers. If somebody wanted to, they could have caused FB to print at way higher prices just by hitting some of the quotes that were out there at the time. There's always the possibility that someone is going to come in and do it. It doesn't cost a lot of money, and it can significantly impact the overall psychological feeling of that market.

Are you a fan of ISO orders or not?

You know, if they were used for their purposes I would be fine with them, but they're so abused. They were supposed to be used to try to mop up liquidity, like if you're buying more shares than exist in one particular exchange. The ISO order prevents the order from routing the balance to another exchange. The ISO orders are used a lot now by some HFTs that don't want to get direct feeds from other exchanges. They only want to get the direct feed from say NASDAQ, BATS, and EDGE. They just use ISO orders all the time so as to ensure it will only execute in the exchanges where they know the prices are.

With regards to the Knight trading glitch, did you have a lot of clients who were able to capitalize on that?

I know people that saw the obvious in large cap stocks that were completely mispriced and they just jumped all over it.

I read about people complaining that sometimes they try to hit a specific ECN or exchange for, say, 500 shares, but they only get a 100 shares, the rest just moves. This is a little different from the routing issue we talked about earlier. What is going on here?

A lot of things like that go on. I hear that a lot.

I understand that they can pull away when the order needs to be routed out. What happens when it's the same exchange?

According to the book *Dark Pools*, there are special order types that allow them to do that. When you see 500 in one exchange that could be five different lots of 100 share orders. It might be that they're flickering in such a way that the 400 is not always there, and it happens to be when your order got in there. Or they saw your order coming in for 500 and they just canceled the 400. I've seen that looking at order book data, where all of a sudden a big order comes in and for some mysterious reason, and a lot of orders, even some that were there for a long time, get canceled. It leads me to believe that they're seeing that order somehow.

Some traders I know use some ECNs or exchanges like EDGA or BX in order to sit at a limit order and get hit first, because they offer a rebate or low fees for liquidity takers. That way you can get ahead of other people in the same level. Do you think it's a good idea?

As long as it holds, yes. But I've never seen something with more footnotes in my life than in these fee schedules from the ECNs and exchanges. The fees depend on the order that's routed, where it's routed to, the size of the order, the type. If that changes all of a sudden, you'll have to adapt.

To me this looks like a way for retail or professional traders to subpenny everybody else at the same price level by offering a rebate for liquidity takers and thereby getting some type of price priority over others in the same level.

That sounds like a good idea.

What are the main differences between the open and close periods?

Oh, the open has really wide spreads. It really doesn't take a lot of capital to affect the market open. We saw that on Knight Capital when they had their error on August 1. What I believe happened was that their test algorithm was randomly buying and selling all kinds of stocks. Some stocks opened down 4 to 5 percent and stayed down and vice versa. If it had not been random and it were all to the downside, for example, it could have brought the whole market down. In the first fifteen seconds of the open, the bid ask spread is just phenomenally wide. At the close, there's a whole additional liquidity there, especially in the E-mini contract and the larger contracts. They do game that last millisecond of the day. People that are not collocated and don't have speed the last ten seconds probably want to be out. But there's a lot more liquidity in the last fifteen minutes.

What are the games that they play right before the close?

The last millisecond of the day belongs to the fastest player. They can affect the set the close of the market and affect things like options that they want to get out of. I've seen them flood the SPY at the very close and send it down by 15 cents. They'll get it back and forth by 15 cents in the last milliseconds of the day. In that very last millisecond, anything goes.

It's like massive tape painting?

Yes, there's such a huge volume of messages in that last millisecond that sometimes it takes a few seconds to print out on the tape. You don't really know what happened in that last millisecond unless you have absolute state-of-the-art processing. You get an immense flood of information.

Some people say that at the open the spreads are really wide because the HFTs don't like risk, but I also think that maybe they're trying to make more money off the retail orders, market orders, that are hitting the market.

I think you're right. We see the bulk of these flash crashes happen at the open. In the first minute of trading, there's a high percentage of them. I think they know that some people don't know the dangers of market orders. They don't have time to worry about it, and they get their market orders or even limit orders that get taken advantage of. We did a study and found there was a gradual erosion in the first fifteen seconds since 2006. Spreads have gotten wider gradually, and things have become much less stable. If somebody really wants to affect the market, that's the time to do it.

What are your thoughts on the mid-day period?

We see a lot of algo testing going on around eleven in the morning and one or two in the afternoon. We see significant market moves during that time on no news at all. Maybe they're testing to see what it takes to perturb the market. And they come out of the blue.

What do you think happened today in crude oil? It had a tremendous sell-off.[23]

It wasn't an algo gone wild. It wasn't somebody trying to scare the market. Maybe there some kind of news that slowly got disseminated and nobody had an advantage there. It was a very slow rolling move. It took a minute from when it started to when it reached the bottom. You didn't see any spikes or any telltale signs of anything other than a large number of participants shifting their opinion on oil.

---

[23] Nanex ~ 17-Sep-2012 ~ Crude Oil Drops
www.nanex.net/aqck2/3586.html

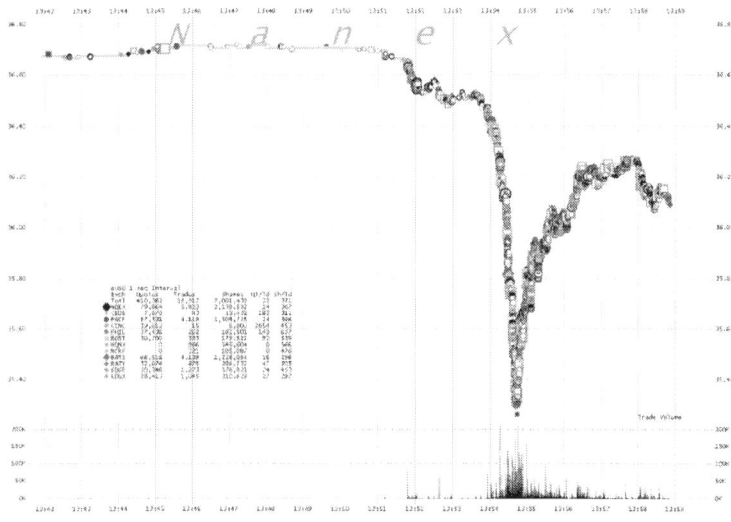

Crude Oil. Source: Nanex LCC

With regards to the flash crash, who do you think lost the most there?

Probably Waddell and Reed. They took a pretty big hit. They got substantially lower prices for those E-mini contracts than they would otherwise. Some retailers definitely got hurt. The ones that had drops in their stocks that weren't big enough to get canceled. There was a lot of frustration that day, people trying to get executions. I know somebody that was trying to get SPY fills from Fidelity and it was hours before they were finally filled. I heard that Goldman Sachs made a lot of money in that afternoon.

Do you know how? They bought the S&P 500 E-mini at the lows?

Yeah, trading the E-mini.

Some people say that the old market makers would back out from chaotic times just as the HFTs did on the flash crash, so there's no difference. What do you say?

Well, I'm not so sure. When we reopened from 9/11 a week later, that's when you had market makers stepping in there and holding the market up. You had the expected gap down open and then it traded higher. It wasn't like in the flash crash where there just wouldn't be any buyers at all.

Do you think the exchanges and ECNs should make the special members have some kind of firm obligations instead of just making whatever market they want?

I believe they just need to stop this nonsense of being able to cancel orders when they see real buying or selling interest. There's a big difference between requiring them to step in front of a moving train and making them step away every time there's a slight breeze because they know they'll be a little bit more profitable. Just require them to honor their quotes, for example. If they tried to pull this type of trick in the pits, nobody would trade with them anymore or they'd get a black eye or both. This game of hiding behind being anonymous and pulling quotes because they can — especially with the speed of light is in their favor — is just wrong. If the exchanges were too look ahead to the future, they'd realize this.

What kind of advice do you have for traders and investors dealing with these crazy markets?

Learn as much as you can before you jump in, and don't try to compete with groups that you're not on an equal footing with. Don't try to compete with HFTs.

November 2013 Update

The last time we spoke you were optimistic that regulators would crack down on a lot of the advantages that the HFTs have. How's your assessment now?

It's like a roller coaster. It really is hard to say. Every once in a while I'm hopeful, but it seems like they take one step forward and one step back. The last big hope was when the CFTC fined Panther Energy Trading for placing large fake orders, but they didn't follow through with others, so...

What do you think of the SEC getting the Tradeworx system with that whole MIDAS thing?

What they put out is an abomination. You're averaging data for the whole day when lots of events happen in less than a hundred milliseconds now. Even if you average for a whole second you won't see a lot of what's going on. I remember Greg Berman saying that these flash crashes weren't caused by HFTs, and he was going to show us with the data. They still haven't shown us anything. And they won't, because the data can't back up his claim. They also haven't updated their site in six weeks. That's a long time.

This year, you've brought attention to the fact that HFTs are getting economic news before everybody else. Do you think they've been doing this for a long time and they only got caught now?

Yes. The thing is, I don't have a problem with that. I do have a problem when they're doing it in secrecy. In fact, what we found was that once people knew that Thompson Reuters was supplying the Consumer Confidence Index earlier to some folks, the explosion of market trading stopped. It went from hundreds of thousands of shares traded in milliseconds to less than one thousand. It was like night and day. Nothing changed with the news. Nothing changed with them getting it faster. The only thing that changed was that everybody knew that it was happening.

So if there's a perception of unfairness, the volume just disappears, and no one wants to play anymore?

That's right. They won't participate when they know it's unfair. Take what happened with the Federal Reserve in the FOMC no-taper announcement, for example. That whole thing was about doing it secretly. It was so secret that the Fed didn't even know it was going on.

Do you think they did this because the time difference was so small that they just thought nobody would notice?

Yes, I think they thought nobody would notice it.

You rated the NYSE Twitter IPO an A. I noticed that the OTC markets were shut down that day. I remember you said that the BATS IPO was manipulated. Do you think they shut down the OTCs because they wanted the retail volume going into Twitter stock, so it would look better to the investment banks?

No. The OTC is so small. It's a rounding error compared to the listed markets. There's not enough going on there to make any difference.

Lately there have been some fines over layering the quotes and showing fake sizes. Do you think that game is going to end? I still see that a lot in small-cap stocks.

It's happening more. This is the roller coaster I was mentioning earlier. When the CFTC investigated Panther Trading in July for doing just that—putting large fake orders in one side to drive the market to their orders in the other side—they were fined so much so that they were shutdown for a period of time. That would be disastrous if it happened to, say, Goldman Sachs. It was a monstrous fine and totally unexpected. The natural thought was, well they're going to do this with everybody. Now that they have this hammer, they're going to find some nails to use. For a period of time after the Panther fine came out, there was a definite change out there, but after a month or two it just started to creep back in. Just last week we saw somebody putting this order of 20,000 in one natural gas contract. Normally, anything over 100 is big, 1,000 is just huge, 10,000 is unprecedented, and this was a 20,000 contract order! I didn't see any fine for that. If I was the regulator, I could find out who did it within one hour.

Do you think this game will ever stop?

If I were the regulator, I would fine the bad guys and that would be it. Right now, it almost seems like the bad guys are too big to jail, and maybe that's what is going on. I can't answer the question because the whole thing just defies logic.

Do you think the Twitter IPO was smoother because it was in the NYSE, and they have a better system compared to the NASDAQ?

NASDAQ was trying to use the same order book software logic to do two vastly different things. They were trying to use it to do, essentially, a Dutch auction in the opening cross then instantly switch to the regular auction system for regular trading. When they couldn't make the switch from one to the other, that's when it failed in the Facebook IPO. NYSE doesn't do that.

Does NASDAQ still do that?

I don't know. I haven't looked close enough. There hasn't been a big enough IPO on the NASDAQ in quite a while. So I don't spend time looking at this.

What are your thoughts on SMART routers from retail brokerages?

Well, I've seen the results of them. I've had large institutional firms share their trade date with me. These SMART routers are not as smart as the HFTs that are trying to trip them up. When the NBBO flutters, say, a hundred times a second, some of these SMART order routes get shutdown; some get delayed.

We spoke a little bit about that the last time. The HFTs try to overload the servers so that the time it takes to send an order to different ECNs and exchanges changes, and since the SMART router is counting in a stable relationship they kind of misfire and are exposed. The HFTs can cancel and make the person pay more.

It kind of builds a momentum train longer when you've got pent-up demand. The more pent up you can get the demand, the bigger the bang when it comes out. This is just one of the many strategies going on. Another one is just to try to detect if there's a large order coming. If somebody is trying to split up a 10,000 share trade and hit ten different pools of liquidity — if they can trip it up and expose the order — they can pull their bids and offers in the other remaining pools. If you think of these milliseconds of delays in human terms, it's like a whole hour. A lot can be done in that period of time.

So, instead of using the SMART router, a trader might be better off using direct routing to a specific pool, taking that and then assessing if he wants to buy and sell more?

You really have to experiment a little bit. You have to be very careful of never really exposing your order size if you want to buy or sell a lot. You can use time too, algos can forget about things after a couple of seconds. I've seen one algo that was trying to sell a lot. He hit the market hard, and after a couple seconds that bid book was almost completely recharged. Now, things change. After a while the algos get smarter and that might not work anymore. So you might have to change it up.

You mentioned that you have some products that you sell to your clients. I didn't understand exactly what it is that you offer. Is that like a direct type feed of market data?

A lot of our traders are not trading in the subsecond time frames. They're longer-term, so we provide a real-time data feed that contains almost anything traded in the United States — options, futures, equities. We also have archived data for people that want to go back in time and check how things traded. Pretty much all of the statistics that we publish comes from that.

What is the advantage of your data compared to other places?

The advantage is being able to use the data immediately. As a programmer, sometimes you do all the hard work of dealing with different types of data, APIs for futures, equities, options, etc. They can change over time too. We normalize that so you don't really have to think how to decode. That's all done. We do it in a way that allows you to write an algorithm that works on historic data and use the same exact algorithm in real time. We also compress the data about twenty to one, which allows much faster work with that data.

How did you come up with your charting style?

Two of the things that I specialized in are compressions and graphical display of the information. I've been doing this since '86.

You had to come up with a whole new charting system because regular charts just wouldn't do it?

Yes, it's a big challenge trying to put all the different kinds of information together in a way that's not just a cluttered mess. With these charts, we tried to bring out information that wasn't apparent.

Last year the *Wall Street Journal* and Haim Bodek exposed a lot of the special order types that the HFTs have. Which do you think is the most abusive order type out there?

Given that I'm not in the trading side, I'm really not an expert on that. I would rather rely on what I've heard from other traders. Again, like the stuff about early news releases, it's not so much the fact that it exists as the fact that's done secretly and not widely disclosed. If the way they roll out these orders types is requiring people to look for fine print, or they're not disclosing it unless you belong to the club, I would have a problem with that.

You want them to disclose and be transparent about this stuff so that the people who participate and don't use these order types can avoid playing that game?

The best markets are the ones that are the most transparent. They have the most diversity of participants — people trading on different time frames, methods, news sources, etc. The only way you'll get diversity of participation is if all these different players know exactly who's doing what and who has what advantages. It's OK for some groups to have advantages, as a long everybody else knows what those advantages are. It's fine for people to get the Fed news early, as a long everybody knows what's going on.

In that day of the Fed FOMC no-taper announcement, gold was moving way before everything else. What was that about?

My best guess is that this information got leaked out of the Fed. It had to be a leak, because the machines bought with such abandon that they had to know. They were all-in, and in Wall Street they rarely do that. Quite a few people had to know that information. It wouldn't surprise me if some of those leaked to someone else, and that's how it ended up in gold. In other words, there were probably a dozen people who knew it. It probably wasn't as closely guarded as it should have been. One of those people leaked to someone else.

Why do you think they chose gold specifically?

Because it's international—it trades around the world. They might not even have bought the COMEX or CME gold. They might have done it in Europe or in the Middle East. Then it was arbitraged into our market.

Do you think they did this because if the leakers got caught it wouldn't be easily traceable to whoever was behind the trades?

Yeah, they probably went to the place that was the easiest and most anonymous. It only showed up in our markets later. I haven't looked closely at that. Maybe it's something to investigate one day. That's my feeling. Gold always seems to be involved. If anything is going to have a tell early or have a fake-out early, nine times out of ten gold is going to be a part of it.

If they'd bought the S&P 500 futures, it would be so obvious that everybody would want an investigation?

Yes and you can only trade the S&P 500 futures in one place.

And it's easy to trace the orders and trades too, correct?

Yes, it's quite easy to trace.

According to some reports, the profitability of HFTs is going down. Why do you think this is happening right now?

Part of this is the fact that the rules are being followed closer now. For example, we don't see as many locked or crossed quotes as we used to. But a big part of this comes back to the issue I talked about earlier, which is that people are becoming aware of what is going on. If people know the advantages that are going on, they're going to adjust accordingly.

The low hanging fruit's gone. Their costs skyrocketed too, because every time you move things faster, your costs go up exponentially. You have to have really talented people to run ten-gig-networks, for example. We are getting to the cutting bleeding edge, as we like to call it. It's extremely expensive all around, and the cat is out of the bag.

Do you think there's hope for a fairer market, because they're going to start to go out of business, and they'll be unable to do as much lobbying and pushing for advantages and things like that?

Yes, you could be right. The market's becoming aware of all this might end up doing more than a regulator ever could. It's a shame that we pay for these organizations, the SEC and CFTC. We've got these rules that are clear and easy to follow, and it's frustrating when they don't apply them evenhandedly. Capitalism doesn't work unless you have the rule of law.

In the OTC markets, the SEC has been very aggressive in stopping frauds and scams this year. What do you think of this new chairwoman of the SEC? Do you think they mean business this time?

I think the new boss is the same as the old boss. If she wanted to show us she was serious, I would have expected a lot right away. Take the whole Mark Cuban trial, for example. I actually looked at that data very closely. I spent a couple of days investigating it. My take away from it was that the stock manipulators who were behind mama.com were complete frauds. They should have been investigated. Mark Cuban was just a victim of all that. The SEC went after the victim. It didn't make any sense to me at all. I was surprised that it was allowed to go on like that. It didn't take much reading to realize that they were going after the wrong people. They essentially gave the mama.com people immunity for their weak testimony against Mark Cuban.

They fined the NYSE over the fact that they were delaying the data on purpose. Is that still going on?

Yes. I published a paper after the SEC had the rollout of MIDAS in which I said that the one thing they should look at immediately was the quotes from the consolidated feed. Then they should find their counterparts in the direct feed and compare the time stamps. That's how we found the NYSE delay. That's how they're going to see that the delays are much more frequent than anybody realizes.

Do you think the SEC doesn't understand a lot of this stuff because they have too many legal experts and lawyers on their staff?

No, they have the trading and markets division. Greg Burman says he knows what's going on with markets much more than Nanex does, for example. He told a group of institutional investors that Nanex doesn't know what they're talking about. That would seem to imply that he does. I would say that they're very aware of what's happening, which makes the next question even more difficult — why let it happen?

If you were asked to take his job would you take it?

I would do it for free for a year, but only if they applied the law to whoever I found to be the bad guy, no matter who it was.

So if you accused Goldman Sachs and they didn't fine them, you would step down?

Yes.

What about that Goldman Sachs issue with the options in the NASDAQ. How come they had their trades busted?

What's so odd about that is that when NASDAQ had their outage one week earlier, one of our customers was arbitraging equities and options. The BBO stopped, and he was thinking the price of the stock was X. He'd gotten on in the options side and was working his order in the equity side, and it kept coming back — failing because the price actually moved. NASDAQ wasn't printing out the quotes anymore. He ended with only half the side of the arb. He immediately requested the CBOE to cancel his options side because of the equipment failure in the equity side. They didn't let him out. They said the equity didn't go out until 12:20, when in fact the trading stopped at 12:20, but the quotes stopped at 12:10. It was a small trade, less than twenty contracts, but two weeks later they helped out Goldman Sachs — who obviously should have known better — get away with destroying with the whole price discovery process. That got them all busted. That makes no sense.

If it was Knight Capital that had done that, would they have busted it?

In my opinion the only reason they didn't bust Knight trades last year was because they weren't cleanly delineated. You couldn't say, "All trades above this price, or bellow this price." It was a mix. It was impossible to say they were going to cancel some trades but not others. That's why they didn't cancel Knight's trades. I believe they would have if Knight had done all the trades in one side above or under a certain price. The CEO even called Mary Shapiro's private cell phone that evening. He wouldn't have made that call unless he thought there was a chance of a cancel there.

Do you think the exchanges are in urgent need to update their hardware?

Yes. The thing is they spend all their money on the direct feeds, not enough on the consolidated feeds, which is the one that retail and dark pools gets access to.

Lessons from Chapter 5

1. Don't try to compete in ultra short-term time frames. As Eric explains, the delays both from the data feeds (most people get the slow consolidated feed instead of the fast direct feed) and the human eye (along with brain processing) means that by the time you hit the buy or sell button you're already trading ages after the HFTs have. If there's any kind of opportunity for profit in excess of trading costs, it's unlikely it wasn't taken by the HFTs by the time you act.

2. Levels of intraday noise have increased significantly since 2004. As Eric's study shows, prices have become more noisy and volatile since then. This makes it important to have wider stops. Lengthen your time horizon to avoid getting caught in that noisy chop.

3. Market orders are gamed because the order routers can't send out the order to other exchanges fast enough. The HFTs can

quickly cancel their other orders, leaving you with a partial fill in your intended position. Anything more than a 100 shares is a risky size to be used in a market order. This doesn't apply as much in liquid ETFs such as SPY, but it does in less liquid issues such as small, mid-cap, and certain big-cap stocks.

4. Passive limit orders will be gamed in illiquid stocks. In more illiquid names with a bigger spread, if you try to avoid paying that spread by posting a limit order on the bid or ask, your solution might be worse than the disease. Assuming you don't get penny jumped by a market-making HFT (which is likely to happen a lot of the time), you will still get subpennied by internalizers and wholesalers. What is the solution? **Only trade in these more illiquid issues when they're in play** (when there's big news going on with a lot of retail or big money participation). If they're not, don't trade them at all. Avoid scalping on them because fills are really difficult. If you do trade them, use native hidden orders, that way at least you won't have some of the games played against you.

5. Retail flow can be inferred through subpenny trades. Eric points out that aggregating subpenny trades can tell you what the retail is doing. This might serve as an indicator of which side is likely to be a good fade down the line or what kind of interest is behind the current move of a stock.

6. Lots of HFT games in stocks are about trying to find out which orders are real and which are not. This is why you should never show your hand. These guys make a living off making you pay a few cents more after they know your intentions.

7. The open has significantly wider spreads. It's very important for you not to misjudge your liquidity at the open. If you take a big position through the NYSE opening auction or NASDAQ opening

cross, you'll find that it's impossible to exit without materially affecting the price. You can bet the HFTs know this, because they have access to the opening print volume and the current liquidity level. At the mere sign that some people are trying to exit their positions, they'll make these traders pay. This also applies to overnight positions and trades taken after the opening.

8. The importance of position sizing and knowing how big can you get in a trade. This lesson is related to the last one. In an HFT driven era, liquidity is really scarce, lots of firms have strategies to try to detect big orders and then make these orders get executed at worse prices. **Always know how big a position you can take and try to be on the safe side because you are harmed asymmetrically by mistakes.** You will hurt yourself a lot more by having a position that is 4 times what it should be (given the available liquidity) than one that is 2 times what it should be. You are likely to be harmed by more than 100 percent in comparison (It would be 100 percent if there was not asymmetry) by making the larger mistake due the efficiency in which HFT firms can detect bigger orders and the mechanics of auction markets[24]. It's a much bigger problem to have someone discover your intention to liquidate your position if you are several multiples of the available liquidity because now they can "squeeze" you (whether you are long or short). They can now find the highest price you are willing to pay or lowest price you are willing to offer (your "squeeze price") and get your order done there. With bigger positions there is more time for you to be detected (as you work your order) and more volume to be done closer to your maximum squeeze price. If you didn't understand this lesson, keep reading until you do.

---

[24] In an auction market, the price is set by the highest price a buyer is willing to pay and the lower price a seller is willing to offer.

9. Never show your hand. Be careful with "SMART" order routers, a lot of the time these routers don't even have a Thor like system behind them, which means they constantly give HFTs a chance to cancel orders and make you pay more to get your orders done. The issue is that even if they do, these routers can be gamed by HFTs because they have a set criteria of how to route to multiple pools of liquidity all at the same time. Lots of times they count on a stable relationship in the time that it takes to send the orders from the broker to the ECNs — exchanges. It will try to send the multiple orders in the exact time difference between them so they all hit those pools at the same time (at the millisecond level), taking all the displayed liquidity without allowing the HFTs to cancel their orders. When the relationship changes (due to tricks such as quote stuffing, essentially bombarding an ECN or exchange with orders and modifications), the router can backfire and end up exposing your buy or sell interest. Another issue with these smart routers is that they sometimes will hit dark pools first before going to displayed exchanges, some of these dark pools might be tipping off HFTs about incoming orders and this will allow them to cancel and make you pay more. How can you deal with this issue? That's where lesson 10 comes in.

10. Direct routing can be pretty effective when trying to move size. If you're trying to work out a larger order, try directly routing to an ECN or exchange that's displaying the larger size. Take it out and see how the price reacts. As Eric says, sometimes by waiting a bit, you will see some recharging of bids and asks, which allows you to continue to work your order. It can be a costly mistake to try to get out of size all at once with a SMART router. You could be better off using direct routing to certain pools in order to avoid showing your hand. If you must use a SMART router at least make sure it has a Thor-like algorithm to try to prevent exposing your

hand to HFTs, the difference between different brokerages smart routers can be enormous, you would be surprised how often these routers don't even have that basic technology. Experiment with both and see what works best for you.

11. Gold can provide you with tells or clues of incoming economic releases. Due to its international nature and liquidity, gold is used by people who get leaked news. It's likely to have happened in the FOMC no-taper announcement. The folks who get the data ahead of time, in an effort to hide their activities, will buy gold in Europe, Asia, Middle East or any market where they have anonymity. Due to arbitrage, that buying will show up in GLD, CME Gold, etc. Anyone who read correctly the gold rally on the FOMC no-taper day could have made millions buying the S&P 500 futures, all legally, since this is simply a speculative opinion about a public price.

Chapter 6

Mitch Semon – The Veteran Stock Operator

Mitch (twitter @mitchthemoney) has been trading for a really long time. He has a lot of experience dealing with all kinds of markets and has pretty much seen it all when it comes to stock trading.

After working for a decade as a market maker, he made the move to prop trading, initially using other people's capital to trade. I didn't notice it during the interview process, but as I got into transcription and editing, I realized that he'd been a bit guarded about sharing too much information about how he trades. I suppose this is normal during tough times in the markets, and it further reinforces the main lesson from chapter 9. Even being a bit guarded, he did provided significant insights and lessons that I found helpful.

This interview was conducted in January of 2013.

When did you decide you wanted become a trader?

I'd just come out of college, then I got hired at OLDE Discount, which was a discount brokerage firm. I worked at OLDE for maybe ten or eleven years until I got moved to H&R Block, and then we got bought out. After 9/11 they didn't like the risk of that firm, so they eliminated their trading force. I was a market maker, like a New

York specialist, with them for ten or eleven years, and I was actually the head of the listed equity desk for last year before they shut it down. Then we got laid off. I didn't really want to move to New York, Florida, or Texas. I decided to start trading on my own. So I've been doing it probably for eight or nine years on my own now.

So you were a standard market maker back then?

Yes.

How do you see the computers that do that job right now? They seem to make the markets, but they don't have the obligations that you guys had.

That's the problem. The spreads used to be large. Then we went to teenies, then to pennies, once it got there it just wasn't worth it for the New York specialist anymore. So what that did was to make the market thinner, take volume away, like the NASDAQ now. These computers put bids and offers in, but they're not really making markets. They're not ready to stand by whatever they're showing. The computers now are just throwing stuff and moving it, putting the bids and taking them away really fast. That's why we have more things like flash crashes now. There's no one ready to step up when liquidity dries up. Before, a market maker would step up. These days there's too much risk and not enough profit. It's not worth it. For me, that's the biggest problem with the electronic trading now — they're not there to stand by a market. They're interested in making a profit. But a market maker's job was not only to make money, but also to make a good market.

Back then in the '90s, was it easy to make the markets and make money every day?

For the most part, yeah. When we made markets, we had order flow also, which helps make you money, because you it helps in capturing the spread. And we had somewhat bigger spreads, especially on the NASDAQ where they had different rules. They could do whatever they wanted. On New York, it was pretty well written what you had to do. It was pretty easy to make money every day.

When markets went to decimals, did you immediately give up on the idea of making markets and try to develop a new strategy?

No, because I was with the company. We were still making markets, and it was still pretty profitable. We did a report from before they shut us down, and it showed how profitable we were. It was still profitable business, just not as much as in the past. And like I said, we had 9/11 and a few things that made the risk outweigh the rewards, because there were lawsuits starting to happen at that time due for people not getting prints or people doing funny things with the orders. Not necessarily at our firm, but just street wide. H&R Block bought us out, and they didn't know the risks involved, they didn't want to delve into it and figure out if it was risky or not. You still could have made it in market making back then, but it was getting harder, and the profit margin was getting squeezed big time.

And what college did you attend?

Oregon State. I was in finance.

Do you think the knowledge there helped you?

It helped a little bit, but I think it's more of a personality trait than anything. I think you can't really learn how to trade. You know, it's kind of in your blood to trade or it's not. I don't think it's something you can pick up by reading it in a book. It takes a certain type of temperament and frame of mind to be able to do this.

After they closed down the trading division there, you moved immediately into a prop firm?

I traded on my own a little bit with Ameritrade. I had a no-compete clause for one year, so I couldn't go anywhere else. I traded in that period, taking longer term views of the market. And when that time expired, I actually went to two other firms. Short-term trading prop firms.

What was the main reason that you wanted to go prop? Was it the leverage or being able to be next to other traders and learn from them?

We were working for companies at that time — prop firm for the company, trying to make money for them. So we were using their money. And that was the main reason. If you do blow up or you do have an issue, it's much easier. It's not your own cash.

How long did you have the advantage of trading on their cash?

Probably a couple of years. I did it with two different firms, and it probably lasted a total of two years, probably about a year each.

And back then, what was the way to make money?

A lot of time, I pull up a lot of stocks by sector. And whatever news is out, you find a hot stock and you find some of the laggards and the others in the same sector. So if somebody had good news, you pulled the whole sector and just traded off the stocks and didn't quite pick up the same momentum that they had.

Like sympathy plays?

Right, yeah. Sympathy plays. It was a hot news of the day strategy. I was basically a high frequency trader back then. The market is very different now. It still wasn't as computerized as it is now. A lot of big levels would have a sell stop, so they would blow through whole numbers. You could put these sized bids in. When it hit the number, it would gap. We still had gap prints, which we don't have anymore. So that was an easy trade to make, quick money.

When did you start to notice that the markets had become more difficult?

Markets became more difficult in the last two years for sure. Two and a half years.

So you had a ten-year period in which it was good for you?

Seven to eight years.

Why did it become more difficult?

Two reasons: the computers and the volatility. Volatility is what all day traders live for, and when the volatility has just gotten killed like it has, it's really hard. And then you add the computers on top of that. It seems like they're controlling these thin stocks out there.

So after Reg NMS, you didn't notice anything. It took a few years for things to get harder?

Right, yes. But like I said, we had huge volatility at that point, which still made it easier for a trader to make money.

It was mostly momentum trading, what you were doing?

No. I usually did revision to mean. So when something got too far oversold one way or the other, I used to trade.

Is it like STZ today?

Like RIMM this morning when it just sold off hard. When it accelerates in the downside, I start buying small and as it gets lower you buy more and you profit on the way back up. That's how I used to trade a lot.

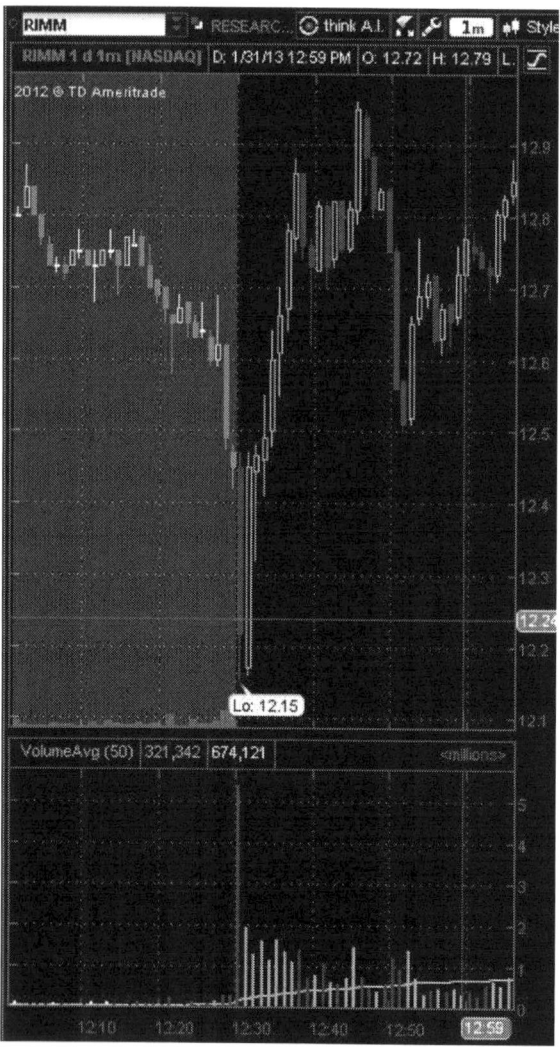

Source: Thinkorswim platform

A lot of traders say you're not supposed to trade mid-day, but sometimes I find that if there's news, it becomes a good opportunity, ike STZ. It's mid-day, but it's down a lot, and it's probably going to bounce.

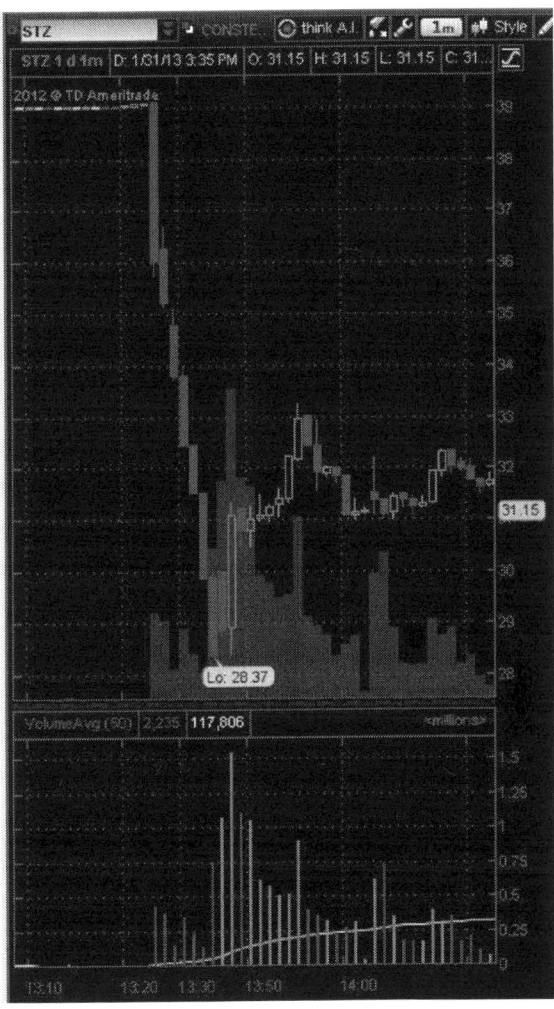

Source: Thinkorswim platform

Yeah, I played that a little bit today. A lot of it these days is picking news stocks because you need the volatility. If you don't have it, it's really hard to trade in this market, because these computers can just move the stock back and forth. Unless you have strong conviction about the position, it's hard to keep it. I'm trading more now on breakout levels, 200 moving average, finding levels that will give me more conviction in what I'm doing. Before I use to trade the momentum, oversold or overbought stuff and took the other side. With the computers, it's more of a trend thing. You have to go with the trend more.

Given that you do these news plays, don't you find that it's worth it to invest in more expensive news services?

When I'm trading the news, I'm trading more to see the stock. I'm not quick enough to see the news and understand it. As soon as the news hit STZ, they already moved the stock a ton. Same thing with earnings. As soon as it hits, they move the stock and you have to figure out if it's overdone or not. Hearing the story first is great if you can do it, but everybody gets the story at the same time, and the computers are already doing what they're programmed to do.

So you're not trying to compete with them in that game?

They're way faster than I am, and they're going to understand it faster. What I'm waiting for is for the computer to make a mistake, like in STZ today, where they just take the news and keep beating a stock down. The computers feed off themselves because they don't know what's going on. They just follow the momentum.

Do you use Twitter a lot to get a sense of what is going on?

I follow some people on StockTwitts to get a sense of what they're looking at, what they're doing. I don't tweet anything, but I do follow some people just to get an idea of what they like in the market. Helps me find some trading ideas. It also helps me with research so I can piggyback on other people's research. If someone says some levels are breaking out, I'll pull up on my chart and see if it's something that I'd like to pull into my watch list for that day.

When you gave up on market making and moved to retail or prop, were you profitable right away, or did it take awhile?

No, I've always been profitable. Of course, there are days that you're not. I've probably had a couple of months in my ten years that I was not profitable, but the rest of them I made money.

Do you think right now is probably the toughest time for someone to start?

Yes, this definitely has been my toughest time in twenty years, mainly because the volatility is low and the markets are being run by the computers. It's a double whammy. As I said, right now you have to play news stories, and it's hard to decipher exactly what the news is and how it will impact the stock in real time, so you're taking a little more risk.

So you found that your time frame had to be widened out a bit? You can't get in and out so quickly?

I do both. I try to not carry stuff overnight, because you never know what can happen, but I definitely do sometimes.

Do you backtest your strategies?

I don't do any backtesting.

You just learn on the fly?

I traded as a market maker for ten years and did it on my own for another ten, so I know what I see when I see it. It's hard to teach somebody, it's a matter of being in the market for so long.

Are the any similarities between the current market and the markets back then?

This is kind like what we saw in the NASDAQ during the tech boom. Back then the market makers would just keep stepping away, because the stocks were just going nuts. Everybody would just keep buying and the market maker would just keep moving his bids and offers up so the stocks would just move insane amounts. I think we see some of that in stocks these days.

Do you think because you had all those years watching the markets, you built up an instinct that tells you when something is overextended, it's too low, too high, etc.?

Right, just watching, you can get a feel for the market. You have to put in the time. If anyone is thinking of getting into day trading, they have to just sit and trade a dummy account for a long time just to get a feel for it. The people that are jumping in right away, they might get lucky a little bit, but it's hard to be right consistently.

Do you make most of your money at the open?

Open, the close, and the after-hours.

After hours for earnings and things like that?

Earnings, news, or just market making. Sometimes you find people who to have to get out of positions, and I'll take the other side. I do it in stocks that don't have a lot of risk.

With regards to executing orders, do you find yourself being screwed over by the computers many times?

You can see that if you put an order in, you get front run a lot, usually before the open and after the close. Sometime they'll penny jump you.

One thing I noticed is that in the premarket they use a lot of EDGX to make markets, because they know you can't use a hidden order with that route, so it prevents some tricks a trader could play on them. Do you use stuff like hidden orders?

I will use a hidden order if I want to buy some stock and there's an order in front of me and he keeps penny jumping me. I might go ahead and put a hidden order, but I don't do that a lot.

Do you take liquidity most of the time?

I do both. We get paid to post an order on most exchanges, so it's more beneficial to post instead of lifting, but obviously, in the news stories and trades like that I will lift, or if I want to get out of something, I'll just hit what I see. In other types of trades I'll post.

In these news stories, sometimes I find that it's good to post. Like in STZ, it was already down so much that sometimes it dropped more, hit you, and then bounced right back.

Right. Another thing I do because the market is more momentum driven is to use buy stops or sell stops.

In those days where the markets just keep going, it looks so easy to make money. You just buy the dip and cash it. Is it really as easy as it looks?

It's easy if you can do it. As I said, I tend to be more countertrend so it's hard for me. I'm having a harder time in the last year. It's a slow creep up, and I'm just not used to doing that. It does look easy. You see a lot of those people on StockTwitts, or whatever, that do go with the momentum. They're just buying with small size, so they don't get rid of it if it does pullback, and then they let it run.

Do you think this is a sign of complacency—that everybody is so comfortable with the markets and buying the dip that we're headed to a crash or volatility expansion?

I think we could be, but a lot of that has to do with the Fed just pumping up money. All the stocks are just propped up by money. When the Fed puts that much liquidity in the economy it has to go somewhere. It's going to bonds, which are headed to a crash, and they're putting in stocks, which over inflates its true value.

In 2008, when there was a lot of volatility, did you do well there?

Yes, that was my best year.

You just shorted bounces?

I bought sharp moves down and shorted large up moves.

You believe it was easy in that year because there were so many fund managers in the market distorting prices?

Right. It was the movement, for one thing, and because there were so many different players and lots of disparities in the market.

These fund managers seem not to care about a few cents. Does this benefit the day traders?

Yeah, these fund managers just don't care about a few cents. The machines are different. That's what they're playing for.

Sometimes I see intraday that, at a key support or resistance level, a fund manager will be sitting there with a huge order. Aren't they just giving money away doing that?

No, because if they have a level that they want to get in or out at, they don't care if they're wrong in the short-term. For instance, if a manager wants to get STZ at $32, he doesn't care if he buys it. It goes to $31.75, and he had to overpay a bit. If he wants to buy a million shares, he can just post at $32 and sit there all day until he gets his size done. He knows where he wants to enter the stock. He's giving away a little bit of money, but he's also happy he got the price he wanted. That's what his goal was. In the long-term, 20 cents doesn't make a difference for hedge funds.

Can a human take advantage of that, or is it just for the computers?

If you know the guy is there and he has an order, he's usually not going to show that kind of size. We used to have people on the floor that would give us an idea what the order books looked like.

What is your take on subpenny trades?

They need to get rid of that. There should be no off-exchange trades. It's hard enough with a one-penny, and it really doesn't provide much price improvement.

What other advantages you believe should be stripped away from the HFTs?

Off-exchange trades is the main one. I can sit in a stock as best bid and ask, and I still see plenty of volume going through off exchange, and I don't get those fills.

Through all of the years in your trading and in prop firms, what's the biggest characteristic you noticed in winning traders?

The biggest characteristic is that they knew how to take losses. It's easy to make money, but it's hard to take a loss. If you see something going up and you like it, you buy it, but what do you do when it turns? Do you double up? Do you ride it? That's the hardest part — knowing when to cut your losses and limiting your losses.

Do you think it's easier for you because you have a long history of making money? A new guy doesn't have that confidence, and he might have bills to pay, so he has to deal with a bigger psychological pressure.

Yeah, I had ten years as a market maker and many years using other people's money before I had to use my own money, and by then I knew I was a successful trader and I could do it. If you're starting out, if you make money, that's fine, but if you lose, it puts you in a hole and a bad mental frame. It does make it a lot tougher. You might step off what you normally should do, try to make it back. It's similar to what a gambling addiction would be. If you're behind, you might start pressing your bets, and that's a bad way to trade. If you have a big loss one day, that's life. You just have to go back to your normal trading and not try to recoup it all in one big swing.

Are you confident that you'll continue to make money in the next five and ten years?

Yes. It definitely has gotten worse, but I assume the volatility will pick up some. I don't think it will pick up anytime soon, but I believe the markets will get a bit shakier if the Fed will quit flooding the markets with money.

Are you concerned that the computers will get so good that they'll start to take profits away even in longer-term time frames?

No, value wins out always. If a stock is worth X, it will get there. If you like a stock and do your homework, the value will shine through eventually. What the computers do is take stocks that people like, such as Apple, and when everybody is pounding it higher, the computers extend that run a bit more than what it should have been. You essentially have a bit more boom and bust.

So they just exacerbate daily volatility?

In certain stocks, yes.

And the edge lies in fading these extremes?

Yes, it's hard now without other people in there, because liquidity is thin. The computer doesn't know that. It just knows that it went up, so it wants to get long. And then it goes up more, and then others want to get on. You can see that, when it's really thin and nothing else is happening, the computers control the stock. They'll throw fake bids and fake offers to make it move around a little bit, but for the most part, there's not a lot happening. Most people take the lunch time off, because there's not a lot happening, but when there are news plays, its worthwhile trading. It's the same thing with the market in general. Back then the down period during lunch time is like the whole time today. We used to have a lot more volatility in the open and the close.

Some people are concerned that the computers can tell when there's an area full of stops and they can trigger that to mess with people. Do you think they do?

They do.

Do you get stop hunted sometimes?

Yeah, they'll go down to trigger something they see. I believe they pay for that. I think they see that ahead of time. That's for sure something they're doing.

So you don't use hard stops?

I do use some ARCA or NSDQ stops, and they'll still trigger then, but sometimes you have to use them. In super thin stocks I don't use them, because they'll go there and trigger them on purpose. In more liquid stocks it's not a big issue.

How much of your trading is instinct compared to logic?

Probably 70 percent are breakouts, moving averages, news, etc., and 30 percent is just gut.

Do you use moving averages to figure out what other people are thinking?

I use them to know some breakout levels. Whether it's right or wrong, they do move the stock. Fundamentally it doesn't make a difference, but technically it does. Stocks react to that, the computers react, Twitter and day traders do too. It's a self-fulfilling prophecy kind of thing.

Which MA are most people paying attention to?

I don't know — 30, 50, 200 day.

So you don't use intraday MAs? You use daily MAs?

Yes, for important support and resistance levels. I have friends that do use intraday MAs, but I don't.

Some traders I know found that moving away from one-minute charts was useful in an HFT-driven market. Is that something that you found as well?

No, I just use one-minute charts.

Do you pay attention to longer time frames?

I'm watching basically the same stocks every day so I don't need to, except for news stocks, for those I will pull up a longer-term chart, because you don't want to be in the opposite side of something that's a big move. For the ninety stocks that I watch regularly, I just know from watching them every day and seeing what their ranges are.

So you have a set of stocks that you watch every day and try to learn from. Then every once in a while you'll put a trade in?

Yes. I'll also trade whatever the news is, whatever is hot or is moving. These stocks I'm not as familiar with, so I'll need more information from longer-term charts.

Do you think that by watching those same stocks every day you accumulate knowledge that gives you an edge over other people?

Yeah. You know the general range of what the stock does. If $1 or $0.30 that is the normal for it, you get more comfortable taking positions when it reaches one of those two bands.

For instance, on the Knight debacle day, REE, which normally trades in a narrow range, just quickly dropped over a dollar and kept bouncing 20 to 40 cents and selling off. I liked being long down there and made really good fast money without much risk.

Do you use the Level 2 to predict, to make decisions? Or does it not matter anymore?

It doesn't make that much difference, I do use it and watch it, but there's a lot of BS too. They put stuff then take it away. I use it, but it's not as indicative of what it used to be.

In the old days you could use it to predict a lot of moves, right?

Right, that's what the computers are doing now by paying to see all of our orders ahead of time. They see the orders, and they're front running. Back then, if you saw a big bid or offer somewhere, you'd sit in front of it and have a stop to lean on. You could make money if it went up, or lose a penny if it went down. Now the books aren't what they used to be.

Would you say the same thing about tape reading?

Tape reading is more of a feel thing.

Do you think there can still be an advantage there?

Yes, there's definitely an advantage there. You can see if someone keeps refreshing and the pace at which they're doing it, and you can kind of see when they get cleaned up. Let's say a stock is down a lot. When you feel the seller has been cleaned up, you want to be back in there, because it will probably bounce.

So you try to get a sense if there's a big fund that's liquidating or accumulating?

Yeah, it used to be a lot easier. It has gotten a lot hard in the last couple of years.

Sometimes it seems that you can tell a big fund manager is liquidating just by looking at the chart. You see a stock with bad earnings going down over quite an extended period of time, and it hardly bounces. Could that be an indication?

Right. Like I said, most of the fund managers, if they have a target or something has changed in their perspective, they don't care what the price is. They'll just get out of their position. If they don't like earnings, or they were expecting a certain amount of growth, if it doesn't achieve what they want, a lot of times their whole view on the stock changes, and they just want out.

I think I saw that the other day on AAPL after earnings. In the middle of the day, it just went straight down with hardly a bounce.

It looked like easy money. Just short, and these guys will continue to sell.

Yeah, before it used to be different. Now it's easier to go with the trend, because you got the computers, the funds, the day traders — everyone is doing the same thing. It becomes like a self-fulfilling prophecy. I'm not as used to those plays, so it's harder for me to get onboard with that. I'm more of a countertrend guy. I'm trying to adapt to that a little bit. You have to keep adapting to these market changes. You have to try new strategies, new ways to trade.

During earning season though, it gets a bit better, right?

Yeah, there's more news, volatility, a little more movement in the whole market. Earnings season definitely helps.

With regards to reading the news and interpreting it, doesn't your finance background help on that?

It does, but I don't try to pretend to be smarter than all the funds out there. I'm probably better than most of the day traders, but for all the mutual funds and hedge funds that have positions and are reacting to that news immediately, I assume they know more than I know. Also, the news we see is not exactly the real news. You can see news stories that are wrong. Some are fraudulent, and some are stated incorrectly.

What kind of machine setup do you have?

I'm not really tech savvy. I have three computers, eight monitors.

Why so many?

I have my platforms that I trade on two, six have charts, and one of them has news as well. I have Fly on the Wall, Briefing, StockTwitts, so I can see what news is coming.

Do you trade inside a prop firm or do you trade from home?

From home.

You don't find that it's worth it to go to the prop firm?

I'm on Skype all day with people that I used to trade with at OLDE, so it's like sitting next to them. It definitely helps to have people to bounce ideas around. It's also good to have more eyes to see when something is moving. If I didn't have that, I'd probably prefer to go to a prop firm.

In the period that you were in the firm, did you learn a lot from others?

You definitely learn, but everyone has their own style and their own risk tolerance. You can see someone make $100,000 every day, and you think all you have to do is to mimic him, but you have a different risk tolerance and it just doesn't work. Sometimes you try to do what others do, and you just don't have the same feel for it, because they have a different style of trading. You can learn stuff from others, but you can't just trade like somebody else.

Why do you think you were able to adapt to changing conditions while lots of other traders weren't able to do?

The biggest thing is that you don't want to get too stubborn. Take your losses and move on. The markets are constantly evolving. There will always be something new. You have to adapt, otherwise you'll be left behind.

Do you think it helped that you were humble about the market?

Probably, because I've seen it all happen. I've seen plenty of people blowup, have big losses, and end their careers. Seeing that definitely makes you more aware of what can happen. It also makes you a bit more risk averse, which can hurt your profits too. During the Internet boom, I didn't care to play any of those stocks that people were making a killing on.

What's the biggest loss you ever had?

My biggest loss was working for a firm. A big loss is usually something that moves really quickly, so fast that you can't logically get out of it. Like on STZ, if I was long at $39 and the news came out, and it was at $34, $33, and then I bought more and it then went to $32, $31, $29 — it's too fast and I wouldn't be able to take a loss at that point. I'd be stuck playing my average instead of doing what I should be doing, which is cutting the losses after a certain amount no matter what. If a trade blows through those limits, it's hard to do that, you're nowhere near where you wanted to take your loss.

I believe I lost $200,000 for the firm once. We had a minicrash. I was long on big name stocks, but the market makers were backing away. These big name stocks were dropping a buck or two bucks with every print, kind of like a flash crash.

During these flash crashes these days, I find hard to trade, because you don't know if there's news out that you are not aware of.

Right, right. If it's an individual stock, it's a lot more risky. If it's market-wide, it's a little easier to handle, because you know it's probably an exaggeration or a matter of computers chasing computers. In a single stock, you just never know what the news could be.

Do you step in every once in a while in a specific stock in a flash crash type decline?

Yeah, like STZ today, you have to pick your spots and start small. Normally you shouldn't average in a bad position, but in this case you're just saying it's an overplay on something and you average in. You just don't want to get too big too fast.

During the mid-day, do you just sit and wait for the news plays?

I actually try to walk away from my computer. I trade from 7 to 11 in the morning (EST), then come back at maybe 2:30. I try to take that mid-day off unless the market is active with news, maybe the Fed or something. I find that I get in trouble if I sit at the computer during the mid-day.

In the premarket, do you trade the ARCA/NSDQ premarket or mostly after BATS and everybody else comes online?[25]

I trade right from the start, the ARCA/NSDQ premarket.

Usually news plays as well?

Yeah. I'll put bids in stocks that I like. In premarket, some people can get nervous, and sometimes they'll sell it quite a bit away from where the real market is simply because there's no liquidity. In that case, no liquidity is a good thing.

You just try to capture the spread a little bit there?

Yes, try to capture when somebody gets nervous about the market or they don't like their position. Every once in a while I'll get hurt because there will be news coming out that I didn't know about, but for the most part I just try to capture that wider spread than there is during the regular trading day. Same thing with after the close.

Sometimes you can catch people in the ex-div days, if a stock goes ex-div for $1 and you put an offer at where it closed and get hit while in theory the stock should trade $1 lower than the close.

---

[25] ARCA and NSDQ pre-market session start at 4AM EST while BATS, EDGX and a number of ECNs come online at 8AM EST.

What kind of advice do you give to a novice or struggling trader right now?

My biggest advice is just sit down and study the market for a while. Do test trading. Don't put real money until you're comfortable with what you're dealing with. When you do go with real money, start small and learn to cut your losses. Take whatever you can afford to play with, and don't use more than that. If you want to be around, cut your losses well before you hit your personal limits.

Why did you decide that you wanted to trade equities instead of something else?

I don't know. I wanted to be an investment banker when I finished college, but then I got into trading and I liked it. It fits my temperament and my style. I enjoy what I do. It doesn't feel like a job; it feels like fun for me.

Over the years that you traded, did you have a lot of strategies that you discarded?

Yes, like I said, the markets are constantly evolving. As long as it's working, I don't try to change it, but when it starts to slow down, like right now, I try a few different strategies.

Do you use top-of-the-line, expensive software for charts and everything, or will anything work?

I use QuoteTracker, which is free, and it does a pretty good job for the charting. I use Bigcharts for longer-term, but you definitely need good charts and good news services.

US markets have pretty low volatility right now, but have you ever thought about trading different global markets where volatility is higher? Maybe Europe or somewhere?

We thought about that, but I've watched this market for twenty years. I know it pretty well. I'd be open to that, but I'm not there right now, because I don't have the need for it.

Lessons from Chapter 6

1. The ability to take losses is the most important characteristic Mitch noticed in winning traders he saw over the years, and he's been trading for over twenty years. Chapter 11 provides some advice on how to improve your loss-taking abilities.

2. When the markets are not really providing good opportunities, you have to focus more on news plays. They tend to attract retail traders, fund managers, etc. This provides you with an opportunity to interact with non-HFT order flow. They cause volatility to rise as well.

3. After a big loss, don't try to make it all back in one swing. Go back to your normal trading, and build your account back up. I know it's hard to do. People get addicted to progress and growth. Having a big loss is quite a setback to a rising P&L. The natural human instinct is to try to fix that by continuing to play larger. That's a mistake, because you will be trading bigger when your mental capital is the most depleted. (Large losses are mentally destabilizing even for great traders.) Your judgment will be at its worst, but your risk exposure at its highest. This combination simply doesn't make sense.

4. Try to develop your trading style so it becomes more robust. This lesson applies to solid winning traders only. Mitch mentioned how he is more of a counter-trend trader and was struggling to just

jump in trends and ride them out. He was making an effort to adapt to that however. The lesson is to try to develop your trading skillset so you can be great at a few things (your main strengths, these are the ones you nail with large size) and at least good at the rest (where you play with small to medium size). If you are a short seller, try to push yourself to buy more stocks even if it feels strange, if you are a long based trader try shorting more. The same can be said about trend following and reversion to the mean traders. We all had setups and trading situations where we highly suspect something is about to happen but have a hard time getting in because it's not how we are used to trade. By pushing yourself to trade in these situations you will get more comfortable and develop a more robust trading skillset, you will be ready for different market conditions. The stability of your trading income is likely to improve as well. There are plenty of periods where your main strengths don't come into play due market conditions, by having a robust skillset you can still make money while you wait for these conditions to improve.

5. HFTs and electronic trading cause momentum to be more persistent and overshoot. Computers can exacerbate these trends. You can profit by jumping into these trends and using a trailing mental stop, or you can wait for them to get really extreme then fade them. For fades, the ideal entry point is when the price action starts to accelerate in the direction of the trend, like in the RIMM trade.

6. Avoid stocks that are controlled by HFTs. They tend to be small and mid-cap stocks that aren't news plays. They have larger spreads and tend to be illiquid. The price action is much noisier. You will get tested a lot, and it will be hard to keep your position.

7. Be careful with hard stops. Mitch believes HFTs can see where they are because they have access to the order books. They're OK in liquid issues (like GE or liquid ETFs like SPY).

8. Have a set of stocks that you watch regularly. This will help you get familiar with their ranges, typical behaviors and patterns. You'll develop a sense of how they'll act on a particular day, and you'll be able to tell when they're overreacting or when they're cheap compared to everything else. This can be quite profitable at the open, because that's where a lot of the temporary price distortions occur.

9. Leaning on big orders is a dangerous game these days, since HFTs will often put fake size on the Level 2. In the old days you could try to be in front of that order, knowing it would provide an out for you. These days this game is way more dangerous. Even if the order is real, the HFTs will know when that order will get cleaned. Then they'll take out the rest of that order and several levels below that before you even have time to blink.

10. Big money managers usually don't care about 20 cents or so, and this provides an opportunity for day traders. The key is to put yourself in situations where you're interacting with them more and with HFTs less. Since these guys have to get their orders done, if you can anticipate how they'll act, you can profit. This is what academics miss about winning day traders when they claim they are just lucky coin flippers, they are actually really good at extracting profits off these big money managers by using tools like charts, L2, tape, orderbooks, etc.

11. Try to keep contact with a group of traders through Skype so you can bounce trade ideas off each other, share breaking news, and learn from each other's mistakes. You might also notice some

methods other good traders are using to adapt to changing market conditions, and this can speed up your own adjustments.

12. In bounce plays, average in slowly with small size to start. The computers can exacerbate these trends, and if you get in big too fast, you could face a devastating loss. The STZ trade provided a good example of that. The stock declined from $39 to $28 in about ten minutes. This is different from averaging down, because it's all part of your plan, and it respects position size and loss limits. By averaging in you can make a mistake or two in terms of timing and still be ok, when you buy all in one shot you leave a lot of room for you to get hurt.

13. Walk away from the computer mid-day. When there are no great plays around, try to leave your computer. This is especially important to struggling traders or people who lack discipline.

Chapter 7

Wayne Kulcheski — The Trend Fighter

One of the first things I noticed about Wayne's (twitter @trendfighter) trading style is how his mind seems to be immersed in the idea of mean reversion. It's as if his mind works in such a way as to give him the confidence that price contrarianism is the way to go. He frequently uses terms like *never, it's ridiculous, always,* and *forever.* These types of strong opinions seem to support him mentally when he has to fight trends in the markets and put a big position against the price action.

Trends can be powerful. They can capture people's imaginations and greed, which can frequently result in financial ruin when they reverse. It takes a certain mindset to resist falling for them. Wayne possesses that mindset, and he's a true contrarian.

At the same time, he's a longtime winner at trading, and anyone trading for so long is also mindful of risk management and the importance of knowing when to get out. Wayne balances the strong mindset and beliefs necessary to be skeptical of certain trends with the ability to pull back, protect trading capital, and live to fight for another day.

This interview was conducted in August of 2012 and updated in November of 2013.

What made you want to become a trader?

I guess the initial attraction to trading was to make as much money as humanly possible. I guess the sky's the limit if you can get a handle on it. I was always fascinated by the markets themselves. Of course, being able to create your own schedule was quite appealing. It gives me the chance to have a life other than working nine to five every day.

Which year did you start?

I started in 2001.

So you came after decimalization?

Yeah, they just switched to decimals, and they had the big NASDAQ bubble collapse, and we were just close to the bottom of that.

When you started, were you comfortable with short selling right away, or did you have to adapt to that?

No, I was comfortable right away. I just considered it the same as buying, really. I started at a prop firm in Canada, and they didn't really educate their people a lot, but they gave us very strict guidelines. We were only allowed to lose a few pennies per share. We just tried to make a few cents every trade, over and over again. At that time it was a little bit easier because, even though it was decimals, there were still spreads, and on top of that there was a lot of activity in both sides of the market.

Were you profitable right off the bat or did it take some time?

It actually took two months for me to become profitable. In order to get a full-time position in this job, a person had to make $5,000 net. I believe in my third month I ended up making $10,000 or $11,000, and I've been profitable ever since. I worked at that firm for maybe three years, but the profit split just wasn't enough. We were making between 35 percent and 50 percent of our profits. It was much better for me to go off on my own and get a better deal where I would keep more of my profits. That's what I did, and a bunch of other people in the office did the same.

Why did you go to a prop firm in the first place?

Primarily because I was twenty years old and I didn't have a lot of money to get started — the $25,000 minimum required and all that. I saw an ad for a prop firm that didn't have that many requirements, because prop trading was new at the time. I applied to all of the branches in my province, and I got a call the next day from a branch that wasn't in my home town but I moved there. If I was older and had more money I would probably have started on my own, but at least this firm provided an access to the market without me having to pay any commissions, so it was helpful.

Do you think that starting at prop and having contact with other traders helped you gain a sense of what worked and what didn't?

Well, because we were all new at this and no one had that much experience, it did help to talk and brainstorm with other people — trade off other peoples' ideas. It did provide us a good base to start to trade in our own styles and help each other. It was beneficial, for sure.

And back then, the main strategy was just scalping — buying at the bid and selling at the ask?

Yes, that was basically all we did. I started trading simple stocks too. I didn't go around on different stocks or follow trends or currencies/commodities. I just stuck with trading Cisco, Sun Microsystems, Intel, stuff like that. It was relatively easy to make money scalping, so there was no reason to venture into anything else.

When did you notice that this type of trading stopped working?

You know, even to this day I still do a lot of scalping. I have a few different accounts that I trade by different strategies. It's harder now, because the market has completely changed. There's not as much liquidity in the market. There are a lot more institutional orders and dark books that I can't really take advantage of. We can't get access to those fills. Whereas before, all of those fills would have to be delivered through an ECN or through the NYSE, now they're just these big blocks of stocks that just go off at these crazy prices. It's very hard now to get in and out of decent sized positions.

Yeah, just today I had an issue with a stock. I put a hidden bid, and a bunch of orders were going to hit me. Before they did, the HFT filled me for like twelve shares. He found out where I was, and he went to the level, got filled for all the market orders, and I was stuck for twelve shares.

Yes, that happens a lot of the times. You get pinged for 12 shares or 100 shares. It's hard, because I can tell you that so many times during the day I have a decent size position, and let's say I have an offer there to sell at some level. The number of times it comes right to my price and stops there — it's ridiculous. It's almost as if your order will not get executed unless the HFT guy can get a better price than your order. It's like no one is going to buy your 10,000 shares at $9 unless they know they'll get $9.02 or $9.05 or whatever, because they know the order flow.

Can't you use native hidden orders to try to disguise your hand?

I use hidden orders all the time. I use iceberg orders all the time. I also have access to a few dark books. I have NITE dark book and Credit Suisse dark book. These two are excellent sources of liquidity because, essentially, if you're trying to sell a stock, if you're trading Apple at, say, $600, and the spread is 20 cents, what you can do is put an order on the cross finder to sell. You're not displayed anywhere. Apparently nobody knows you're there, and you can get price improvement. You can get filled on the far end of the spread if you have the order in. Sometimes, you'll see trades going on the offer in the ECNs without filling you in the dark book, but almost every time, you get an even better fill in the dark book.

Is this solution of accessing dark books available for most people?

No, for anybody who trades through retail, through IB or Scottrade, there's no way to have access, but through one of the platforms I use, I can route through the dark books, but I only have access to a couple, and there's a lot of action going on in the market that I don't have access to — lots of action.

So how are you able to scalp these days? Lots of traders say they moved away from that in recent years because they just can't compete with the HFT programs.

Over the last three years, a lot of the traders I know have stopped trading, mostly because they can't make money or they consistently lose money. I would say scalping has become tougher, but I'd say all types of trading have become a lot harder. The usual technical patterns and indicators that we used to use don't really apply anymore, because the problem with the HFT is that if you're in just a random stock, making a market, trading it, and let's say some news hits, by the time that happens, the HFTs have repriced the stock, deciphered the news, and know what the new price is. So if it was trading at $14, it will just trade to $15 instantly and then trade millions and millions of shares. This all happens before I even get the news or know what's going on.

I've got news feeds, I've got Squawk Box, I've got everything, but by the time I get it, the HFTs already know how much things are now worth. Before, you'd have news and it would slowly get disseminated, you'd see gradual buying, you could jump on and ride the wave. Now there's no wave, just a big spike, and that's it — done. Sometimes the HFTs overreact, so you can make money taking the opposite side of the trade because there's no time to get on the trend. A lot of the times you have to bet the other way. I have a scanner that scans for HFT programs. That gives me a bunch of stock symbols and tells me how many trades and how many quotes were put in that stock at that second. I can see there were 250 trades in that last second, so I know there was HFT activity there. I can go to that stock to try to figure out what's happening, but it's difficult. Another problem is that all of the news that's been driving the markets in the last six to eight months are from Europe, so there's no possible way we can get the news before somebody else does.

You mentioned that scanner for HFTs. That must have triggered a lot during the Knight trading debacle, didn't it?

That scanner is separate from my platform. All it does is give trade counts. It doesn't tell anything else about the stock. If all of a sudden I see the lights in the stock, I know there's something going on. I can immediately go over there, but by the time I do, I still don't have the news. But at least I have an idea of what's going on.

The Knight trading issue was the best thing that happened to human beings. That day was great. I had it on that day, but I didn't use it. I didn't even have to, because when it happened, I was on Skype with about four other traders. I had an overnight position in NOK. The market opened, and I was watching NOK. I was seeing millions of shares going through the buy side and I was thinking, this is crazy. What's going on here? Then my buddy told me the same thing was happening in DD. So I looked, but I thought he said DE. Well, when I looked at that, I noticed it was happening there as well. So all of a sudden, we started finding all these stocks. We had a list of ten or so.

We knew within about thirty seconds of the open that there was something wrong. After thirty seconds we started shorting these stocks. After a minute we shorted more. We shorted for the first five minutes, and I said to these guys, "There's something seriously wrong here. Why is it this not turning off?" Because most programs have a stop button—something that will turn it off if it goes wrong. You never have a program in which there are twenty-five or thirty minutes of constantly buying. Usually, if a program screws up, within ten seconds or even two seconds it stops. There's no opportunity to make money, but for whatever reason, this thing was just buying forever.

All of us shorted every single stock because we've been trading forever. We knew these were not correctly priced stocks, and they were going to come back down. We were all pending negative tens of thousands of dollars, but it didn't really matter. If I'd had more money and more buying power, I would have shorted more because it was free money. After thirty minutes, they finally shut this thing off. Everyone started to learn who screwed up. The second that program shut off, all of our stocks collapsed, and we all got paid.

The problem is that if you've been trading for as long as I have, if you've lived through trading halts and all of this other garbage, if you cover those positions, you run the risk of having a serious problem. In a lot of cases the exchange will break the trades, but they'll only break one side of your trade—the entry. If you cover on the way back down, on every single stock you were short on, you're going to be long. So that day I had no choice. I had to sit in all of these positions. I had to stay in short DE, NOK, etc. I took some profits, but I had to wait the whole day for the NYSE to say it wasn't canceling any trades. As soon as I got that OK, I covered everything.

Couldn't you hedge with an ETF or SPY?

You could always hedge, but why hedge when you're up thousands and thousands of dollars with zero risk of going back up?

You started shorting those stocks even without checking the news? You just knew it was wrong?

I knew there was no news. Everybody knew. Every single stock was printing millions and millions of shares, a hundred shares at a time, nonstop. And the market wasn't moving. It was flat at the time. There was no movement except in these hundred stocks. You had zero risk of losing money, because if these stocks were priced $2 higher than where they should be trading, even if the market had a small rally during the day, it would never go enough to make me lose money. I was up so much money per share that it didn't even matter what happened to the market. So there was no reason to hedge, no reason to trade. In a situation like that, one second you'll be down fifty grand, and as soon as the program stops, you will be up one hundred grand. That basically happened in a matter of seconds.

Did you do well in the flash crash as well?

The flash crash was a different type of animal. I was not at my trading station at home that day, but I was trading. We did well, but nothing like on the Knight day. The flash crash was a little bit scarier. I kind of sat back because the whole market was collapsing, so I didn't put the type of risk on that I normally would. Fear was the big factor. I still held some stuff against me and made money on the way back up but nothing special.

The last few weeks are the best example. I don't know if you read ZeroHedge. It talks about how the market has been the least volatile it's been in ages.[26] We're in the S&P 500 with a four-point range, which almost never happens. What happens in any stock is that it becomes so efficient by the programs that it doesn't even move. It just consolidates into nothing. They'll keep it in the range of 5 cents or whatever. I often question how a high-priced stock can stay in a 10 cent range all day. It's impossible.

Even if PCLN or CMG had earnings, they gap down like $90 a share, and then they don't move after that. It just sits, and it has a $1 range all day. That would never ever happen before. There's no way a stock would gap down a lot and not move the rest of the day. Now it's a matter of all these programs going through the earnings. They now think it's worth X, and they're all in agreement that it's worth X, so by the time everyone goes for lunch, the stocks don't move anymore. It's almost like the people are happy losing $90 a share, and there are no new buyers or sellers. Things are so efficient that people like me disappear, take time off, etc. Then everything

---

[26] http://www.zerohedge.com/news/complacency-5-year-highs

becomes very illiquid. It's very difficult to get out of positions, so you get a massive move to the other side where everything gets very inefficient. All of a sudden you'll be down eighteen points in the S&P 500 in one afternoon, and no one knows, why and there's no reason other than that somebody needed to get off some stock. Before it was easy to sell that stock, now it's not so easy.

Another problem is the fact that what's moving the market is in Europe. By the time it opens here, the market has been repriced. It opens down six, seven, or eight points, and then there's nothing for us to do. That's a change from 2008 when everything was US based. Now I almost wish I was trading somewhere in Europe, because I think there would be much more opportunity. Basically, everything I learned about reading charts still exists. I base a lot of my reasons for getting in on charts alone. So even though the moves in the market are far more extreme and far more violent than they were before, and a lot of the times things get overextended, I find myself doing a lot more scaling into positions now, rather than just getting in at one price, because a lot of the times I'm too early. If something is going down, I'm too early buying. I'm countertrending almost all the time.

I believe that if I missed the down move, all the moves will be overextended. Same on the upside — the more violent the move up, the more I short. Today I was trading BIDU. This stock got downgraded this morning. It was trading at $120. It was $134 the other day. Someone downgraded it, and now it's down $118, $117, $116, $114, $110. That was the low. There's no choice but to buy the stock. For someone like me there's not even an option; you have to buy that stock. I'm not going to market make it. I'm going to hold it because the move was way overextended.

Do you find that sometimes the time of day matters? You'll see these extended moves off the open and they reverse in the afternoon?

In this case, the news came out in the morning after the market had already opened, about two hours intro trading. Throughout my entire trading career, what I've seen is that if I look at one hour increments of the entire day, 90 percent of my money is made in the first hour of trading—even more so these days. What happens in the first hour is that you have all these imbalances, all these buy and sell orders. All these people come together to have a party, but the problem is that it ends very quickly, so everything quickly reprices. The HFTs reprice things, then by 10:30 EST, things start to slow down. Then I just sit back on my Skype with my buddies and wait for random events. After the first hour, there's really not much to do until the last hour of trading.

Do you find that when there's news, there are opportunities even in the mid-day time frame?

There are always opportunities when there's news, always. But a lot of times it's hard to make money, because the programs have already gotten the news and repriced the stock. But sometimes we do really well. I'd say almost every day there's a takeover rumor of some kind. And as soon as the news hits, the stock rallies, and I short the stock. One time you're going to lose because it's going to keep going and going, but 90 percent of the time, the stock just comes right back down for the rest of the day. The other day we had the BBY news. The CEO was going to take the company at $24. The stock opens at $23, and that's simple. You just short it, done. That is nice. We do have these simple trades every once in while in which it's a no-brainer.

How did you do during 2008?

Best year ever. It was great—an extremely volatile market. In any type of trading, you could make money hand over fist. At that time I made most of my money in Bank of America, cheap stock, huge thick levels. It doesn't take that much to make a lot of money if you have 250,000 shares and you make 5 cents. That's 12 grand. You could do that in five minutes. I wish every year was like that. Even though there was HFT in the market, there wasn't as much. On top of that there were hedge funds, institutions. I mean everyone was in the market. The volume was super high. The liquidity was there. You could get in and out for as many shares as you wanted. Will it ever come back? Of course it will come back, somehow, sometime. Everybody is worried about the programs ruining the market. I'm not saying they haven't, but if you think what happened last time will never happen again because of lack of volume and lack of liquidity, no—it will happen again. It might be even more violent and extreme than last time, because every time you have a superefficient market, no movement, nothing, and everything is fine, you always breakout of that range. The more efficient it is, the more inefficient it becomes when something does happen.

So I'm hoping in the coming weeks and months it will happen. Everybody's got debt up to their eyeballs, and if the market goes up because of inflation or down because everybody's got so much debt, makes no difference to me. Either way it's not going to stay like this forever. Another reason the market is so crappy is not because of HFTs. The entire world is flooded with money, with 0 percent interest. It doesn't create that much volatility in markets because everybody is at 0 percent. There's really nothing to do. For bond traders, there's nothing to do,[27] and you just buy and hold forever. Once things shake up a bit, things will start to move. I'm not worried about that at all, because I have a good grasp on what these HFTs do, how they work. I'm pretty sure that even if I'm one of the 15 percent of the traders left, I'm going to do fine.

You mentioned your great results in 2008. Were you just riding the trends or doing something else?

I was just riding the trends, the news. I do like to go countertrend trading. One day they banned short selling. It was the best thing in the world. The market would gap down four hundred points, and it's the best buy ever. That's the morning you just come in with your full buying power. You buy everything and just wait fifteen minutes.[28] Stuff like that would happen all the time in both sides of the market. You just had random financial stocks in the middle of the day start to get sold off for no reason. Mid-day, you could just sit there and buy. If you had a large account and were willing to put some risk on, that was a free money year. All of us knew that the government just wasn't going to let this slip away. The market wasn't going to go to zero. Right when they announced that they were going to do QE, you had to buy it. You had to invest all your money in stocks. It was a no-brainer. There were stocks so cheap it

---

[27] An interesting piece of data that demonstrates what he is referring to are fixed income margin requirements. Requirements for Fed Funds futures went from a little over $1,000 in 2009 to about $300 or so in 2013.

[28] What Wayne is probably referring to here is the fact that without short sellers, prices will frequently overshoot to the downside due to absence of short covering. This provides traders the opportunity to buy highly mispriced assets.

was ridiculous. I look back now and think, why didn't I do this or that? I regret so many things, but what can you do.

So you made quite a bit of money buying in 2008. Where you doing bounces and stuff?

Yeah, sure. Obviously if you were positioned short before this happened, that was great. We participated on both sides. I start every day at zero, so I'm ready to go. It don't matter on any given day if that market is going to go up or down. Yes, I have some position on the side, but even though the market is coming down as violently as it was in 2008, there was a lot of money to be made on the upside.

Did you max out your buying power in October 2008 when things just kept falling and falling?

October 2008 was probably one of my better months. During that time I tried to get as much buying power as I could. I can't say I caught the bottom. I wasn't long at the bottom. I wish I was, but I did start to put a lot of money in the market shortly after the bottom. Even though I might have missed the bottom by 10 percent, it didn't really mattered.

Do you do a lot of backtesting?

I don't do any backtesting. All I do is to look at my charts, and they're all one-minute charts. I keep everything super simple. Everyone looks at a million indicators. I don't use any. The only things I have are a couple of moving averages—volume and one-minute candles. I have a few longer-term charts, like sixty minutes for another account that I do some investing and swing trading in, but for my main trading I use one-minute charts. All I look for are price and volume and similar technical patterns,—double bottoms, triple tops, breakouts, simple stuff. A lot of the times these days you get these ridiculous fluctuations off the open, so if that happens I'm there always countertrading. Literally within two minutes you can be out and make a decent amount of money, because there are some wide ranges off the open. You're fighting with programs to get in the position, but as a long you're not in super big size, you can get in and out all of the time. You tend to look back and think, why didn't I hold or I could have gotten a better price, but you're still going to make money.

Do you find yourself taking liquidity more often that adding it?

Yes, I probably do about 500 or 600 trades a day. I probably take too much liquidity. I do around 1.5 million shares a day. In 2008, I probably did about 5 million a day, but now there's no volume. I do take a lot of liquidity to get into my positions, and I try to scale out of my positions by adding liquidity. Unless I'm in trouble, I do try to provide liquidity. But I do pay a hefty price in ECN and SEC fees and all that.

When you try to get out by adding liquidity, do you try to choose the best ECNs for rebates and things like that?

A lot of times now, because there's nothing going on in individual stocks, I trade a lot of SPY. There are some ECNs that get hit first in every stock, no matter what, and the reason they get price preference and hit first is because of their structure. There's no other reason. The HFTs know this. If you're an HFT program and you're not providing liquidity to the dark pool, you're going to hit EDGA, and you're going to hit BX first, because you get paid.[29] Then you're going to hit the rest of them. If you're sitting there, you have a much

---

[29] These ECNs have an inverted model where they pay or cost nothing to take liquidity but charge for adding liquidity.

greater chance of getting hit because you're using them, and they pay others to take liquidity, as opposed to the situations where people have to pay $3 per 1,000 shares. In SPY, because it's attached to the ES futures and because it's the entire market, of course I'm going to throw out BATS or EDGX or something that will throw me a credit, because in the SPY, if they're going to take a price level, they're going to take anything and everything that's there. They don't care about .003, but in some stocks you have to be very selective in which ECNs you use now.

You said you do 500 trades per day. Is that all manual, or do you have some automation going on?

No, I'm completely manual. I trade fairly large positions, and I usually only carry maybe two to three positions at a time. I don't trade thirty stocks at once. I'm usually focused in one or two stocks. My favorite situation is a stock that's $3 to $10, fairly big float, news play, and I can trade in and out all day. Those are a bit hard to find these days, but that's the ideal. There's nothing better to me than that stock that I can get in and out of with 10,000 to 20,000 shares over and over again all day and make 5 to 10 cents.

You usually make 5 to 10 cents?

Depends on the price of the stock. Like today with BIDU, obviously I wasn't trying to make 5 to 10 cents. I was trying to make 2 bucks, but when I'm trading the spiders, 5 to 10 cents all of the time. Just over and over again.

So you didn't find it necessary to expand your time horizon due to the HFTs?

It all depends on the situation. I'm not going worry about the HFTs, because if there's liquidity and there's volume, I'm just going to continue to trade the way I always do. I've just got to be a little more selective in my entries and exits, because no programs are going to front run you for 1 penny when they can make 30 more cents. You're going to get your fill no matter what. If you continue to scalp in something that's not very liquid, you're never going to make money. You're going to lose money for the rest of your life, because you can't get in and out, and they know you're there.

Even with the hidden orders?

Oh yeah, even with hidden orders — doesn't matter.

Do you think they're selling the hidden order books to the HFTs?

Because I use dark books, and because I use hidden orders, nothing would surprise me. One thing I really hate are flash orders. I use a lot of EDGA because it's essentially free, but they do what we call flash orders. Do you know what they call a flash order?[30]

Yes.

That I have a serious problem with, because by the time I blink, they show my hand, and they can choose if they can fill it or not. Many times if they see the order coming for a large amount of stock, the level just disappears, and it reprices and I get no fill. That bothers me a lot. If you're going to get filled, and if you have 25,000 shares and you hit sell and they buy it all in one shot, you know you just screwed up. Because if it wasn't going to go up, they'd never have filled you. You get filled when you're wrong.

---

[30] A flash order is the controversial practice where some ECNs will allow some HFT firms to see orders coming down the pipe in a ECN or exchange. This allows HFTs to change their quotes, cancel orders, or trade in a way that benefits them.

By the flash orders, they know the order flow. So if I've got a big position, a lot of times I'll never try to get out of all of my position, but sometimes I do. That's why at the end of every decent sized move, you see big candles and big volume. Everybody's panicking to try to get out. Then you will get an effect like a railway track — one big down candle and one green candle side by side. It's all order flow. They know what people are up to, and they just back off. That's how the flash crash basically happened. That's how those stocks during the Knight debacle started pushing up that morning. They got so high because everyone would just back off. No one will give a fill when somebody is trying to buy millions of shares 100 shares at a time forever. No one will sit there and sell. They'll just ask for a better price.

Does stuff like subpennying hurt you too?

Ah, subpennies are horrible. If I could participate in it, it would be great, because when I started, I used to be able to shave on the Level 2 on NASDAQ and ARCA and everywhere. This drives me crazy. If I'm trying to buy 10,000 at, let's say, $25.30, so many times I'll hit my hotkey. I'll buy at $25.30. The thing will print two times my exact share lot at $25.295 and $25.30. I get the thirty print, but somebody else made the half cent, and that's what they do. That's their program's job — just to make the half cent over and over all day long. That drives me nuts. In stocks with the very large levels, like Bank of America, it's very hard to sit there at the whole number with your order pending watching halves go off all day long. And it's not even just halves; it's shaved to the 99/100th. It's ridiculous. So, yeah, I would say that hurts. I hope sometime, somehow, we're able to participate in that again. I'm able to participate a little bit on the shaved prints using Credit Suisse, but not like these guys can do.

Do you think there's an edge in being able to watch the subpenny prints going on in the tape and predicting the order flow?

You know, you can definitely predict where the order flow is going by watching the tape. There's no doubt about that. It's very easy to do, very simple to do. But the problem is that it changes in the blink of an eye. One time they'll be swiping all the midpoints orders and the offers at the same time, so you know there's buy side going on. Then, seconds later, it will be all midpoints, and then all orders will be on the bid, so it's very hard to determine even what side of the market the bids are on, or the midpoints or the shaves. It's very hard.

One thing that does happen very often now, way more often than ever before, are block prints though ADFN. If you look at your time and sales, you have all the prints, and there will be ARCA, NSDQ, BOSX, and there are these prints that go off as D or ADF or whatever. ADF is *alternative display facility* network. It's every other system. All the dark books are ADF prints. They're basically outside of the exchanges, outside of the ARCAs—anything that you can't see.

So now you'll see these block prints. For example, today on BIDU, it went from $120 to $111, and all of a sudden—and this is the best thing ever—you'll see that there's a big print at $111.70 for something like 50,000 shares. How the hell did somebody get 50,000 shares? There's no market for anyone.

I can't get even 3,000 and this guy gets 50,000. And this is another reason why I bought BIDU today, because I saw big prints at $111. There were no big prints before $117 today. There were some of these at $117 or whatever, but when somebody is taking positions of 30,000 to 50,000 of BIDU at $111, and the stock is down $10 on the day, no one in their right mind would short the stock there, and no one would sell either. You have to be an idiot to sell down there. So you got a pretty good indication of a good trade on your hands, even if it went $1 against it or even $1.50 against me, it wasn't going down much more. I mean, it could. Anything's possible, but you got a good indication when somebody is putting 50,000 blocks in there and there's no market to get in and out of that much.

If you really wanted to get out of that much stock in the market, you would be dead. Big prints happen a lot now, and they usually signal some type of momentum shift in the market or in that particular stock. That's another thing I never used to use but that I use a lot now. I have a time and sales window that only finds big prints. You know that almost every trade these days is 100 shares. It's stupid. Nobody buys more than 100 or 200 shares. Ten years ago, the average trade was something like 900 to 1,000 shares. HFTs and HFT programs don't trade at 10,000 to 20,000, so when somebody's trying to buy at that amount, the HFTs know, because what all they do is put 200 orders for 100 shares.

So in that situation, with the block trades, you had someone panicking, trying to get out, and somebody who knew something just took the whole thing?

You know, that's the thing. I don't know where these prints come from, because I don't understand who would take the other side of the trade. One thing I know is that if the market is super illiquid, and it's a hedge fund trying to move a position, that's a different story, because if they lose $1 or $2 in a stock that's plummeting $12, they don't really care, especially if they're long forty points lower. They couldn't care less. I never really understand who takes the other side of the trade, because somebody has to sell that. They have to match those shares somehow. Even yesterday — this was the best ever — we had a big correction in AAPL. It was down something like $20. I'm sitting there at the open, and I like $650 to buy the stock, because it was just at $674 the other day.[31]

I like the stock there, so I'm looking at the Level 2, and there's a guy sitting on the L2 at $648.50. He's sitting there and displaying 65,000 shares, and if you ever looked at AAPL, nobody displays anything. It's mostly a 100 to 200, maybe 1,000 the odd time. But I swear to god, a lot of the time these guys put these orders because they know they're going to get filled. I see this every day. 65,000 shares, relatively close to the open, and he's filled 648.50 for every share. All at once, he gets filled on everything. The low of the day is 648.13, and then the stock goes up $20 in a straight line for the rest of the day. This happens all the time. So I look for these types of trades as well.

So tape reading is a key part of your success?

Yeah, I believe it is. It's a lot different from the way you use to read it. I don't understand how these guys do it. It has to do with accumulating and distributing shares. That guy put that order there knowing he was going to get filled. I'd say 90 percent of the time I see these orders, they get filled. I don't know how, I don't know who fills them, but someone does. Before, when these orders used to get filled, you would think, oh, my god, the guy got taken; the stock is going to collapse. And it would collapse. Now it's not like that. You never ever short a stock with somebody showing a huge order. You always go with that order. Before it was different. There was some follow-through.

How were you able to adapt to the changing market conditions and make these adjustments over time?

---

[31] This is a good example of his mean reversion mindset.

I don't know. Trust me, I'm not making nearly as much as I was making before, but I'm definitely not losing, and I have no intentions of finding a new career anytime soon.

I've got a good group of traders that I'm constantly in touch with. We have a Skype chat that we're on every day, so even though I'm trading by myself at home, I still have the influence of other traders that are really good and that have made money in the last ten to twelve years just like me. But it used to be that traders would make $5,000 to $6,000 a month, or $10,000 a month. Those guys are all gone. They were only making that because it was so easy, not because they understood the market or because they understood what was happening or could read charts very well.

When I started trading, our office would hire ten guys at a time, and eight guys would make money. Toward the end of my stay there, four years in or whatever, three or four would make money. And honestly, now if you get ten people to start trading the way I learned to trade, I guarantee you there would be zero that would make it. You might get one the odd time, but you're not getting anyone making consistent money. It's impossible. From the beginning I liked to take risks, but I would always keep my losses very tight. The main reason I'm still around is that I don't mind punching out of the stock when I lose $20,000. I have no problem with that, but someone else that's looking at this loss will let it turn into $30,000 or $50,000. They'll lose forever, because sometimes these stocks never come back. You get into a position, you think you're right, and you never give up. The guys who trade like that are all gone. I do believe that as a long as you know how to manage your losses and take them, the profitable trades will be there, and they'll take care of themselves.

That's characteristic of your Skype friends as well?

Yeah, for sure. I have another good friend who's going through a rough patch. In 2008/2009 he was making money hand over fist. He's never been as strong as other people, but he understands the market. He's a very good trader. But what happens is that our nice free money, our easy trades, are not there anymore. So what happened to him was that he got into trouble, only because when he gets into positions and the stock goes against him, it will go by so much that there's no chance he can ever make money on the trade. If he just sticks to what we were always taught, get out of the losers quick, he would be fine. On a day-to-day basis, he'll make money. He'll make $1,000 a day, but the problem is that when he loses, he'll lose like $6,000 to $7,000, so it takes him quite a while to make it all back. One trade can cost him two weeks' worth of work. He's not making the big trades. He's making small profits because we went back into making smaller profits as a result of these markets, but he still will not get out of the losers.

You mentioned swing trading. Is that a big part of your profitability?

I have another account that I do a lot of swing trading in, and last year (2011) was the first year that I didn't make a penny day trading. I made up for it by swing trading. I have a million excuses for it. I didn't really have a house. I was building a house. I had no office, so I was trading from my laptop, and the markets were garbage. This year, I'm in the house. I have an office set up. I'm having a good year, but I think last year I learned a lot about swing trading and the differences between that and day trading and the mentality it takes to do it versus what I'm used to doing. So I got a lot of education and experience, and I'm actually doing really well with the swing trading these days. These positions I hold from two hours to three days, something like that. That made up for my other account last year that I made $0 on. This year, both accounts are doing really well. When I do swing trade, I prefer futures, I really like to trade gold and silver. The odd time I'll trade stocks as well. Like today I got some BIDU options. I like to trade AAPL. I like the bigger stocks. For scalping I prefer the lower-priced stocks.

Did you find that as the HFTs started to suck liquidity out of the market, you started to trade more big caps and avoided the small cap stocks?

When the markets were really moving, I was trading all of the financials. I like cheaper stocks with thick levels. I'd say more than going to big stocks, I've gone to ETFs. I much prefer trading the SPYs, IWM, GLD. If I'm trading stocks and there's not much going on, then for sure I will be in the big caps.

How important would you say are your instincts compared to reading charts?

I'd say probably fifty/fifty. I do take almost all of my trades based on charting. That's the only thing I know, the only thing I use. But sometimes, like today on BIDU, I had to go with my gut. I've been trading long enough to know that if someone comes in mid-day with a downgrade, and the stocks is down $10 bucks before the downgrade and $10 bucks after, there's no way I'm not going to buy it every single day every single time. There are things I've seen happen over and over again that I don't need a chart for. I don't need anything. I just know that it's going to work out.

Do you think these downgrades and upgrades are similar to the takeover rumors and things that you can just sort of fade?

They're very similar. It depends on the situation too. Now that I've been trading a long time, I know all of these companies too. If it had been a different company, or if the guy had a better explanation of why he was downgrading it, I might have thought differently about it. I do try to read into the news to understand what's going to make a stock move to a certain extent. Takeover rumors are a little better because there are random takeover rumors every day. It's ridiculous. You get these and you know it's never going to happen, so you just short and that's it. How many of them work out? And how many of them work out that day when somebody calls it? So when something goes up ridiculously on that kind of rumor, of course I'm going to short it. It's an easy trade. Upgrades and downgrades are a little bit tougher. I need to read in and see what's going on.

What do you think happened in the BATS IPO?

I don't know. I really don't have an opinion there. Maybe sabotage? I like BATS, but I have no idea what happened.

Do you trade IPOs at all?

Oh yes, of course. I love IPOs. Unfortunately we only have the opportunity to buy IPOs, which really sucks. I only scalp them though. I don't try to swing trade them. A lot of the time, what happens in IPOs is that there will be violent candles in there, but there will be a whole number where there will be support. So let's say an IPO price is at $17 and it opens at $18. There might be support at $17.50, and of course at $17 they'll buy it forever[32]. They have to defend the IPO price. When it breaks the IPO price, it's very weird the way they trade, but it's very methodical. It will go down 50 cents. You buy some, then it bounces. It's very strange, but you can make a lot of money trading them, especially if you get in a good one. But

---

[32] Wayne is referring to the underwriters who will frequently support the IPO price.

I can't think of one that's gone up a lot since it opened. What I like about them is that there's a lot of volume, and if there's a lot of volume, you have a much better chance of making some money.

On the other hand, the Facebook IPO was a complete disaster. Probably the second best day I had this year. It's amazing how much money you can make in these things.

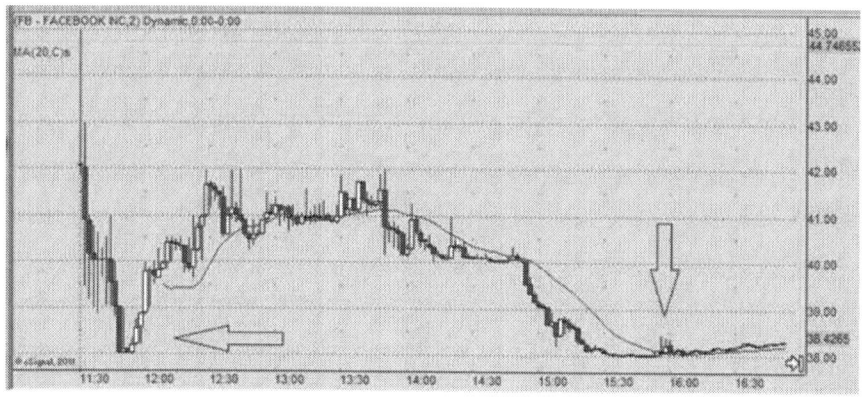

FB IPO. Source: Esignal.

Buy at $38.01 and sell higher?

Yeah, that's what I did. I bought something like 60,000 shares at $38.05 and sold higher. It opened at $40s, or whatever, but it was a total mess. It was supposed to open, but it didn't open. One thing you could do on FB that a lot of people didn't know was that you could route orders through Chicago 20 to 30 cents lower than the best bid and get filled. You could immediately flip it out for 20 to 30 cents, over and over again, until it got close to $38. When it got there, that game was over. For some reason that was one system that was taking orders and giving fills out cheaper than the rest of the market. For whatever reason, when they trade through the Midwest or Chicago, there are always block prints and orders that go through outside the market. I don't know why. It's not outside of what the trading range would be. I believe the reason this happened in this case was because there were a lot of people who had millions and millions of shares of the stock, and these institutions didn't care about 30 cents at that time, because they were trying to get off 10 to 20 million shares of stock or even get short. Don't think that people can't short IPOs. That's bullshit. As this was happening, they didn't care about 20 cents, because they knew they were going to get out lower. As you can see now, the stock is worth much less. It was free money for them.

Does this underwriter strategy of supporting a price create a lot of free money situations? I saw something like that the other day in the MANU IPO.

I didn't trade the MANU IPO, because I was out of town, but my buddy did a similar trade at the $14 level. Manchester United is the biggest pile of garbage ever. I don't know why anyone would ever buy that stock. I don't even understand why it's even listed. I don't know how, but my buddy got short the stock. He borrowed from I don't know who, and he was shorting every time it went up and covering at $14, but he was hoping for the big move through $14. I don't know if you were watching, but when it broke $14 in the first day, it dropped something like 50 cents really fast.

Which news source do you use?

My main news comes from Briefing. One of my buddies on Skype uses RanSquawk audio and also Benzinga.

You have the kind of setup with five monitors and stuff like that?

I actually have twelve.

Twelve?!

Yeah, I've got two different trading platforms going—my swing account and my main trading account. And a third for Briefing. Also one for imbalances, HFT alerts, and then eight monitors for charts.

What kind of hardware you have?

My computers now are about two years old, but when I bought them they were the best of the best. Monitors are standard. They're fine. What's funny is that I actually use the oldest keyboards in history. I don't use anything wireless, because I don't trust it. The keyboards I have are the old clunky ones with F keys, because those are the keys I use for entering orders, now they have these fancy ones without F keys. I probably should buy half a dozen more, because sometimes keyboards around here get broken. Sometimes anger get the best of me and keys go flying.

What kind of advice do you give to new traders?

Start out small—something like 100 shares. Don't worry about the money you make in a day. Just try to make 20 to 30 cents a day, something like $20 to $30 a day after commissions, whatever. But the only thing that will ever save your life is how you manage your losing trades. You have to exit the losers. It's tough out there. Everyone is trying to go after profits that are super small. Spreads are small, and volume is light. There's not as much money available to be made. It's not just us, it's the HFTs, the specialists, the hedge funds—everyone's profits are down. Any trading firm, any time frame, profits are down. So it's a very hard environment to get into trading. Anyone who can get into trading at this time and make money will do very well in their career. It's the hardest time to get in. To have a future in trading, this is the best time to get in if you can figure something out that works, because honestly, I don't think it can get much worse than this.

Before I started to research this market, I didn't realize how bad it was for people trying to add liquidity to the markets.

We always joke that we're the liquidity providers of last resort. In the old days, there were so many people doing that. They were just providing liquidity, bid offer, get in and out. It was great. If something big in the world does happen, if there's news, and stuff starts to move, there's not going to be anybody standing in the way. You'll see moves in stocks than you've never seen before.

Do you have a plan for when something like that happens?

Because the markets have been such garbage and there's not a lot of money there and its summertime, I haven't been trading too much. We weren't really ready for the Knight situation, because if we were on our game and making a lot of money, that day I would have been trying to find buying power from anyone to short millions and millions of shares. One of my friends has a huge buying power, but he only used like 20 percent of it. Even I didn't use all of my buying power, because I was a little scared. I haven't seen this type of situation before, so it's fine to say you have a plan, but it's a lot different when it actually happens. You don't know exactly what is going to happen. The flash crash was to the downside, and it affected the whole market. Knight was to the upside. No one thought the stocks would go up in a glitch. So, of course I have a plan. If we flash crash again, I'll buy everything. That's the only plan I can give you, but it depends on what the news is. If there's no news like on that day of the flash crash, then yeah. I'll buy everything.

Do you read a lot about regulations and rules like Reg NMS?

I don't care about that kind of garbage. We've adapted to all kinds of rule changes, bans on short selling, etc. My profit margins are small. On average, I don't make very much per share, so provided they don't add a trade tax or stamp tax, I'll be fine, because all of those other rules everyone will just adapt to it. It does suck that if a stock goes down 10 percent you can't short on a downtick anymore, so we even have strategies that are geared toward stocks that go down 10 percent. We've adapted to all the rules just like everyone else.

I noticed that these stocks that go down 10 percent and trigger the uptick rule tend to have some predictable moves after it. Is that something that you noticed as well?

It depends on what kind of news there is, but generally, yeah. If it's a large company—I believe even BIDU today triggered the 10 percent, which makes me even more attracted to it for a long. It's one of my rules. If the company is good and the news is not that important, I'll always buy when it reaches the 10 percent.

Because the short sellers can't whack the stock anymore?

Yeah, exactly. You have one variable in your favor at 10 percent. You look at every trade, and it's all odds. That one variable makes the trade that much more attractive.

November 2013 Update

How would you rate this year in terms of profitability compared to last year?

Worse. A lot worse.

Would you say that's because of the VIX coming down more and the Fed keeping everything stable?

It's very hard to make money when the VIX is at lows and interest rates are 0 percent around the world. There's just nothing to do, unless you bought the stock market at the beginning of the year and held all year. Then you would be doing fine. Intraday trading is pretty bad right now.

Being long stocks, buying dips, etc. Is that something that really isn't your style and you struggle with that?

I guess. Maybe mentally I think the market shouldn't be up here. I'm biased. I would never in a million years buy the market here and invest.

If the market turns, you think you can do well by being short biased all the way down?

I probably won't be short all the way down, but at least there will be a lot more volatility, a lot more swings in the stocks I like to trade. I don't like to go trade GOOG and PCLN. They're so expensive and very thin. Some of the lower priced stocks I like to trade — I hope they'll come back into play with some bigger swings intraday.

I recall you made good money on the Facebook IPO. Did you trade the Twitter IPO?

I did trade it, but it was very boring. It was basically a nonevent. It opened way higher than it was priced at. It didn't do a hell of a lot. It had a quick move up to $50 but I was never going to buy at that level. I wouldn't buy it now. Maybe I would do it if it went to $20. Without being able to short it that day, it was useless.

The underwriters were doing something similar to FB in the $45 level of TWTR. They were trying to support it. Did you try to pull that move again of buying support and selling a little bit higher?

No, I left it alone. I didn't even attempt to buy it. I did work though. They always try to defend a certain level. The opening price was a good place to do it.

What was your best day this year?

My best days this year have been trading gold. The few times gold had violent moves down, I was pretty heavily short. Those paid me very well. I'm kind of looking for gold to have one more move down.

Were these big trades in gold just day trades, shorting breakdowns?

Actually, they've been mostly in the futures market with sell stops. Most of my trade ideas in gold start to happen while I'm in bed. I just put a sell stop in at a level where I believe there are a lot of stop orders. I just try to front run those orders and get in. I wake up before the pit opens in New York. A lot of times the move already happened before the pit opens in New York. When gold is down about $20 before the pit opens, usually it just continues the whole day. So I just stay in the trade for the rest of the day. Holding time is something like one day, a day and a half, that sort of thing.

Do you think a lot of those moves in gold happen overnight because it's such a global commodity with international liquidity and you just never know when somebody will decide to puke his position in the Asian session or something?

Gold definitely slows down after New York closes, but it's one of those things that when it's moving, it really pays to trade it almost any kind of day. Right now it's not. So in between New York and Asia it's useless. There's no reason to trade it.

What would you say was your worst trade of the year?

It was at the beginning of the year. I was trying to catch a bounce in the Japanese Yen. I got in very early, bad price, averaged down. It ended up costing me quite a bit of money.

I actually hate the Yen, but I just thought the move was way overextended. To this day, the Yen still haven't recovered.

These type trades — bottom plays — would you say that this is a quite risky way to trade and you have to have a lot of experience to avoid big losses doing this type of stuff?

Catching a bottom is very difficult. It's dangerous. It's something that I do quite often. I wouldn't advise other people that are relatively new to trading to do it. I always have a reason why for buying at certain levels. I always have the levels I'm interested at. It's a risky strategy for sure.

I noticed that in a lot of these sell-offs after the block trades, it becomes very obvious that the stock is going to bounce. Before the block trades, there's a lot of stress in the trade, and it's hard to profit. But after, there's a lower stress opportunity. Is that something you noticed?

Yes. These block trades continue to happen. I still use those quite a bit. I don't know why and how it works, but it seems to work.

Maybe it's because there's a big seller, and when he gets taken, the market stops being distorted to the downside and it returns to normality in the form of a bounce?

More than likely that's what it is. The only problem these days is that you don't actually see the seller. You don't know who it is. Maybe the HFTs know or somebody knows. It's not like before where you could visibly see sellers on the screen on the offer. You're looking at nobody most of the time these days. I do believe that the algos that are in the buy side keep fading until they're ready to take that order. I'm pretty sure that's what's going on, but you don't know until after the fact. That's why you wait for that volume. Wait for the big dip, for the mini-flash crash, and then take the opposite side of the trade.

It's nice, because when that happens, you might be underwater in the trade briefly, but if you're in small you can actually scale into a pretty decent position. Once it starts going in your favor, you can actually buy or short more if it's an up move. I always like to average into a winning trade.

Would you say that in these bottom plays the time element is important? I noticed that if you try to play ten minutes in, it's usually a bad idea. Fifteen minutes too. After twenty-five or thirty minutes or more, it starts to work more effectively.

Basing that off what, the open?

The time from where the sell-off started.

Yeah, because a lot of times what these guys do, especially in the futures it's a very classic move these days, is that it makes a low. Churn it for half an hour, retest the low, break it by a couple of ticks, and then rally off that low. It's never as easy as spike down, low of the day, and rally from there. They never make it that simple. I agree that the bottom ticks take a while to form now.

Would you say that your countertrending style is harder to apply in this current market?

I would say it is, but I would also say that any strategy is difficult in this market. I don't know of anyone making money hand over fist. I don't even know automated guys making a lot these days.

Did you trade TSLA a lot this year?

Yes, actually, I traded quite a bit this year. Obviously I did quite well in the short side recently. I never lost any money on the way up. I was short in the $170s, and that ended up working pretty well.

Every time that stock makes a big move in one direction, it seems that it goes in the opposite direction, so I would imagine that you would do well there.

That's one I've done all right on. I'm kind of sad, because that's one where I bought this morning at like $121, sold at $123, and watched it go for $6 more.

In the premarket it was at $116. It seemed that it was a good entry there for a lot of people.

If I'd gotten up earlier in the morning, I probably would have grabbed some at $118 or something. It was already at $120 by the time I got up. I guess there were some headlines this morning in the premarket that moved it up off the low. Nothing would have been better than if that thing had flushed down to $110 at the open. I would have bought for sure, options and stock.

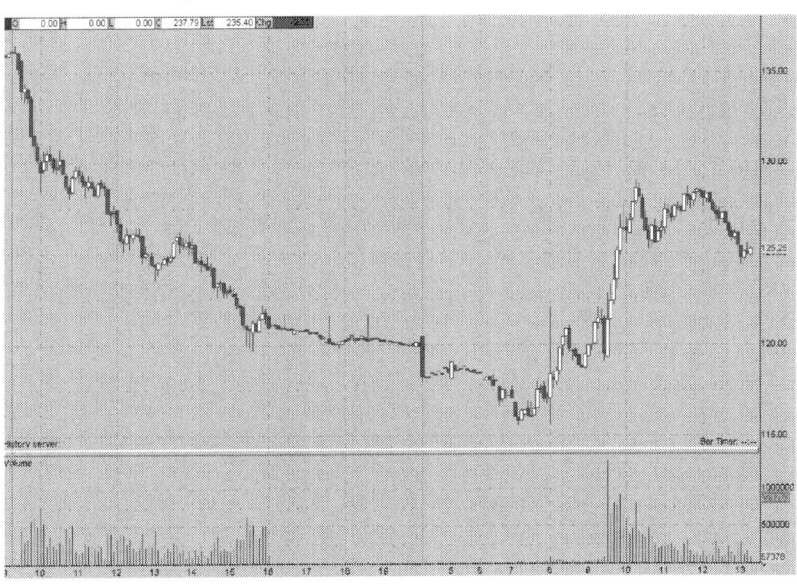

TSLA 5min chart. Source: MBTrading Desktop Pro

Do you think any big move in TSLA is usually a good fade?

This one in particular was, because it went down from $170 to $120 in a hurry. That's a pretty significant move. It was giving up about two-thirds of the up move from the breakout of $90 or $100 or whatever. It had to be interesting for some people to watch for the long side.

Chart courtesy of StockCharts.com

With regards to Fed days, do you try to be alert on those days for some big potential trades?

I always liked Fed days, but lately they've really sucked because rates are at 0 percent, and they're going to stay there for a long time, and the QE is not being changed and everybody knows that. Fed days have been horrible for the last three years except for the last two meetings. Those have been really good. The only reason they were good was because the market anticipated that they might start to taper, and Bernanke came out and said they weren't going to. That caught the market off guard a little bit. Rates aren't going up for the foreseeable future. If they start to taper though, then I'll start to short a lot.

The market now seems that it's run by the Fed. When they start to taper, then my guess is that the top will be in.

Do you think that when this train starts moving to the downside, it will be a little like gold in that it drops but it's still a good short?

Usually no. Usually there's a time to get in the long side as well. When the market is going to make a significant reversal, you have to get in before others. The market always goes down ten times faster than it ever goes up. You have to be very careful if you're shorting the market after it started to roll over. The bounces are violent, there's nothing worse than having bad timing in the short side. The long side is a little bit more forgiving.

Do you trade a lot of the small caps? The GOGOs of the world are doubling and tripling lately.

Those stocks I actually like. I've looked at GOGO but haven't traded it. Recently I traded ICLD. I play close attention to a lot of these stocks with low floats that double and triple, because a lot of these companies are in need of cash, and they raise cash into these moves. Again, obviously I like to be on the short side. I do get in the long side of these plays, but if I feel like they're going to do an offering, I don't play as long.

How do you manage your risk in these low float momentum stocks?

I won't hold overnight in those stocks ever, either side. That alone is pretty much the risk, because usually both announcements of offerings and news are done outside regular trading hours. Intraday, I just keep it tight. I've got a stop 10, 20, 30 cents away from my entry.

Buying the dips and selling when it breaks to new highs works well in those.

Are you trading even less in the mid-day now because of this lack of volatility?

Everybody I know is trading less.

Do you wait for the breaking news to trade in those times?

I'm always waiting for news, but even the news has been slow. There's not much going on. Fannie Mae and Freddie Mac have been moving lately, and I played those some, but it's difficult to trade these pink sheet stocks.

Do you think that volatility expansion that you mentioned in the first interview is going to happen next year? The Fed is supposed to taper soon.

The problem with that is that now you have Janet Yellen saying that they might never taper. Honestly, I don't know. I think they'll have no choice, because they can't keep buying $1 trillion a year in open-market buying forever. They keep buying and trying to create inflation and get the economy going, but I don't think it will work even if they doubled the number. When it does happen, it's going to be even more interesting than 2008 I think.

How do you come up with the stocks you're going to trade in a specific day? Do you have a scan, friends that are throwing tickers around?

Both of those. I have a news feed. We have Briefing, Benzinga. I also use the volume list for NYSE and NASDAQ. Once I get about half a dozen stocks in play for the day, I probably have thirty to forty charts on my screen. Some of them I change every couple of days, some of them I trade all the time. Usually it's off one of those two feeds or the volume scanner.

And you're always in touch with your friends on Skype?

Yes, most of the time. At least a couple of guys.

It's like a private chat that you guys have?

Yes.

If someone launched a Bitcoin ETF, would you be excited to trade that?

Oh, fuck no. I'm not into Bitcoins. No thanks. They remind me of tulip mania, the dot com bubble, etc. Don't get me wrong, I think they can go to $5,000, but I'd rather own gold and silver.

But wouldn't they be a great day-trading vehicle both in the long and short side?

Oh, they would be a great day-trading vehicle. They go up and down 30 percent in an evening, so yes, that's true. The problem is the market is very illiquid, hard to get in and out. Spreads are wide. If you have an account with one of these bitcoin brokers, the commission is ridiculous. You can never do what I do. Sure you can make swing trades on it, for example, but I don't think it would have a lot of participation if they created something like that.

Do you trade around short seller reports like Muddy Waters, Citron Research, TheStreetSweeper, that kind of of stuff?

Sometimes. The thing with these guys is that the stocks they have recommended, like Z, QIHU—if you took those trades you'd be dead. Even HerbalLife (HLF) from Ackman—you would be totally dead.

I think Z doubled.

Z has doubled. QIHU probably more than tripled. HLF I think it tripled as well.

This has to be the worst short selling of all time, right?

It's difficult. Right now it seems that everyone is happily long. When everybody is long and they say the market is the best and you should sell all other assets, I like to do the opposite. I don't like the fact that everyone loves stocks. Like I said, I wouldn't be buying stocks here.

You don't invest the profits that you take out of your trading accounts in stocks in anyway?

No, I don't have a lot of stocks right now. I own a few things, like NBG, which is like a lottery ticket. I own coffee futures. I have the Japanese market in the long side, but that's about it.

You mentioned that even the algos might not be making that much money. Do you think that the profitability of HFTs have peaked and now they're going to start to struggle?

As volume decreases, everyone struggles — HFT, humans, etc. Once volume picks up, it will be interesting to see how the algos react, because it won't stay like this forever. I don't know if we'll have a flash crash or what will happen once stuff starts to move, but I would expect the algos to make quite a bit of money once volume returns. This market could even get violent to the upside. Usually at the end of a bull market, if you want to call it a bull market instead of a Fed program, it gets violent to the upside too. I'm ready for anything. I just want something to happen.

How would you play a blow off top?

If it starts to show that it wants to put that sort of top, I'll be long every day, because that's when they really put the boots to the shorts. We are not there yet. Every time we go to new highs, we just kind of grind up. Other than a couple of days where it just outright ripped — mostly around the stupid government shutdown, which was scenario where it was a no-brainer long — it's a slow move up.

It seems that the only scenario where this market goes up a lot is when it comes from a sell-off.

Yes, as soon as people start committing to the short side, that seems to be about the time things just turn around violently and it goes back up.

It's like one giant TSLA.

Yeah, until it doesn't work anymore. Then all of a sudden everybody wants out at the same time. The charts are yet to indicate that we're going to roll over yet, and when it does happen, I think there will be plenty of time to get in. I can definitely see a 10 percent correction, and that's already 180 ES points or something, back in the day, 10 percent wasn't that much, but we have almost doubled from those days.

Maybe trading it like TSLA is a good idea because the stock tanked from the top, but then it rallied it back and made a lower high in the daily. At that point it was a great short. Perhaps waiting for that lower high on ES is a good idea.

One thing that I really like on a weekly or daily chart is some type of new high bar and then a week that closes bellow the low of that high week. It's the high of the year, all-time, whatever, then you have a week that closes bellow the low of that high bar. Then things start to get interesting. That did happen around the government shutdown, but you never ever short that, because the government won't be shut down forever, and they won't default on their debt either.

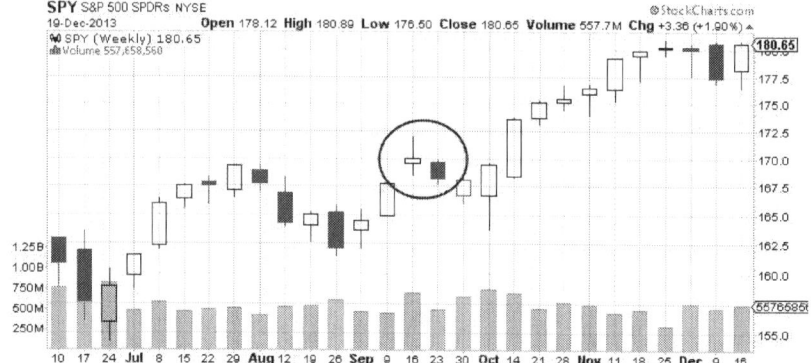

Weekly Reversal Bar. Chart courtesy of StockCharts.com.

I noticed that some traders are good at buying breakouts and some are good at shorting them, but I never met anyone who'll do both very well. Is that your experience with your friends as well? Did you ever meet someone who can do everything well?

Some people are good at taking AAPL and trading it every single day. Other people, like me, want to trade a chart they like. I don't care what market it is—futures, stocks, currencies, etc. You have to have your own style. I don't even care if you trade a stock like SIRI and try to make one penny a share all day long. It trades fifty million shares a day. Lots of people do it.

Would you say that this year it was really important that you cut down your mid-day trades, your marginal trades? And if you hadn't done that, you would have lost some good money?

Yeah, I would say so. I've been struggling with the close lately. For some reason I've been wrong consistently, and I got caught short a few times.

I've been caught short there too a few times.

Even when it's a perfect setup and the market is totally weak, it's still never as good as a good short. I haven't run the stats, but I don't know how many times we have closed at the lows of the day this year. Maybe it's happened only ten times this year. That's how ridiculous this is.

Maybe it's not working because it's a perfect setup and everybody is shorting it.

No, nobody is really short. Not that many people are short. That's the main thing. Everybody is happily long. It's not like they're squeezing people to death. If everybody was short, we'd be getting some really violent up days, and we are not. I hope that's how the market does top. I hope it goes to 2000 next year—really quickly.

Do you do a lot of trading in the premarket and after hours?

After hours lately has been garbage. There's nothing going on. Sometimes when there are earnings out, it's OK. Premarket is OK when there's economic data out, but I don't really like trading those time periods.

Lessons from Chapter 7

1. Risk control despite strong views. Wayne has strong views on the markets, trading and HFTs, yet he still talks about how important is to take losses, not letting losers get out of hand. He also

mentions that he was careful during the flash crash and the Knight situations. It's always better to be careful than to be broke.

2. Big moves tend to end with big candles, big volume, and block trades. During panics or periods of euphoria, markets can easily overshoot. The HFTs will punish people when they're selling or trying to buy by offering worse prices. This can result in an end move that's composed by a big candle and a big volume bar.

The volume can be the result of the block trades Wayne talked about regarding his BIDU trade. It's a bit of a mystery who's behind these orders, but for example, when a stock has a major down move and you see a big volume bar with big block trades, you have to ask yourself, does the guy who bought this entire sell order in one shot know something that others don't? It can easily be the case that he has access to special information. He knows of other news that will come out later in the day (Wall Street research can frequently leak before it is made public), or that he simply knows it's a good value down there. In my experience, these big volume bars and big block trades also indicate that whoever was selling in a panic finally got taken, and now, without that selling pressure, the path of least resistance shifts and there's a better chance of a bounce.

The time element is important as well. It's not often that you see something tank a lot, bounce back, and that's it. Usually the momentum takes a while to reverse. In my experience, buying bounces off ten-minute sell-offs is quite dangerous in stocks, unless it's a quick scalp. After twenty to thirty minutes or more of selling, there's a better chance you actually have the bottom.

Bounce plays are difficult. They're definitely not for people without experience.

3. Adapt to changing market conditions. Wayne talked about the fact that when big orders got done it used to mean that the stock

would continue in the direction of the trend, but these days they signal some type of momentum shift. He observed the market long enough and recorded enough observations in his mind that he noticed changing patterns and was able to adapt.

4. Surround yourself with great traders. During the Knight Capital glitch, he and his friends instantly knew there was something wrong with the stocks the program was buying. As a result, they were able to have their best day of the year. If you weren't experienced enough, you would just think those stocks were acting a bit weird or maybe that there was some kind of news, but he has a ton of experience which, combined with the knowledge of his Skype friends, made him confident the moves were unjustified, enabling him to score a big profit.

5. Be careful in mid-day. Wayne makes most of his money off the open and into the close. He waits for special situations during the mid-day period. Due to even fewer volatility and meaningful events in 2013, Wayne decreased his mid-day trading even more. He says it was an important adjustment in order to remain profitable.

6. This is the hardest time ever to start trading. This is an important lesson, because it can be both a good thing and a bad thing. The good thing is that it provides the opportunity for a trader to hone his skills and learn how to trade in the hardest markets he's likely to face. As Wayne put it, "Anyone who can get into trading at this time and make money will do very well in their career." The bad thing is that you can't get lazy. You'll have to work hard, study hard, and improve yourself every day. Profit margins in the trading business or the investing business are all down. If you don't make the technical adjustments for the HFT era, have the discipline to cut losses and follow good risk management rules, you will wipe out your profit margins.

7. You have to leave room even for great trades. Wayne talked about how great the setup was for his BIDU trade, yet he also mentioned that the trade would have been good even if it went $1 or $1.50 against him. He also talked about this in the Knight trading situation, when he and his friends just kept on scaling in the trade. They were all down a lot at some point, but it all reversed when Knight shut their program down. The lesson here is that you have to leave room for trades. The level of HFT noise is quite high these days.

8. Scalping still works, but the game has changed. If you scalp in illiquid names you will get killed. The HFTs know you're there and they're going to take away your fills. You're supposed to scalp in issues with a lot of volume and liquidity, like ETFs or big cap stocks with thick layers.

9. You have to be careful about which ECNs you use in individual stocks. Some ECNs like EDGA or BX get hit first because they provide a rebate or now fees for liquidity takers. This provides the opportunity for someone sitting on a limit order to be **effectively ahead of others in the same level** due to the financial incentive. It's a way to subpenny the next guy, even though you're not an HFT. You can get filled when you would otherwise not by using the right ECNs instead of being too greedy for rebates.

10. Trading IPOs can be quite lucrative. It gives a trader the opportunity to interact with retail flow, capitalize in glitches, trade predictable patterns, or take advantage of artificial support levels that are the result of investment banks trying to support the IPO price.

11. The TSLA trade. The TSLA reversal off the premarket sell-off provided a good example of an overextended stock. TSLA is already

a stock that tends to move back and forth a lot. That, combined with the drop from \$180 to \$115 in a short period of time, high short interest, and pre-market action made it a solid setup for a bounce play off that overextended drop. The fact that it accelerated to the downside pre-market signaled some kind of capitulation panic that presented the opportunity to enter a good risk/reward trade.

12. Trade less. If your style is not really matching well with the market environment, you have to trade less. It's easier said than done, but if anyone is serious about their trading career, this adjustment could be the difference between a profitable month and a losing one. Wayne's style is suited more to environments where things aren't just a stable uptrend "buy the dip" ride, he makes a killing during bigger volatility days or days where trends fail. Because he realizes the current market doesn't play to his strengths he uses his discipline to trade less and waits for the right spots to remain profitable.

13. The Weekly Reversal Bar. If you want to get a sense off the big picture, look for a reversal of momentum with the Weekly Reversal Bar pattern. First there's a weekly bar that makes a new high for the year or all-time high. Then the next weekly bar closes bellow the low of that bar. This weakening of the price action indicates a potential start of profit taking.

Chapter 8

Anonymous — The Former Winner

This trader was really struggling when I interviewed him. He had made some good money in recent years but then gave it all back in some instances that he recalls in the interview. Why did I decide to include his interview in this book? Simply because I believe there's a lot of be learned from failure. Most traders fail, and I believe being able to understand why that happens is a key factor in becoming and staying successful as a trader.

Most trading interview books only feature "successful" traders. I put successful in quotes because later on you find out that some of the traders ended up failing and you never get an analysis of what happened. What are some of the mistakes they made, lessons they learned, etc.? This chapter is a reminder of why you have to stay humble, why the markets are so dangerous. If you don't pay attention to the basic fundamentals, the market will take everything you have, and it won't even say I'm sorry.

This interview was conducted in November of 2012

When did you decided to join this business?

I started probably four or five months before 9/11.

Was it hard in the beginning?

Yeah, starting out is difficult for probably any trader. It's hard to expect to make any money for the first six to nine months. If you can come out even, that's probably pretty good. I learned how to read the markets a little. I was trying to scalp for 10 to 20 cents — with 100 to 200 shares.

You started in a bear market. Were you comfortable shorting selling?

I don't think it mattered, because trading back then was so much different from now. I didn't take any risk. I would do a lot of spread trading. I would buy Exxon and sell Chevron against it. Buy one Pharma stock and sell one against it. Also, you couldn't short on a downtick. You could see that there was someone coming in trying to short the stock. I traded mostly NYSE stocks. You could see the specialist's book and find out that someone was trying to sell the stock, and you could get in front of him a little. Problem was that sometimes the specialist would hold the order and you wouldn't get filled. Now you have the HFTs. It looks like they provide liquidity, because the spreads are narrower, but if there's a scare in the market they'll just take away that liquidity and there won't be any.

Back then you were just scalping, providing liquidity, and playing the market maker?

I used to trade Viacom A with the Viacom B. I would manually put orders all day long, 10 cents above and below the best bids and offers, and then go to the B stock if I got hit in the A stock. It was very little risk, but it was a lot of work putting orders in and out.

Back then in the NYSE, you could get price improvement. If an institution came in and bought 50,000 shares, the stock might print

$1 up, and you could get filled $1 up. Now, wherever your order is, you get filled there. That makes it difficult for the day trader now.

Why do you think this happened?

Probably because the HFTs led to the end of the specialists, plus competition from the Island, ARCA, Instinet, etc. I used to trade a lot of NYSE stocks just for the price improvement.

How long did these easy-money days of market making last? When did they go away?

Probably around 2006 I started to take a lot more risk. I started to trade almost like a hedge fund. I would hold positions for three days, a week, etc.

So you went from having no overnight trades to having to do them?

Yes, I started to have unhedged overnight trades.

You used to carry Viacom A hedged with the B—things like that?

Yeah.

You mentioned in the pre-interview that you had a good 2008 up to October.

Yeah, there was a ton of volatility there. When the recession was really hitting, politicians were doing all kinds of things. They voted against TARP, and then a week later they voted for it.

How did you give back your profits?

I gave back all of it in October. Right when the politicians got involved with TARP, the financials started to get crushed. I got caught long. I didn't think the markets would go down as much as they did.

How did you make the money in the first half?

I was playing countertrend, but I was really pressing my winners. When most people would take profits of 30 to 50 cents, I would try to ride for $1 to $2 of gains.

Letting the winners run as much as possible?

Yes. I got hurt at the end of 2008 and in the flash crash of 2010 as well. I tend to be overleveraged when there's value. A sports bettor likes to bet more if he thinks he's a 60 percent favorite to win. I would try to treat stocks like that. Problem is that if you get too leveraged you can't afford to let it go against you very much.

So you think you made a position size mistake?

For sure. Position size mistakes, leverage mistakes. I also got involved with options and 3x ETFs. Starting in 2007/2008 I was working thirteen hours a day. Although I was putting in that many hours, I wasn't doing the due diligence that a trader needs to do in terms of understanding risk/rewards of specific trades, keeping notebooks with charts, tracking where I was making money or losing money, times of the day where I was doing well/poorly. I just kind of got away from the fundamentals of being a good trader. I had no game plan like I should have—having exit points or saying if I lost 3 percent or 5 percent, I should be out.

A lot of traders make most of their money at the open and the close. Was that true for you as well?

Most of the volatility is around the open and in the last hour of the day. I have stretches where I'm making all my money in the first hour and losing money in the last hour. Sometimes I'll over trade in the middle of the day and get stopped in a lot of trades because the market just goes back and forth, and I waste a lot of commissions.

Yeah, I've done that a lot too. Do you have a theory on why the open is better?

Well, there are a lot of people sending orders around. A lot of times, stocks will just open up at extremes.

So you can fade the extremes?

Yeah, you can just trade against it. You can also see stocks in a range, and if it breaks out of that range in the first fifteen minutes, you can go with that range.

How would you describe your style?

I would say I'm countertrend.

Have you stopped using limit orders?

When I'm getting out of a long or buying to cover, I'll use them, but to get into a position I will just use a market order.

I'm trying to do more technical trading nowadays, looking at charts, moving averages, support and resistance levels, etc.

Do you have any memorable trades from 2008?

I remember on October 4, it was a Friday, the market opened way up, but then it reversed and went to lows. I'd planned to see the Red Sox with my family, and I knew I was supposed to get out of my long position. It was an outside reversal day, and that was a bad sign for the following Monday. On Monday and Tuesday, I lost everything I'd made in that year.

A similar trade happened when the S&P downgraded the US credit rating in 2011. In that week there was a big open, and then the market reversed and went lower. Five days later the market was lower by fourteen hundred points or so.

I remember that.

I got hurt badly in the week of the S&P downgrade.

What do you think was your mistake in the trade?

It was a big outside reversal. The markets opened way up and then went straight down. All week I was thinking the market was overextended and I didn't get out of stuff.

You were overleveraged there?

I was way overleveraged.

You said that in 2009 and 2010 you did quite well, made a million dollars combined, how did you do it?

I played everything.

You mentioned sports betting and poker. You have a background in that?

I play Texas Hold'em, and I have a friend that gambled professionally as a poker player.

Do you try to look at the market from a similar perspective?

Yeah, you try to find the value in what you do, and if you do the trade a thousand times, the profits come. The more often you can do trades that you presume to be profitable, the better the chances are that you're going to be profitable according to the law of averages.

When you're going to do a trade, why do you sometimes prefer to express that view with options rather than the underlying?

You know what your risk is with the option. You can get a little more leverage, but mostly you know how much you can lose.

What hurt me in that downgrade situation is that I had some put spreads. I sold some and bought other strikes lower. At one point I sold my puts but kept the short.

Was it the same as 2008?

No, in 2008 I didn't sell options. I just bought calls and puts.

What happened in the flash crash situation?

We were probably down about three hundred points and I bought the market. Greece was having riots. It's different now. When I started, all news that moved the market was what happened in the United States. Now everything out there affects the market.

It sucks, because I can't go negative in my account. Once it gets there I have to close the position. I was forced to take some major losses.

Have you always been a prop trader?

Yes, always.

Do you think there's an advantage to being a prop trader because you're around a bunch of other people you can learn from and see what works and doesn't?

I think there's an advantage there. I really haven't in the last four years, and that probably got me to take a lot more risk than I should have. There are some offices, though, where people don't want to share any ideas, or you might have a manager that will try to steal your system. When I traded Viacom A and B, I was away for six months and traded from home. When I came back, all of a sudden I saw a lot of people trading Viacom.

Do you do a lot of news trading? Try to quickly get in a trend after a piece of news hits?

I will try to. I have some news services that I pay for. Sometimes it's good, sometimes it's not. I may get the news quicker than other traders, but I'm not getting it quicker than other people.

I remember I was trading TEA a couple weeks back. There were rumors of someone potentially buying the company. I bought the stock, I sold some, and then I bought back in. The stock went bellow from where I bought it, so I decided to sell. Within about two minutes they halted the stock, and the news was that they were being bought out.

Normally you'll find that late in the week, especially on Thursday, there will be all kinds of rumors. About 90 to 98 percent of them are false. Those are people trying to make money in the weekly options.

In these weekly options, there's what I call options vigilantes. They try to hold the stock at certain whole dollar levels on Fridays so they can collect the premium on both sides. It's like AAPL all of a sudden only moves in a $1 range on a Friday afternoon. All the premium in the calls and puts goes out. I see that a lot on Fridays. The markets make their move after the open and all of a sudden it spends four hours going nowhere.

I interviewed a trader who plays against takeover rumors. He shorts them and makes money that way. Do you play both sides or just buy them?

You can play both sides, but the risk is like in the TEA situation. They can halt the stock and you have no chance of getting out. You have to figure out mathematically where the value is. In that trade, if you shorted, you would lose $3 a share. You have to figure out if in the winning times you make enough to make up for that loss. If the trader makes money, then he probably does.

It's really rare, though, to see a buyout in the middle of the day. I can't remember the last time it happened.

Sometimes if the deal is in process and the rumors get out there, they'll rush the deal, but yeah, usually they'll happen in the mornings after a weekend. They work on it in the weekend.

The other day, NFLX had rumors, and then the news came out that Icahn had a 10 percent stake, and the stock rose a lot.

I believe the rumor was that MSFT was going to buy NFLX, but it was actually Icahn buying a stake.

Yeah, there were MSFT rumors on it.

Do you backtest at all?

No, not normally. I usually just call a friend that has all the applications for it. I recently looked at what AMZN and AAPL did on and around black Fridays and made some money that way.

Did you learn your technical trading by trial and error or from books?

You can read books and then do trial and error on it.

Of the technical that you use, which is the most useful?

I like the 50 and 200 moving averages. Also the outside day reversal that I mentioned earlier, where a stock opens higher at or going above the previous day's highs and then turns back and goes below the previous day's low. AAPL had an outside reversal day to the upside last week, and it just kept going for a few days.

What kind of equipment setup do you have?

I use five monitors, a dell desktop, and an HP laptop. I'm actually shopping for a gaming computer now that can handle more monitors. I'm probably going to get one of those Alienware gaming computers with the i7 processor, gaming graphics cards, etc.

Do you use the trading software of your firm?

Yes. I use Lightspeed.

Do you find that it does make a difference using some software compared to others?

Yes, sure. Some platforms are more customizable, do different types of orders, etc.

Which news services do you have?

I use TradeTheNews and Fly on the Wall.

I've used TradeTheNews and found it much better than Fly. Why even have fly?

Well, TradeTheNews costs me $300 or so a month and Fly $30. On Fly, in the morning they have a list of upgrades/downgrades and things like that. Usually I want to know earnings dates so I can have less risk.

What is a good trade that you put on recently?

I caught the AAPL move up recently for something like $15 a share.

Do you think, because it has some much hype and news, AAPL becomes more inefficient than something like IBM for example?

Yes, it's definitely one of the most hyped stocks out there. In my experience this stock will go a lot higher than you think, and it will also go a lot lower. I tell people that if they're trying to buy it when it's down to wait, and then when they want to buy it, wait again, but in the next time you really want to buy it then do it. AAPL is tricky, because they have a ton of cash and the PE is low.

Do you look at the L2, TS, and stuff like that? Is there an edge there?

I look at it, but in stocks like AAPL, there's so much volume that I don't even bother looking at it. I believe the L2 was much more useful years ago than it is now. I have it, but I don't look at it as much. It's better in stocks that aren't as volatile. You can see that there are a lot of stocks at a whole dollar mark. It's hard now, because people hide all their orders. The thing with these computers is that they can probably see where the orders are hidden, and the stop orders, etc.

What kind of advice do you give to people that are starting now?

Try to understand the risks and rewards when you go into a trade. Don't do trades because you're bored in the middle of the day. Keep records of where you're making your money and where you're losing your money. Hold yourself accountable to stops and taking losses. If you're trading with $10,000, stop yourself at $500 of losses in a position, and be done with trading that day.

So discipline that is the number one advice?

Yes, don't take off things you're making money on, and don't let your losses run. It should be the other way around. Don't add to losses either, unless you're scaling in with a specific stop level. I've been trading for nine years, and my struggle is when I become a little cocky or arrogant. Then I have a bad day or two and want to make it all back. You have to treat every day as a new day.

Did you discover edges in the market by trial and error?

Yes, trial and error, writing down what works, what doesn't work. Certain things that might work for a year suddenly won't work the following year. You have to recognize certain patterns. If you're a new trader, try to play the trend rather than fight it.

Even in a year like this year, where markets aren't trending much and vol is low?

For a new trader it's probably better that the vol is low. He won't freak out, and the risk is a little bit less. Sometimes the market doesn't move anywhere for four months and it will be awesome for me. I would trade where I thought something was oversold or overbought, so I would go against the trend. A low vol market is very good for that. Sometimes when the market is really volatile, I would find that I wasn't doing well, whereas people with algorithms would be doing very well.

I took a $10,000 account, trading 100 to 200 shares to almost $1,000,000 in a year. A lot of that was luck.

Why was it luck?

I didn't have a good system but I had instincts for the market. Sometimes I'm very stubborn. I'll play a reversal but not put a stop in, and I'll take a much bigger loss than I should. In that account I would play 100 to 200 shares, then take it up to $15,000. Then I had a little bit more leverage. Sometimes I was able to parlay those gains into pretty good gains, then all of a sudden I would have over $100,000. Then it became a lot easier to make money. For many years I did very bad right in the summer. I would still not take summers off, because I was immature and stubborn.

Do you think your style is profitable and you just have to bet the right amounts and stick with your stops?

Yes.

Lessons from Chapter 8

1. The importance of appropriate bet sizing. Even though this trader has a background in sports betting and poker, he failed to incorporate one of the key elements of betting games — appropriate position sizing. In gambling, there's a formula — the Kelly Criterion. The Kelly gives you the perfect mathematical amount that you can bet for maximum long-term growth of your trading stake. It's a key sacrilege to go above your Kelly, the results of doing so are a quite disastrous, as you can see in this chart:

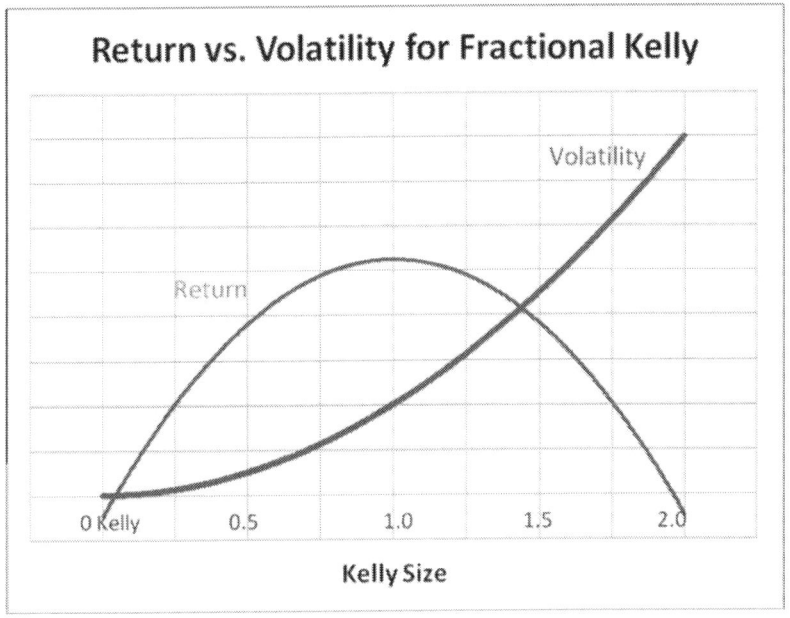

Source: drbobsports.com

What is striking about the Kelly is that if you bet less than the optimum amount (1.0), you'll cut your returns, **but you'll cut your volatility by an even greater amount**. To quote the article from drbobsports.com, which is the source of the chart:

These graphs illustrate the long-term power of using Kelly sizing to increase one's bankroll over time, and beg the question, "If Kelly betting will lead to such incredible returns, then betting double or triple Kelly must lead to even higher returns!" Referred to as "overbetting," this misguided notion is one of the reasons that so many +EV sports bettors go broke just like their square compatriots. **It turns out that someone betting 1.5 Kelly has the same expected growth as someone betting 0.5 Kelly, but with tremendously wilder upswings and downswings, and much more risk**. Betting 2 Kelly actually has the same expected return as not betting at all: exactly zero, and betting more than 2 Kelly has a negative long term expected growth **even if you're making positive expected value bets**, and your bankroll will eventually fall to zero!

In conclusion, Kelly sizing is in fact, as has been stated several times, the point at which return is exactly optimal.

In addition to the dangers of overbetting, the Kelly Criterion also has large swings compared to flat betting. For example, a given positive expectation wager that compounds at 10 percent per time unit will eventually double, and of course grow to infinity. However, since the swings with Kelly betting are so large, **the initial bankroll actually has a 1/3 chance of being cut to half its initial value at some point before doubling**. To an academic, this is immaterial, since they can keep their eyes on the long run expected growth. **However, to investors who are often investing money for a shorter period of time and expecting immediate and consistent returns, this relatively high short term risk and volatility is unacceptable**.

However, because variance is exponentially related to return, we find that cutting the bet size in half causes only a nominal reduction in expected growth, **but square roots the variance**. In other words, if we were to bet one half Kelly unit on our 10 percent per time unit (with full Kelly) proposition, we would grow our funds at a slightly slower rate of 7.5 percent per time unit while our risk/variance/volatility would be the square root of what it was previously. **To use the previous example, we would now fall to 50 percent of our starting bankroll only 1/9 (rather than 1/3) of the time before doubling it — a much more tolerable level of risk for the average investor**. (Emphasis mine)[33]

Does that mean that the Kelly is an appropriate number to use in trading? Absolutely not, because unlike a lot of gambling situations, you don't know the exact odds and the world is full of fat tails (even without overnight risk), in addition the standard Kelly formula might not be appropriate for a trade that has multiple different scenarios for gains and losses (unless you tweak the formula).

What it does mean is that even if you're confident in your position, if you overbet you could easily have long-term negative returns even if the trade itself has positive expectation. If you overbet some but not as much, you'll still make money but with higher volatility than a small risk would create but with no additional profits! (But with plenty of stress and smashed keyboards.) It's nice to estimate probabilities and see what your Kelly is in a particular big bet you want to make simply just so you know where your risk should *not* be.

---

[33] http://www.drbobsports.com/essays.cfm?p=5

Example: If your Kelly is 10 percent of your account, you know that losing 10 percent is too much due to errors in estimation, black swans, halts, flash crashes, etc. You probably should bet half the Kelly or probably even less.

Betting a much smaller fraction of Kelly is the relaxation zone, because you're getting the most bang for the buck in terms of dollar-return/volatility ratio. Getting closer to the Kelly, you're starting to get more profits but your room for errors in estimating your true probabilities is smaller. And your equity will fluctuate more, **so you'd better be mentally tough enough to handle the losses**.

Betting too little can also be a problem, because you leave money on the table; **however, this might be the only way to trade for people that are prone to tilting and revenge trading**. This trader is the perfect example of someone who needs to stick to the relaxation zone. Take a look at the chart again. The start of the volatility curve is where I would say the relaxation zone is. It's probably where most traders should stay in.

This former winner routinely made mistakes in terms of overleveraging, sometimes risking the entire account. This guarantees a long-term negative outcome even though he might be trading a positive expectancy discretionary system the entire time.

2. Lack of exit points. The trader himself acknowledges he didn't have an exit point for a lot of trades he made. Because there's no maximum loss for a lot of his trades, he would frequently face gigantic losses, which guarantees massive volatility and possibly long-term negative account returns. As several traders mentioned in this book, the ability to take losses is the most important skill for a trader. Having an exit point is crucial so you know when to exercise that ability. This ability can be developed, and I describe my personal take on subject in Chapter 11 in the section titled "The Boost Your Discipline Mini-Course".

3. Minimize outside distractions. The trader mentioned having a big long position without a stop in the market in October of 2008 and going to a Red Sox game.

The market had put an outside reversal day, which to this trader meant it was going lower. The fact that the big trade was a loser up to that point, combined with the distraction of having to leave the trading desk, meant that the trader had to take the loss. If you combine that with the technical input of the outside reversal, then it was a no-brainer to close the trade. He ended up holding that and gave back all the profits he'd made that year.

4. Divergence from the plan and trade style. The trader mentioned using options as a way to manage risk, because you know the most you can lose. He was in some put spreads in August of 2011. He then decided the market was oversold and sold his puts (but kept holding the short put part of the spread, a naked short). This left him without a hedge, vulnerable to a huge loss, and completely diverging from the whole idea of using options in the first place (limited losses). He diverged from his plan then lost one million dollars over the next days after the S&P downgraded the US debt.

5. Keep detailed records. The trader himself acknowledges that he failed to keep track of his trading, what was working, what was not, the times of the day he made the most money, storing charts, risk/reward of specific trades, reviewing mistakes etc. If you're struggling, keeping detailed records can make all the difference in your career. I use the free software Evernote for all my record keeping and would recommend other traders to do the same.

Chapter 9

Anonymous — The Secrecy of the Bot Destroyer

I was pretty excited about the possibility of interviewing the following trader. I was told he was quite aggressive and pretty effective at not just making money off market participants in general but also specifically from HFTs, that he was some kind of bot exploiter.

He was pretty skeptical about doing a phone interview. He told me in an e-mail, "I have some concerns about divulging information, and that is why I need the questions to be e-mailed. This will assure I give you the best answers I can while protecting my interest. I obviously won't be handing out free lunches to your readers. I will do an interview, but I want to be very cautious about the information I give. Send me some questions, let me look them over, and we can do a phone call." I then e-mailed a series of generic questions I use to get an interview rolling. Lots of times the interviews just take a direction of their own, and I don't stick with set questions, but for a general start they're useful. Turns out he didn't even answer give me substantive answers to the questions I sent. He answered them quickly without providing much information. I followed up with him, trying to schedule the phone interview but he never accepted it.

Why am I including the interview in the book? First because there's some information in his answers — not a lot, but it confirmed some of other answers given by other good traders. The second reason will become clear in the lesson summary in the chapter's end.

This interview was conducted in August of 2012

What made you want to become a trader?

Lifestyle.

How long did it take for you to become profitable?

Six months.

What made a difference in turning that around?

Learning how things worked. When I began trading, I started with $5,000 and didn't know what ask was.

Biggest difference of back then to right now, which strategies stopped working?

It's more difficult for individual traders to make money. Back then if you got into a losing trade, the market would bail you out with short term reversal. Back then the motto was, if you ain't fading you ain't trading. I've seen a lot of million-dollar-a-year earners who got used to this and didn't change and lost most of what they had earned over the years.

How has Reg NMS changed your strategies?

Well it certainly hasn't made the market less fragmented. It has given HFTs and other professionals more advantages and angles over most. I try to adapt to the environment. If there are structure changes, you must change your strategies to adapt.

Since you have been trading for a long time, how has the market changed for you since the rise of HFT and algos?

Scalping is harder. Getting into and out of positions is more challenging. The biggest argument for HFTs is that they tighten spreads, but that's not exactly true. There's no depth to the liquidity. If you send an order for more than a 100 shares at a time even if your size is allegedly concealed, you move the market more than you would have putting on the same size in the past. Spreads have actually widened for anyone who does over a 100 shares.

How did you do during the 2008?

I did great.

How did you do during the flash crash?

Not as good as I should have.

How do you see the market evolving for short-term traders over the next ten years? Are you concerned it will get more efficient and that edges will close out?

Edges always change. Keep learning and hunting and you'll find something new. Sometimes you know there are edges and you can't take advantage of them. Dig deeper. Find a way to take advantage of them. I was short a stock last week, and I got a buy-in, so I had to cover. I tried several brokers to find shares. I found them and got short again. This company will be out of cash and gone in six months.

Best days?

$200,000.

Worst days?

$32,000.

How often do your strategies stop working? What a kind of cycle do you face?

Constantly.

Are market orders a sucker play?

Not always. If I'm really busy with more important things but I want the stock, I'll send a market order. I only do this on thick volume stocks though. I personally wouldn't do it with anything under a couple million a day average volume.

Did you extend your time horizon?

I would say I've added extended time horizon plays to my play book, but more importantly I've been more strategic about getting in and out of positions. The way to think about it's this is that HFTs are like parasites and you're the host. They do not want to buy a stock unless you want to buy it. They don't want to sell it unless you want to sell it. So just know that when you send an order, it will have three or more times the impact on the market than it used to have. So buying 100 shares is like buying 300 shares. Your impact is intensified when getting in and getting out of positions, and for many traders that slippage was their entire earn.

How do you know when to pull the plug in a strategy that you're running?

You check the data, check that the story is intact, revaluate, and trade accordingly.

Do you think limit orders have weakened and marketable limit orders have become more important because of subpennying and penny jumping?

I take liquidity 90 percent of the time now. In the past, I provided liquidity 90 percent of the time.

Given the disadvantages of limit orders due to subpennying, in which situations do you use limit orders and in which do you not?

Subpennying is the scam of the century. You're essentially being forced to provide free insurance to those who can step ahead of your limit order by a subpenny. They know if the market moves they can dump the shares on you and lose almost nothing. Because of this, I only put in resting limit orders if I'm building a big position over a period of time where I anticipate getting fills at multiple price points.

Is there any edge in watching subpenny trades for predicting short-term direction?

Not for me. I see no point in that. You can't enter a subpenny order, so what are you going to do, jump in there and pay their spread and trade with guys who have a tremendous edge on you entering and exiting the trade? I'm out.

What other advantages do HFTs and algos have over the traders besides subpennying?

Speed, commissions, exchange favoritism. If you ever want to see something interesting, follow the Clearly Erroneous Execution trades daily. You'll see some outrageous rulings. I've seen a $60 stock trade down to $58 on a mini-flash crash and NASDAQ, in their own words has said, "Pursuant to Rule 11890(b), NASDAQ, on its own motion, has determined to cancel all trades in security." And the very same day, just an hour or so later a $5 stock trades up to $20, and NASDAQ says this: "NASDAQ has reviewed the transactions under rule 11890 (b) on its own motion filing involving the security XXXXX executed between 13:31:00 and 13:32:00 (EST) today and has determined that all trades will stand. This decision cannot be appealed." If you inquire about this they'll tell you there are no firm rules, only guidelines, and it's at their discretion. Makes me think it that who's on the advantageous side of those executions will determine the outcome of the ruling.

What kind of equipment do you use for trading? Do you have the latest hardware specs and top-notch, expensive software, or do you try to cut costs?

I have top notch hardware. I do not use a lot of paid software subscriptions aside from data. I have my own written instead.

Can bots be beaten on news trading?

If they misinterpret it they can.

What are some characteristics of winning traders you've seen over the years?

Aggression, resolve, being calculated, and having some gamble in you.

How confident are you in your ability to keep making profits over the next five to ten years?

I've no doubts. I'm a crusher.

What do you do with the money that you've earned but that is not needed for trading? Do you keep in T-Bills or the bank, or do you invest in stocks, real estate, and businesses?

Guns, gold and land.

How important are your instincts? Do you trade off them frequently?

Yes, we call that on-the-gut trading. Most people can't do this profitably.

Did you trade the Facebook IPO?

I bought the open on IPO day and blew it out quickly. I've been trading it regularly and recovered the IPO day loss.

Do new catalysts and volume increase inefficiencies? Why?

Interpretation.

Are the consequences of computerized trading more reversals and overall noise in the price action?

I would say the reversal thing is true currently, but that might change. Overall noise is definitely true.

Do you read more rules and regulations and changes to rules and regulations?

I read a lot. I read more than I do anything else.

Do you avoid mid-day?

No, but I don't scalp it like I used to.

What advice do you have for an average trader dealing with the tough competition of HFTs and algos?

Join them, get a job, or study their weaknesses and take them down.

Lessons from Chapter 9

1. Surround yourself with great traders. Obviously this trader wasn't willing to share a lot about his strategies for a book, but I spoke with some traders that know him personally, and they told me about a bit more about the strategies that he uses. The truth is that people are willing to share much more in a friendship situation or in a small group of people than they are in a more public forum. Why would you give away your secrets to the entire world? If a friend of yours asks about it, then you might be willing to share, especially if it's a trusted friend.

The late motivational speaker Jim Rohn had a saying that is so profound and extremely true. He used to say, "You're the average of the five people you spend the most time with." When you surround yourself with successful people, you can't help but start to absorb their mindsets, tactics, beliefs, etc. I know that for me personally, the idea of making several thousand dollars in a day through day trading was completely out of my concept of reality, but through the process of surrounding myself with great traders, I saw that this was not just common but extremely simple if you apply the principles of good trading, so much so that I started to have those days myself. This was one of the major reasons I decided to write this book. I wanted to learn from the best traders I could find. I wanted to not just understand their technical trading but also their mindsets, beliefs, etc.

There is even scientific evidence that behaviors are contagious. In one very interesting study done by Harvard and the University of California[34] it was found that when a friend of a study participant became obese, the participant was 57% more likely to become obese himself, when the friend was described as a "close friend" the chance

---

[34] http://tinyurl.com/lvkvaut

went up to 171%. Humans are social creatures and we take cues from others as to know which behaviors are appropriate, this is why surrounding yourself with better traders and avoiding losing one's is a key to short-term trading success. The good news is that the study authors say that this contagion effect should hold for weight loss as much as it does for weight gain.

How can you surround yourself with great traders? Reading this book is a great start, because most of the traders were less shy about their own take in trading than the Bot Destroyer, but there are several more options:

- Join a prop firm, not just so you can get more leverage (multiples times the retail leverage limits), avoidance of the PDT rule, and perhaps a better commission plan, but also because you get the chance to hang out with other traders. You can make friends with guys that might be killing the markets for years for large figures. You can learn from the managers there who probably know a lot about risk management since they have seen dozens of people blow up. Don't be shy about asking for advice. Worst case scenario is that they refuse to answer and you move on to the next person.

- Join a chat room. There a lots of day trading chat rooms out there, mostly paid. I never tried the free ones, because I know they tend to attract newbies and people who don't know what they're doing. I'm a member of a paid one, and it has helped me tremendously. By watching good traders alert their trades, you can understand more about what makes them act, good setups, risk/reward dynamics, the loss-cutting process, position sizing, etc. You won't necessarily be able to join the same trade. Usually that's not a good idea, as the slippage will hurt the profitability of the setup, (I say, usually, but that's not the always the case. Some of my best trades were trades off other people's alerts. The thing is, I knew they were great setups, so the move was going to be large.) But by watching good traders in action, you can learn much faster than just by trading on your own. Don't be shy about asking questions of traders through private messages. They'll be more willing to answer you than in public messages. Keep in mind that when selecting a chat room there will be a level of luck and randomness involved. Some of them will be good; lots will be bad. You'll just have to go through a level of trial and error until you find something that fits your style and the good trading principles that are outlined in this book. Don't subscribe for one-year plans until you've checked it out through a trial or a one-month package.

• Get a mentor. If you already know a great trader, try to think of ways you can get him to mentor you, even if it means working for him for free.

• Keep in touch with great traders through Skype. This idea was mentioned by a few traders in this book. They create their own private chat room on Skype. Needless to say, they'll be way more willing to share techniques, setups, and strategies there than anywhere else. Considering creating your own room and inviting good traders there.

2. Risk management. The Bot Destroyer best day was more than six times the size of his worst day. This shows that he has his losses under control.

3. Take liquidity. Even though he's the Bot Destroyer, he still acknowledges all the advantages of the HFTs through subpenny prints, penny jumps, etc. He takes liquidity 90 percent of the time.

4. Backtesting and programming. Even though it's not mentioned in the interview, I'm told by people who know him that he backtests all kinds of stuff. He even said that edges always change. Backtesting is probably a key factor that he uses to adapt to changing conditions. He also mentioned writing his own trading software. Yes, it takes a lot of work, but in this HFT world, where edges are being fought tooth and nail, being lazy about learning to code is not a good idea, especially if you're struggling.

Chapter 10

atticus — The Options Expert

The following interview will be hard to understand for a lot of readers. There are a lot of options terms and strategies that you might be unfamiliar with. I ask you to persevere and try to learn more about it, because this style of trading might fit your personality or you could learn things that will be useful for you.

This trader is very detailed and scientific about his methodologies. He has a deep understanding of options and option microstructure. I first came across him many years ago in the forums at Elitetrader.com (atticus is his nickname). He has run quite a few journals where he outlined daily what his plays were and which option strategies where best for each situation. He has made millions of dollars extracting profits from the markets, so even if you don't understand specifically what he means in a particular situation, try to understand why he was profitable or why his overall approach to the markets worked.

I included several footnotes explaining some of his option structures, if you're already familiar with options you should be able to understand the strategies. If you're not, I would encourage you to read basic free tutorials on the web before tackling this chapter. If you still have difficulties understanding, I would recommend you to go straight to the lesson summary at the end of the chapter. I explain there in simpler language the lessons that I learned from this trader.

This interview was conducted in March of 2013

Why did you decide you wanted to become a trader?

My dad was a mathematician. He retired early from a teaching job to trade on the floor of the CBOE in Chicago. He had me fairly late. When I was born, my parents were in their late thirties. I grew up with the *Wall Street Journal, Investors Daily, Barrons*, etc., around the house. I was also on math track. I graduated high school early, around fifteen. At sixteen I was looking for a job that I could actually do. I wasn't planning on starting an undergraduate program but taking a year off. In the summer I worked as a clerk for my dad at the CBOE. I would run orders from the order desk to him. The pit in the CBOE was different from the CME. It wasn't a deep pit, just a couple of steps. I would reconcile sheets at the end of the day. I would look at the closing prices and see what I considered arbitrage opportunities at the time, but my dad would tell me immediately, "Those are stale quotes." Equity markets don't reconcile at end of the day to a fair value figure. They don't do reverse conversions and conversions and rolls to determine the prices.

I would look at discount arbitrages and deep in the money verticals and so forth. That really sparked my interest, because it looked like it was free money. I quickly learned that it wasn't. This was in 1983. The put market wasn't even ten years old yet. Calls started in 1973 in the CBOE, but you couldn't synthesize a put. It was hard to even get market data back then unless you were at the exchange, but then I decided to start an undergrad program.

While I was studying, I traded using a handheld device called a Quotetrack. It was an FM receiver back then. I was seventeen or eighteen, and my dad loaned me $60,000 to open my own account and trade for myself.

Do you think the fact that your dad was a mathematician helped you get on the right path?

I think so. It helped me understand that options are basically a probabilistic function. You're looking at the likelihood of price meeting X. You're looking at a logarithm distribution, and you can plot that in the chart. Delta, which is the first derivative of the price, is pretty close to the probability of expiration. In most markets, with libor where it's right now, you can pretty much use delta as the probability. That was basically how we looked at it, but that's where the math ends. I did algebra and calculus I and II, but I didn't follow in my dad's footsteps.

What happened to the first account that you father helped you fund?

I took from $60,000 to about $25,000. At that point I just stopped trading. I told my dad that I only had about a third left. He told me to rethink what I was doing and stop for a while, not to trade on tilt and blow the rest out. It took about nine months to do that. In the next summer I decided to come back to trading from home. I bought a new Compaq DeskPro, I think it was a 286 at the time. I had a wireless FM desktop box for feeding the machine with data. I had Lotus1-2-3 as well. I decided to just trade at the end of the day, last thirty minutes before close, looking at the closing trend and trying to do directional bets in volatility.

Back then we had a Reg T margin that was much different than now. The parameters were much more conservative. You really couldn't do a lot of naked writing. I knew a guy at the floor while working for my dad that I learned a few things from. He was one of the largest single name stock traders in the CBOE. I took his advice and sold straddles[35] on Friday at the close. Then I would convert to a butterfly on Monday morning. It was an unwritten rule they didn't even like to discuss outside the trading circles, but the CBOE guys, and to a lesser extent the Merc guys, where very specific when they would mark down their sheets for the weekend decay. Because it's not a continuous market, you don't wake up Monday morning and have the same prices that closed on Friday in terms of vol. They would typically mark down around noon central time or 3pm EST. My strategy would just front run that a little bit, taking the least risk as possible, going to closest to neutral as a could in single name stocks. I would sell ATM straddles in a basket of stocks in the indices, like GE, CAT, etc. On the following Monday I would take the weekend decay or vol mark down.

I would sell vol of something like 16 to 17 percent, then I would pick up about thirty basis points on Monday, buying it back the wings.[36] Or I'd sell the straddle. I would choose the closest wings that would give me a credit larger than the strike width, basically get a free butterfly.[37] If I couldn't get the credit, I'd just buy back the straddle.

---

[35] Selling an ATM straddle involves selling a call and a put at the same expiration and strike price. It's essentially a bet that the implied volatility is overpriced.

[36] Buying the "wings" means that the trader has bought an OTM call and a put. This effectively hedges an ATM short straddle position against all kinds of risks.

[37] A "fly" or butterfly is essentially a strategy where the trader is short 2 options in the "middle" and long 1 option in each "wing."

The rest of the week I would just do data mining. By the end of the summer I had about $50,000 from doing that, so I doubled the account with fairly low vol.

By the time 1987 hit, I was nearly break even in the original account. In '87 I shorted a ton of vol, and then the crash happened. I was on vacation, but we didn't have stuff like Wi-Fi. I was able to get out of my positions but ended up losing about 40 percent.

My dad actually ended up losing something like five million dollars, which was the bulk of our family's net worth at that time.

Did that event make you think the strategy was flawed?

I was only in the market two days a week, the rest of the time I was usually completely hedged, but because I was doing well I took some directional risk that I shouldn't have taken.

The VIX hit something like 300 back then, right?

It did hit some astronomical levels, but you have to understand that those bar charts contain maybe one trade of a guy capitulating at the low, and it wasn't representative of any real volume.

After '87 I decided to go to med school, and I knew I wasn't going to be able to trade actively, so I just traded two-to-three-month positions long-term vol bets. I would basically buy three-month butterflies and calendars to negate my Vega exposure.[38] A long

---

Ex: short 2 100 calls, long 1 120 call and long 1 80 call. You are short volatility in the middle but hedged against tails events.

[38] Buying a calendar involves selling an option in one month while also being long the same strike price option in another month that is after the month of the sale. The trader is trying to profit from differences in implied volatilities at different expirations. A calendar is long volatility because the long portion of the trade has a higher sensitivity to changes in volatility in the underlying than the short portion (in other words, it has a higher Vega).

butterfly is short volatility and a calendar is long volatility. I did a ratio of around one to five, so for each fly I would get about five calendars to negate my Vega, but the problem of that was that I was ramping my gamma, because both are short gamma. I was neutral in vol, but I had massive gamma figures.[39] It was a complex strategy, and my broker only asked about it when I called to put the orders in. I decided to go simpler and sold puts in stocks on which I liked the vol figure and bought puts in the index. At that point the skew or volatility smile in the index, even though we had the crash, wasn't that weighted toward the down and out strikes. In other words, if the index was at 500, the 450 puts weren't trading at a much higher vol than the 550 calls, maybe two hundred basis points more.

So I was trading this short dispersion strategy and making maybe 1 to 2 percent a month with very few drawdowns. I really appreciated the value of being hedged, even though a short dispersion has correlation risk.

Did you always trade from home?

Well, my dad had a JBO account with a trading firm. Essentially he had a market maker haircut instead of Reg T on options positions. He made an arrangement with one of the managers to let me trade the account, and we did really well there. What my strategies needed were looser margin requirements. Something that would cost me about $30,000 to do in a Reg T account would require $4,000 to $5,000

---

[39] This happened mostly because the calendars are highly exposed to near-term price changes in the underlying. Since the volatility "hedge" (that is, the long options part of the calendar) are for expirations many months from now, near term price changes can all of a sudden affect the price of the options portfolio a great deal, ie: short gamma.

in the JBO account. I turned his $250,000 account into $750,000 in the first year. We split fifty/fifty. After tax I had about $200,000.

In the trading firm, did you learn stuff from the other traders?

No at all. I thought I would. There was a bunch of ex-floor traders, market makers and directional guys, but most of them were from the south side of Chicago. They had no aspiration to go to college. They wanted to be a policemen, farmers, etc. They had very limited finance backgrounds, which is fine. My background was limited too, but a lot of them did things I just didn't believed in, such as doing point and figure charting, which is a massive smoothing of the data and I wasn't into breakout systems. I also met a guy that was in med school that I thought I was going to learn from, but I found out he was a complete degenerate. He had no bet sizing methodology. He would literally go all in when he really liked something.

Were you backtesting stuff or just feeling out when you thought something was mispriced?

There weren't a lot of backtesting tools back then. I have what is called eidetic memory. I can remember numbers very easily. I can recite pi out to maybe two hundred digits. I would have a really good memory in the stocks that I followed. I can recall the vol figure that I computed for an ATM straddle and the skew. I could recall the closing prices in stocks that I followed for maybe ninety days back. At some point I switch to the financial futures options and commodities. I was primarily trading options in T-Bonds, corn, beans, crude oil.

What do you think is the biggest difference between those options markets from those days compared to right now?

Electronic trading and the Internet changed everything, because when I started trading, single name and indices stock options spreads were really wide. For example AAPL, the four forty-five ATM straddle for April expiration is about 40 to 50 cents wide, and the straddle is priced at $16 to $17. As a percentage of the value of the straddle the cost is really small. Back in the '80s and all the way to maybe '98/'99, the ATM straddles would be maybe $1.50 wide. In one sense, when I had the JBO with the risk haircuts, even though I had margin treatment I was still buying at the ask or hitting the bid, even though I was supposed to be a market maker. You would have to run your sheets, run what the fair value was. You would have a midpoint in every position, then you would derive what you were willing to pay in terms of edge loss due to the spread. Back in the '80s and '90s, vol was much higher. Most of the names I was trading had volatility above 100. These days vol is very low. You can get in and out with almost no edge loss due to tighter spreads, but unfortunately the vol is very low.

These stocks that had 100 vol, how you would assess they were mispriced? Do you look at fundamental data, news, or something else?

You look at realized vol. At this point we would have DDE links to Excel, and you could pump the data into a spreadsheet. I would just look at thirty-day realized vol figure in the stocks I traded. For example, JDSU was in the $80 to $90 a share range when the markets were already in the downswing from the bubble. You would look at historical vol of maybe 50 to 60, but you would have an implied vol of 120 in the options. That gave me the confidence. I would go 30 to 40 percent of my account in JDSU selling vol. It wasn't guaranteed, but the risk was so asymmetric. The reward would so outweigh the risk. All you had to do was hold it for three days and you'd be up $6 per contract. I remember prior to JDSU releasing its quarterly earnings report, the stock was at $79 a share. I sold the front month straddle at $22.05. There was about three or four weeks to expiration.

After earnings, the stock went up $6 or $7, all the sudden the straddle was at $14. I bought the wings to convert into a fly.[40] At that point the trade was virtually locked up. I made something like $60,000 in that trade, holding for three days. The money wasn't enormous but the edge was. The one thing that kills me the most when I look back at my trading is that I wasn't larger in that period.

I also remember in that in the '99 to 2001 period there was something called RAIS in the CBOE. It was an execution system that if you traded twenty lots or less as a retail client, you would get FIFO treatment. The market maker wouldn't get filled before you. Let's say if we were both at $3.10 bid and $3.30 offer, I would get priority over the market maker. Back then there were no exchange links. You would have about five options exchanges. You would have options in COMS COM or tricom at the PLHX at $3.10 bid and $2.90 offer at the PSE. There was a huge arb there, and I got into that. I would buy in one exchange and sell it in another up to twenty lots. I would have a quick gain in a transaction that would take me about fifteen seconds.

I remember the first week that happened, I was totally unprepared for it. I had a programmer, but I was afraid to tell him about it because he could tell the whole world. I was just executing manually. On the first day of this arb. I made about $180,000, with about $100,000 in capital in an Interactive Brokers account that I set up just for this purpose. Second day was about $280,000 or so. At

---

[40] In this case it was technically not a traditional butterfly (but rather an Iron Butterfly) because it involved being short both calls and puts in the middle but it's a similar structure. Converting a straddle into a fly cuts down the risk of exposure to fat tails or volatility increases.

that point I had to bring people in to execute the orders, about four or five people, and the edge immediately dried up. Exactly one week after this system started it stopped. The markets were still there, but we would not get executed. Basically the OCC and the exchanges froze all the REIS transactions, so that was the end of that arb. About a month later I got a letter from the OCC saying that they were going to try to go after my profits in court. Then I got a letter from Timber Hill saying that they were going to represent me legally. The OCC never got a dime, so I'm very loyal to IB for that.

Did you regret telling other people?

Yeah, totally. I knew that if I'd been more discreet I could have milked it for at least a few months. The problem was that I was getting carpal tunnel syndrome from all the mouse clicking. I was literally executing five hundred transactions, if not more – about a thousand round trips a day. It's very hard to do it manually. I knew that these guys were very sharp, and they would be telling every family member about it, and the people they told would also start talking, and the edge would disappear and it did. I didn't know it at the time, but the guy who started the Archipelago ECN was much bigger than we were in doing this. He was making millions on it.

Was that the last time you saw easy edges like that?

Yes, there are some opportunities to do some reverse conversions in hard to borrow stocks so I could get shares in stocks that were reasonably hard to short.[41] These reversals would pay 70 to 80

---

41 A reverse conversion can be achieved by selling a put, buying a call at the same strike and expiration while also being short the stock. Hard to borrow stocks usually have inflated premiums for a number of reasons, especially in the put side, this strategy tries to capitalize on that by having a credit after the option transactions

percent a year, but they can pull the stock on you at any time. If the shareholders ask for the certificates, they can pull your borrow.

As the HFTs started to show up in the markets, did you have to lengthen the time frame of your trades?

No, it's always a function of the volatility. The lower the vol, the more we have to go out. HFTs work both ways. For guys that are pure stock traders that try to make markets and collect rebates, the HFTs are brutal, because it's so mean reverting. If they put in a bid in a stock at $4.87, the HFTs will see that there's some natural demand, and they'll subpenny the deal. That doesn't happen to me at all. The HFTs actually help me because I trade a lot of stock, so I can hedge an options position. For example, if I'm short puts and I'm short the stock, HFTs help me get a better fill. The NBBO are narrower as a result of HFT interest. Since I'm not a directional trader in the primary market the trade is now cheaper. HFTs for me are great, but I can understand that for guys at stock prop firms it's tough, because you get no swings, as soon as you put an order in and they're subpennying you or stepping in front of your trades you're constantly having to take liquidity and this hurts them. For me, since I always have been a price taker, the narrower spreads actually help me.

So the vast majority of your orders in options are taking the liquidity available?

Totally, all the time. I never buy an option at edge or sell an option at edge. If my methodology is dependent in getting in at the

---

which then is an almost guaranteed profit given that the position is hedged by being short the stock. But of course, as atticus says, it's not easy to profit from because you can get your borrow pulled at any time leaving you exposed to a decline in the stock.

midpoint or bellow midpoint of the spread then it's not robust enough. I can't depend on microstructure. If I'm a four leg spread and the spread is $30.00 x $31.00, my average fill is probably about $30.80. So I'm 30 cents off the midpoint. $30.50 is fair value, I'm paying 30 cents in edge loss or about 1 percent on average.

When you sell options and tails and things like that, are you constantly scared of a black swan? How do you prevent a black swan from taking you out of the game?

I buy what are called "garbage puts." I don't buy a lot of upside protection, because we have the natural autocorrelation on vol in the upside. When prices goes up, vol goes down in inverse proportion. In the downside you need protection. I buy a lot of single name stock puts that are very deep OTM, not so much for the vol sensitivity but for the delta gamma. If we do have a blow up, something that I paid a very low price for could easily go up ten to twenty times.

I'm also not always in the market. I'm not a passive trader that constantly sells vol like a lot of guys do. I feel strongly that if the vol is too low, there's not a duration that I can go out to that will fully compensate me for that vol plus I'm exposing myself to that much duration and market risk. For example, I trade fairly large in the crude oil markets, but I tried to sell vol recently and just could not do it, because it's heavily correlated with stock index vol. So, I'm not always in the market, and certainly my income and exposures go down in low vol markets. These days I find myself buying a lot of close-to-the-money calendars in indexes, single name stocks, and commodities, because it allows me to sell a little bit of gamma and gain a little theta while also being long volatility.

You had that learning experience in '87. How did you do in October of 2008?

I would have to take a look at my spreadsheets. I know it wasn't great. I can tell you how much I lost in 9/11. It was about 19 percent, because Friday before the attacks I got a long signal in one of my Neural Networks systems. I was about 100 percent long in the Friday before 9/11. When the markets reopened I remember it was pretty orderly. It was down 5 to 6 percent, but I thought, wow, maybe I should stay in it. The loss was big though, so I took it.

I heard from some guys that if they get too big in an option, the market maker can tell it and they try to shake the guy out by perhaps manipulating the prices. Do you think that's true?

Oh, it is. It's less of an issue now. There's the sell side that's making the markets—the Citadels, Susquehanna, Wolverine, etc. You also have the buy side, which is primarily hedge funds that are price takers for the most part, that trade huge size. They're not necessarily concerned about manipulation, they just want to get in or out. I remember a firm that I heard about that was trading 30,000 contracts a day in a fairly illiquid series. It turns out that if they lost their entire investment it would have been something like 1 percent of their AUM. I remember in the early 2000s, I was working for a fund of funds. I'd traded a fairly large number of flys for Best Buy. I routed an order to the AMEX, got a terrible fill, then I called a friend of mine who worked in a different number of single stock posts. I said, "Hey, bud, I got a really terrible fill from a broker." He said, "Oh yeah, I saw that trade. I didn't participate, but they were talking about it and laughing about how they raped the guy that sent that order." It was my fault for giving the broker any leeway in the trade.

You mentioned bet sizing. Do you have a mathematical algorithm for position sizing?

I do. I determine an edge in a position in terms of a five- to seven-day look in a thirty-day option or maybe a two to three week in a quarterly option. I determine what my vol edge is, forecasting what is the likely realized vol over that duration. I determine what my edge is in terms of premium and percentage terms, then I apply essentially a Kelly criterion to that. I've it programmed in my iPhone, Android phone, and in my spreadsheets.

Do you go 100 percent of the Kelly?

No. I limit myself to 25 percent of my account in short vol trades, spread out in 5 percent blocks. So I might have a single name position that is 5 percent, an index position that is 5 percent, and so on. If I like something a lot I might go up to 25 percent of my account in any single trade, but I usually try to manage in 5 percent blocks.

Because the Kelly assumes that there are no fat tails, do you think it can be dangerous sometimes?

I have a nuclear risk figure, so if everything blows up, I know how much I'm going to lose. It's hard to do that in the dispersion trades that I do, but I look at things like VAR[42]. If my two standard deviation, two sigma VAR is 20 percent of my portfolio[43], I'll have to reduce it. I monitor that in real time. I might reduce it by a quarter.

The primary risk that I look at, along with every trader that I follow, is our theta figure, because its dollar figure[44] It gives you

---

[42] Value at risk. It's a statistical measure of risk over a certain period of time.

[43] A two sigma VAR, in theory, would tell what is likely to happen roughly 95% of the time.

[44] The Theta of an option or of an options portfolio tells you how much you are expected to lose per day due time decay. Ex: If you a long $500 in calls with a Theta of 25, in theory you're expected to lose $25 per day due time decay.

basically a proportional gamma figure that we derive. If my dollar thetas are positive and are 5 percent of my book in total, that is way too much. I will have to cut it down. Let's say I'm short puts in stocks with long puts in indexes and my theta figure is 5 percent of my book. If it was 2 percent a week ago, that means the stocks that I'm trading are not well correlated, and I'm taking too much risk in the dispersion, and I have to reduce.

I've gotten to the point where the longer I've been trading, the simpler I've made the analytics. The biggest traders I know simply look at their theta figures, so I figured if it's good enough for them, it's good enough for me.

People who use Kelly in casino games usually do one bet at a time, but in trading there are multiple bets, sometimes correlated bets. Do you take that into account?

Sure. Everything is correlated. If I have a 3 percent bet in a single name, a 5 percent bet in an index, a 4 percent bet in a European single name. I don't see much difference between those. The DAX right now is pretty much leading our markets and so is Japan's. If I have a fairly large long delta[45] position in the United States, I would try to counter that with a short delta position elsewhere. The problem with that is that you also have to look at your modality of delta. If you have a short delta in the United States and a long delta in Europe, is the short delta in the United States unimodal? If it continues to go down does my delta position get smaller?[46] Does it become less

---

[45] Being long delta means he is exposed positively to a rise in the underlying price.

[46] This would happen, for instance, if the short Delta exposure was expressed by being short ATM calls. As the price of the underlying declines so will the value of the call, your dollar exposure in the trade will also go down leaving your hedge smaller and smaller.

sensitive or does it increase. If I have convexity to the downside, or positive convexity, that means I will gain more deltas as it goes down. Then I feel like I have a robust hedge. If I'm initially short deltas in the United States, and that delta flips bimodal—it flips sign—I won't consider it a robust hedge. I do try to keep my hedges unimodal. If I'm bearish in one market, I make sure that stays bearish. I don't worry as much about upside modality. If I'm bullish in another market and it flips to bearish after it rallies maybe 5 percent on the index, I will look for the mean reversion to maybe get me out. I make sure my hedges are true hedges. If I'm short delta, I make sure I remain short delta in the hedge.

What do you think enabled you to be able to consistently find edges for all these years you have been trading?

That's where the experience comes in. There's no impact other than experiences. Like I said, it's much easier now to move size. I can get in and out a thousand lots without moving the market more than a quarter point, but the vol is so low that it's just harder to find stuff.

Basically my edge is in terms of discretion, being out when I should be out and in when I should. Right now we are 11/12 vol on the VIX. The VIX figure is actually a strange number. The figure that they apply to the tails is indicative of the volume in the tails, but it's not the primary mover, because most people are trading ATM. It's not like I sit there and sell tails all day long and sell futures, because it just wouldn't be prudent if you consider the gamma of that. So I look at the ATM figure, if you're trading with 10.5 ATM figure, it's very difficult to sell vol in that level or even buy. Realized vol in the S&P 500 is under 10, if I sell or buy 10.5 and I hedge discreetly in the underlying, I'm not going to make any money. There's no edge. I do look at what the dynamic hedging model would produce based on current realized vs. implied vol. If there isn't enough edge that I can hedge discreetly, I don't get involved long or short vol.

It's difficult. It forces you into single name vol, like earnings reports ramp up in vol trading duration (term skew). For instance, if May has an earnings report, you can buy May vol and sell April vol. As the date gets closer and people buy more and more May vol, you can profit. I trade a lot of calendars but only when I see an edge. When I do them, I'm not concerned what the broad market is going to do.

With regards to single name stock, when there's panic, does the implied vol gets consistently too high most of the time?

Sure. Prior to the Dragi comments about bailouts you had days where the VIX would go from thirteen to eighteen, or something like that, without a big sell-off in the markets. You would have this asymmetric profile and you always will, because essentially the VIX is bounded to ten or nine. It's like trading Eurodollars at 99.50. Can it go above 100? I don't think we will ever see that. The VIX is similar. There's a lower bound at around nine. If we drop 50 points in the S&P 500, we would see twenty-two on the VIX. Would I be selling twenty-two on the VIX? I probably would but not in the index, but in single name stocks, simply because I think there's less risk and better compensation. If the VIX is at twenty-two, names like Apple or Google might be at forty, so I'm being better paid there. I would not see twenty-two vol as necessarily a mean reversion selling point, because if it goes to twenty-two, it can easily go to forty.

I do look at technical stuff, outside reversals. If I was looking at the weekly chart, if I saw a high print of 1570 in the S&P 500 and a low closing print of 1520, there's no way in hell I would be long any deltas or any market. Maybe gold, but even then you can get creamed as well as it can be a source of funds for injured equity accounts.

The equity markets are perceived to be small compared to FX or debt. They are, but the notional risk in equities drives everything. All of the psychology is really based off the equity market. The cab driver, the guy at the local bakery, everybody is looking at equity prices. I look at the equity markets as the sole barometer of where we are headed. Right now it looks great.

Because vol is so low, is it a good time to buy it, maybe long-term vol?

There are very few instruments where you can get paid to hold. You can buy calendars in the VIX or some other vol instrument. The problem with that is you're short variance. Let's say you're technically long deltas in the VIX. Now you have modality again. If you're long deltas to say sixteen VIX and we are at twelve. Then we have a day where the ES is down thirty to forty. We are going to have eighteen VIX. All of a sudden you're no longer long vol. There's no vol exposure. You're short so many deltas that there's nothing you can do about it. There's no hedge to it. It's essentially a write-off unless you can get back to neutrality on deltas.

There are very few things right now that you can do that you get paid to hold, so I'm not looking for that necessarily, but if we had an outside reversal day in the chart, or Bernanke swearing off of QE, I would probably be long vol regardless of what the print was, but we are so concerned with what could happen that any blip in the market is backstopped. That's the danger of buying vol here, especially in the VIX, where you have an artificial curve based on absolute levels of volatility. Lots of times you see manipulation on the curve on settlement day.

I look at ATM vol I look at twenty delta risk reversal, which would be the twenty delta put over the twenty delta call, and I also try to determine what the skew is. Right now I don't think it pays to be long vol into the summer months. Cyclicality says we're going to be slow here. If I had to be long vol I would love to be long vol in China, Singapore as a proxy for China, the Nikkei, and definitely in the DAX through some kind of synthetic calendar, long back spread/short delta.

The fact that you're not paid to hold to be long vol, couldn't that be a good thing? Almost no one is doing it, and maybe it's mispriced because everybody is short that trade.

Yes, it's definitely not crowded. I think people have become complacent due to all the backstops. If you look at Europe, with the confiscation of bank accounts in Cyprus and all of that, it's spooky. It's so difficult to buy vol when somebody just has to say, "Yeah, we don't have to worry about it. We're just going to print more money." When the dollar starts to fall against the euro, that's when it will be time to buy vol, because with all that's going on in Europe, there's no fix. The time to buy it will be when EURUSD goes above 1.30, 1.31. When we see inflation taking effect and that impacts the currency markets, I might start to position trade in vol.

When you trade single name equities, do you read the tape or look at stuff like L2 at all?

I don't look at that stuff at all. I look at closing trends, sector weights, and heat maps. I want to see where the large caps are moving. I look at the breath, relative value. I don't look at ticks or nominal statistics like that. If I see AAPL/GOOG, and I see networking stocks doing well and closing on the highs of the day that might get me to short vol and get long delta. Basically the two trades that I believe exist are short delta/long vol and long delta/short vol. If you want to be short the market in any significant way, you don't want to be short vol. And if you want to be long the market you don't want to be long volatility. That's basically all you can do, and that is all that I do.

Do you use your instincts a lot to try to get a sense of what the stocks are going to do?

I certainly have as much analytics I can in terms of setting up a trade, particularly in terms of bet sizing. I might commit up to 30 to 40 percent of capital if it looks like smooth sailing, but with EU as it's right now, I won't commit that much. Most of the instincts are discretion in terms of bet sizing depending on how the world looks. It's also a function of the fact that there's not as much opportunity. I'm virtually flat this week. I was short some vol in crude oil, and that worked out OK, but I'm very quick to take profits when I can.

In some of these plays that you do, do you use your experience that you accumulated over your career to sense when things are mispriced?

I think I mentioned on Elitetrader at one point, for each ticker that I follow I try to determine how the vol skew looks like in a percentage term.[47] I will also have an over/under on premium, so I know how the vol figure looks like in dollar terms. I will also price the complex spreads out in width, starting with a very narrow butterfly, say ten points wide, then fifteen, twenty, twenty-five. Beyond that point, the wings are so cheap, cheaper than half a point in terms of combined premium, so I stop tracking them. This gives me a relative value in terms of flys. I normalize them for dates as well. It gives me a variance figure, a vol of vol figure. I use a dollar figure on skew in

---

[47] The vol skew tells you what is the difference in implied volatilities between OTM, ATM and ITM options.

the S&P 500 and other indices like NASDAQ and the DAX that gives me a relative allocation level. If the skew looks fat, if there's a large tail convexity, that gives me more confidence to sell vol even if ATM vol is relatively low. This indicates that maybe the tails are fat there might be something fundamental coming up somewhere, but it won't be something that will impact the market for weeks to come. Maybe it will be just something transitory and it will be reverted back.

Any memorable trades from this year or last year?

I had a LEAPS position in AAPL maybe a year and a half ago. I sold vol prior to an earnings report and I was also short delta. I don't do this in indices, but occasionally I will do it in single names if I have a strong view. I felt that AAPL in notional terms couldn't support their valuation with the Android taking up so much market share. It was a fundamental shift. I saw so many people walking around with Androids. When the Galaxy Note came out, which is the Samsung's phone-plus-tablet device, I saw all my friends buying. I was in Midtown Manhattan and I saw like six of them in half an hour. I bought some LEAPS flies that were bearish. They essentially went up four fold after the earnings and the follow-through.

What kind of equipment do you use for trading?

I have the latest 12 core Mac Pro and two 30-inch Apple monitors. I also have some Macs that are dual boots for stuff like Excel. I have a Bloomberg as well. I run it on a Mac with Bloomberg Anywhere.

Does the Bloomberg subscription pay for itself?

I don't pay for it. I have some folks who supply that for me. I can do without it for sure. I use a small fraction of their analytics. Basically everybody in New York is collocated with their Bloombergs with extremely fast connections, whereas I'm far away with a 100Mbs connection. The latency is so high I can't get any meaningful edge.

Are you doing a lot of backtesting these days?

The more experience I have, the more trading I do, the less I backtest. I never put a lot of weight on backtesting. I used to do a lot of microstructure backtesting, seeing how orders would impact my overall results. With the spreads narrow now, I just don't do it anymore.

What do you do with the capital that you don't use for trading?

For the most part I move into cash. I will buy stocks but mostly to trade premium around it, like XOM to write calls on it. I might sell puts if I see a little skew there over the ATMs. As I accumulate premium over a few months, I'll convert them into additional shares. Once I get to the size that I want, I'll start to write calls against it.

What is the best book for somebody that wants to become a better options trader?

Anybody with a limited finance or statistics background should start with John Hull's *Options, Futures, and Derivatives*. With regard to equity options, I'd go with Sheldon Natenberg's stuff. If you want to know how to price synthetics, which are pretty basic math but most people don't know it, there's Allen Jan Baird book on *Option Market Making*. That stuff can be very useful. For instance, if I'm bullish XYZ at $100, I think the stock will be trading at $102, but I think realized vol will drop, given that implied vol is autocorrelated component, instead of trading the synthetic iron fly, I may buy the put fly, because I want my body strike to be OTM at the next expiration, or at least touched.[48] This simply because it provides a microstructure advantage. Deep ITM flys that have a deep ITM short component typically trade wider because there's more risk to the counterparty to trade out of.[49] I look at microstructure a lot when I trade. A lot of decision making is at that level, which is going to be the cheapest or most efficient way to express the trade.

Any last words of wisdom?

It's tough, because people learn about options and feel that they have to take positions, but there's so little juice out there right now. I would say for people who have a stock background, if they can make money there, continue there, and don't go to options. People use to have 4 to 5 cents of edge, now they have a fraction of a cent in edge. Sometimes they feel like they need to go into options because of that. I know guys that trade very large with major prop firms or NASDAQ market makers that left the game for options because they could not beat the sell side. I know guys who made millions over the last few years simply selling puts on bank stocks because they used to make markets in bank stocks. Unless you have a lot of capital and you can sit on your hands, it's just not a market to get into here. The vol is so low. It does not pay to be long vol. It does not pay to be short vol. You're naturally forced to go out of the curve in terms of time. Unfortunately, the longer you go, the bigger the Vegas will be and the more volatility risk you'll have. You can't trade short-term, because there's no juice. You can't trade long-term, because you

---

[48] The iron fly would be short a put and a call in the "middle," whereas a long put fly would be short two puts in the middle. This difference can provide the trader an advantage in certain situations due microstructure even though they express a similar bias.
[49] This provides the trader an additional vol "juice" to capture by selling the option.

have juice but the vol figure is so low. I would not recommend anybody to go into vol trading at this point.

Lessons from Chapter 10

1. Protect yourself against black swans/fat tails through garbage puts. A lot of people think selling volatility is a money loser in the long-term, because occasionally you get hit by a fat tail or black swan and lose a large amount. This definitely can be true if your risk management and position sizing is poor; however, if you protect yourself against such events using way OTM options, you can reduce those risks.

It's important to understand that picking nickels in front of steamroller is not always a bad idea.[50] This can be counterintuitive for people that were trained to look for good risk/reward trades. They see a one to ten gain to loss payoff ratio and naturally are turned off and think people who engage in that kind of trading will lose everything. This is probably correct for 95 percent or more of participants who engage in that sort of trading. This is not the case with the Options Expert. It's pretty easy to prove that a one to ten win loss ratio can be extremely profitable if your win percentage is high enough. The real issue is making sure that ten-unit loss is really ten units and not five hundred during an once-in-a-lifetime sort of event.

Perhaps an example can illustrate this situation. Let's say stock ABC is trading at $50. It then proceeds to drop $20 in a week during a series of bad news. You notice that IV is at 200 percent. You believe that is completely mispriced and this was created by an irrational

---

[50] I understand this statement is controversial but stay with me.

panic by investors. You decide to sell vol by selling the ATM straddle. But what if the stock goes to $0? If you do this type of trade enough times, at some point you're going to get hit by some kind of massive bad news, perhaps accounting fraud or maybe the SEC suspends trading in the stock (after which the stock doesn't trade for weeks, gets delisted and usually opens down 90 percent in the gray sheets market). In order to protect yourself against such an event, you can buy way OTM puts for, say, $15 strikes. You'll still get hurt by the fat tail. After all, your short put position will lose way more than your short call premium, but the garbage puts locks in the max loss you can possibly have. This enables you to have a loss that is consistent with a Kelly criterion style risk metric and thus prevents long-term negative account returns (as well as instant account blow ups).

Selling vol in this manner is similar to running an insurance company. You're taking the opposite side of a bad trade (the bad trade being buying vol), but **you must have a large enough bankroll** compared to your maximum loss, otherwise your equity volatility will be large and you'll possibly have long-term negative returns. This style of trading is not for everyone, it requires rock solid risk management and discipline otherwise one day you can make a mistake and end up facing such a big loss it can set you back dramatically. If you do trade this style always be willing to sacrifice some profit in order to reduce the risk of a large negative event through the use of garbage options.

2. Have a sound position-sizing and risk management methodology. As you could see, The Options Expert had a very specific position-sizing method. He was the most detailed about it of all the interviews I conducted. He limits his exposure to 25 percent of his account in short vol trades, spread out in 5 percent buckets.

He derives how much he should bet from the Kelly Criterion formula, keep in mind that in options it's frequently the case (but not always) that you know exactly how much you're going to lose, so you can get closer to the Kelly percentage in a lot of trades. This is not the case in stock or futures trading, where you can be hit by halts, overnight gaps, etc. For those types of situations you have to be lower than a conservatively estimated Kelly just to be safe.

He uses a "nuclear risk" figure of 15% for a two sigma VAR event (if he notices that it is 20% in his real-time monitoring, he will reduce it to 15%). A two sigma event will happen more frequently that what a normal distribution probability model would tell you but it's important to keep in mind the following things:

A.   He is taking risks based on "account size" not net worth, he has money in long-term investments, cash, etc. His true economic exposure is smaller than that.

B.   Even if he faces a significant loss (say 30-40% of his account in a several sigma event) occasionally (like an insurance company) he can still grow his account quite well. As of matter of fact, the Kelly criterion frequently suggests risking significant % of your bankroll if you have a great system. The key is to have these losses under control.

3. Dispersion trades. If you like a stock and its the vol figure (meaning, you think vol it's too high), you can short its puts and then buy puts in the index. This enables you to win by being right about the stock rising and/or profiting as the implied volatility decreases. You also won't be exposed to broad market situations like the VIX going to 40, or something along those lines. There's correlation risk of course, but at least you diminish your overall market risk. If this position is of meaningful size you are probably better off also buying

some "garbage" puts in the single name stock in order to further reduce your risk. If it's not (if the stock goes down 80% and it doesn`t threaten your account in a significant way) you can probably do without it.

4. The importance of sitting on your hands. The options expert had no problems saying that he wasn't trading much recently, given the lack of opportunities. He says one of the keys of his success is the discipline of being in the market when he should and not forcing trades. As Jesse Livermore said, "It never was my thinking that made the big money for me. It always was my sitting."

5. Use theta as a risk figure for your options portfolio. The theta gives you a dollar figure that you can use to manage your exposure. It's used by a lot of big time options traders.

6. Books. He recommends a few books for traders looking to become better options traders. If you're looking to expand your knowledge in that area, they're a good start.

7. Microstructure. Some options strategies might be superior to others, even though they express a similar bias. This is due to microstructure differences in the backstage of the trades. If you want to improve as an options trader, learning microstructure might provide you with additional knowledge that you might find useful.

Chapter 11

Additional Advice, Resources and Tips

1. Trading Psychology

In this book I tried to emphasize the more technical aspects of trading and not as much psychology. This doesn't mean that trading psychology is not important. Lots of traders mentioned the ability to take losses as the most important trait a day or swing trader needs. I simply didn't want to write another trading psychology book with lots of bumper sticker advice, when market microstructure and strategies have become more important than ever. As far as psychology goes and how to improve in that area, I can provide the following tips some people might find helpful.

1.1. Read *The Six Pillars of Self-Esteem*, by Dr. Nathaniel Branden.

I highly recommend this book to pretty much anyone in any area, even if they don't think they need to improve their self-esteem. The author goes through what he believes are the six keys to enhancing self-esteem that he observed in decades of study and work that he did as a psychotherapist.

Have you ever wondered why some athletes, like Tiger Woods, Novak Djokovic, or Sebastian Vettel, seem like natural winners who would often perform even better in high-pressure situations and somehow get an advantage over others even though their opponents were performing just as well? Sure, they're talented, but in any field there are countless examples of talented players who never reach their full potential. (In tennis, off the top of my head I can name David Nalbandian and Marat Safin) Also, in most fields in the top ten to twenty, pretty much everybody is talented. Self-esteem provides one clue as to why some people perform better than others when they have similar skill sets. A lot of high performance athletes talk about the important of mental toughness and psychology in their performances. Djokovic himself said that whether he goes or not for big shots at key moments plays a large role in his big matches against Federer and Nadal in Grand Slams. He said that as he matured as a player and person, that process got easier.[51]

For a person with high self-esteem, success feels natural. It doesn't produce anxiety to be close to it (or if it does, its level is lower than a person with low self-esteem). Your mind is more relaxed. You're better equipped to perform in the way you trained, because you feel deserving of the success you're about to achieve. A person with high self-esteem is unlikely to engage in self-sabotaging behaviors that can drastically impact the long-term outcome of a career.

I suspect that mental stability (through a good level of self-esteem) is probably one of the major factors why Tiger Woods is so good at playoffs (he's at 11-1[52]). Think about it. He essentially had to play these playoffs against a guy who just played really well, had

---

[51] http://tinyurl.com/lsdsdbq

[52] In a binary format like Golf playoffs where one mistake can cost you the win this sample size is not small. It's far more likely he was a significant favorite in these playoffs than him being a 50 to 55 percent favorite who got in a lucky streak.

the run of his life in a major, yet he would win over and over again. Was it golf skill that made the difference? It's unlikely to be a major factor, because they both had played the tournament and scored the same exact amount! (Which is why the game went to playoffs). And even if skill was a factor, it certainly can't be so large as to enable him to win so often (again, his opponent had the same score as Tiger did on that golf course over the weekend, so he clearly adapted well to the course, and along with Tiger he was the single best golfer out of the entire field).

To me it's clear that it's his psychology that gives him the edge. Because he feels deserving of winning and success, he doesn't get nearly as anxious as his opponents. As a result, his higher level of relaxation enables him to do what he has already trained to do countless times. Meanwhile, his opponents who lack the same level of entitlement feel stressed and are more likely to engage in poor decision making, negative thinking, sloppy execution, and self-sabotage. In a quick format like in the playoffs, these differences can turn a small or nonexistent skill advantage into a gigantic overall edge.

Woods is also 14-1 when going into the final round of a major with at least a share of the lead. When he's playing well, he stays that way. Meanwhile, a player with poor self-esteem might just get into a negative mindset, telling himself, "I'm leading. I hope I don't screw it up." And he might perform poorly as a result.

In trading you can see some people who, due to a lack of self-esteem, would frequently feel undeserving of profits after a certain number (say, more than $15,000 a month). These traders would all of a sudden lose their courage and not take risks they know they should, because they don't like the discomfort of being up so much. They'd rather stay "where they belong," with smaller profits, than grow as a person and reach new levels of profitability.

Other manifestations of poor self-esteem in trading would be taking reckless risks, desiring to be right at all costs, refusing to acknowledge your strengths and weaknesses, refusing to take a loss, gambling, poor planning, among others.

The first time I read Nathaniel's book was when I was seventeen and I was struggling severely with extreme shyness, anxiety, and depression. I'd already tried all kinds of different methods to overcome it (NLP, lucid dreaming, self-hypnosis, and others), but they all failed because they didn't go to the heart of the matter. They didn't changed the day-to-day behaviors that were affecting my self-esteem. In my case it was a lack of self-assertiveness (one of the pillars of self-esteem) when dealing with other people, along with not living consciously enough (engaging in self-deception). For others it might be lack of accountability (the second pillar), they might keep blaming people for their mistakes or just refusing to acknowledge their imperfections. These kinds of destructive behaviors accumulate in the unconscious mind and add up to an overall assessment of your self-worth that comes out through an experience (that is even more than just a feeling) of you being pleased with yourself or not.

That book literally saved my life. After I read it, I immediately implemented several changes in my life and noticed that my self-esteem skyrocketed. I'm forever grateful to the person who recommended that book to me, which is why I'm now doing it myself.

I understand that the word *self-esteem* has lots of different meanings to different people. The truth is that the author of the book does not endorse the mainstream definition of the term as meaning, "feeling good about yourself." Lots of things can make you feel good about yourself, like a drug, a love affair, a quick reckless profit, etc. But they're not necessarily good for your self-esteem as he defines it. He also doesn't believe you can have too much self-esteem as some psychologists think. "It's no more possible to have too much self-esteem than it is to have too much physical or mental health," he says.

A lot of the misconceptions about self-esteem exist due poorly executed "empirical" studies that don`t use good methods or an intelligent definition of the word self-esteem.[53]

Note that in trading, it's frequently said that you ought to keep your ego in check, otherwise you'll end up fighting the market. Nathaniel has a different definition of the word *ego*. He talks about the ego as a good thing. The ego we hear about in the trading world he refers to as "pseudo self-esteem." This is all just semantics, however. There's no conflict between his principles and good trading psychology. I'm just mentioning this so people don't get confused when they read about it.

I probably won't do the book justice if I try to summarize it. If you're serious about becoming the best trader you can be check out that book and do the exercises in it. He also has an audio program "The Psychology of High Self-Esteem," which is terrific.

1.2. Understand, manage, and increase the activity of your pre-frontal cortex.

The key to understanding why the pre-frontal cortex (PFC) is so important to traders is knowing which human activities and

---

[53] Some studies ask people about how high their self-esteem is which hardly qualifies as good evidence of such given how often people deceive themselves and how differently people can interpret that term. These are just a few of the problems with a lot of the studies that are out there.

behaviors are controlled by it. This area of the brain, amongst others, is responsible for:

-Orchestration of thoughts and actions in accordance with internal goals.

-The ability to differentiate among conflicting thoughts, determine good and bad, better and best, same and different, future consequences of current activities, working toward a defined goal, prediction of outcomes, expectation based on actions, and social "control" (the ability to suppress urges that, if not suppressed, could lead to socially unacceptable outcomes).[54]

-Forecasting the consequences of a current behavior on a long-term goal. Controlling immediate reactions to a stimulus.[55]

It is essentially the discipline muscle. I use the word "muscle" as do many neuroscientists because, like a muscle, it strengthens when it is used regularly and it weakens when it is not. Research has indicated that activities that use the PFC increase its size and efficiency.

Sometimes it's very hard to do the "right thing" when it comes to a particular trade or decision because we essentially have two brains.

According to Nobel prize-winning psychologist Daniel Kahneman, we have the System 1 brain (impulsive, fast, automatic, emotional) and the System 2 (slow, logical, conscious, calculating) brain. System 2 is mostly controlled by the PFC. What happens a lot of the time to losing or struggling traders is that because they never really fully developed their System 2 brain, they spend a lot of their trading using the System 1 brain, and this leads to all sorts of career-

---

[54] This information is derived from studies with people who had damage to their pre-frontal cortexes.
[55] Neuroscientist Jordan Grafman Ph.D.

ending mistakes, such as not taking losses, adding to bad trades, oversizing to make the money back, overtrading, and gambling.

If you want to be effective as a trader, you will have to develop and improve your System 2 brain. Learn what helps it, harms it, and what activities outside trading can develop it further. I developed a quick, practical mini-course that you can use today to understand and develop your PFC and make your System 2 brain more effective. If you stick with the course, even if it's a little hard at first, you will notice that difficult things will get much easier as you develop your PFC muscle. Discipline will become second nature.

I'm putting it at the start of a new page so readers can print it out or copy it and re-read occasionally.

The Boost Your Discipline Mini-Course

The key to having discipline is developing your *willpower*, which is self-control, the ability to do or say the hard thing when your emotions want you to do or say something else. The good news is that anyone without brain damage can do it (really, we have an entire area of the brain dedicated to this, saying "I can't do it" won't cut it). The bad news is that it's going to be a little annoying at first because, like a muscle, if it's a little out of shape, it can take effort, but once you get going, it gets easier, just like physical exercise. Even if you don't think you need more willpower, I encourage you to practice activities that boost it. Just as you can't be too physically healthy, you can't be too mentally healthy, either. The sky is the limit when it comes to being in good mental shape.

I would highly recommend you pick up the book or audiobook *The Willpower Instinct*, by Stanford's psychologist Kelly McGonigal, Ph.D. She is one of the three people to whom this book is dedicated. Her work is tremendously practical and easy to understand (something you don't see very often coming out of academia). Her book is filled with techniques and experiments, all proven empirically in rigorous tests and in her in-person course, The Science of Willpower, to boost the area of the brain responsible for willpower, the pre-frontal cortex (PFC). Here are some of her key techniques and understandings about willpower that you might find helpful:

1. Sleep has a large impact on willpower.

2. Meditation can boost your willpower.

3. Being self-critical, harsh on yourself, or feeling guilty increases the likelihood of future willpower failures.

4. An attitude of self-acceptance decreases the likelihood of future willpower failures.

5. Blood sugar crashes can hurt your willpower.

6. Willpower can be restored by being in nature, listening to music, spending time with people you like, and exercise.

Let's go through one by one.

1. Sleep has a large impact on willpower.

According to McGonigal, eight hours of sleep does wonders to recharge the brain and its willpower capacity. In one of the studies, she mentions that it was tested whether adding a five-minute, breath-focus meditation would help people suffering from substance addiction.

The meditation actually boosted test participants sleep by one hour. That increase predicted whether the subject would relapse and give in to addiction in the future. The PFC consumes a lot of energy. When we operate under sleep deprivation, according to research, the body and the brain have their sugar metabolism impaired. The PFC and many areas of the body won't be able to operate effectively under those conditions. The condition won't improve even if you create a blood sugar spike by eating high carbohydrate foods, it does improve when you have a good night of sleep. (For scientific references and sources related to McGonigal's work, check out her book, I don't want to bombard the reader with references most people are not interested in).

In my own trading, I notice that if I had a bad night of sleep, I get impulsive. I overtrade and losses get more irritating by a factor of several times. When you are sleep deprived, it's crucial that you do one of these two things, either take the day off or trade defensively. If you were already thinking about taking a day off to take care of things outside trading, days following a bad night of sleep are perfect for that. Go ahead, deal with your issues, and enjoy yourself. You will be back, fully charged, the next day.

If you do decide to trade though, **decrease your position size and only trade the best trade setups**. It sounds easy, but the fact that your PFC will be on shutdown mode can make following this rule challenging. However, it can literally save you thousands of dollars. On defensive trading days, try to sleep during the mid-day session. This accomplishes two things: first, it keeps you out of trouble by not trading during the least profitable time of the day when your PFC is under-functional, and second, it re-charges your willpower for the close, when you are likely to have more profitable opportunities.

2. **Meditation can boost your willpower.**

Meditation is becoming more popular these days, and for a good reason. Research indicates it provides all kinds of benefits, ranging from lower stress, less anxiety, and better focus, to more creativity and better memory.[56] The greatest hedge fund manager of all time,

---

[56] What Happens to the Brain When You Meditate (And How it Benefits You)- http://tinyurl.com/kszjg3x

Ray Dalio, says, "Meditation, more than anything in my life, was the biggest ingredient of whatever success I've had."[57]

I notice that when I'm not meditating regularly, my trading suffers noticeably. All of a sudden, my brain will lose its discipline and start to seek stimulation. When I have a losing trade in a stock, my tendency is to try to overtrade my way out of it. After a few hours, I notice that instead of putting in ten trades in a day, I did twenty or thirty or something along those lines.

The mid-day session becomes particularly problematic because it is already boring. Without meditation, it is even more boring. It becomes easy to justify some trades and start to overtrade your way into giving back your morning profits. But this habit goes beyond just trading. I'm in a much better mood when I'm meditating regularly than when I'm not. It is harder for me to get irritated, and my tolerance for pain increases (which helps with losing days and drawdowns).

According to research, meditation is a great way to develop your PFC. Yes, it will be difficult at first. That's the whole idea. If you are the type of person who has a hard time doing nothing for twenty minutes a day, then you are exactly the type of person who would benefit from integrating meditation to your life. If your mind just won't stop thinking about all kinds of things, you start to feel silly doing something so boring, and you keep thinking about checking Facebook or Twitter, your brain is addicted to seeking stimulation (The System 1 brain). Stimulation seeking can be extremely harmful to a trading account; it's a hard habit to break, but it is possible if you start slowly and don't try to do too much too quickly. I would recommend starting with even just a few minutes of meditation a

---

[57] Other practitioners include Tiger Woods, Kobe Bryant, David Blaine, and three-time Olympic gold medalists Misty May and Kerri Walsh.

day, then as you get more focus and willpower you can increase to 5, 10 and eventually 20-40 minutes. How do you practice meditation? Here is a simple technique that I use daily and that helps me a lot:

Breath Focus Meditation Technique

Sit down, away from your computer or cellphone (or any other type of stimulation), in a comfortable place. Set an alarm for the length of time you plan to do it. I recommend you start with one to three minutes, so you don't get discouraged. Just stay there and focus on your breath. Just listen to it—the sounds, the in and out. You might find it helpful to say, "Breath in, breath out," if you have trouble concentrating. Listen to your breath, and try not to move or scratch yourself. You might feel an urge to do so; that is your System 1 brain trying to get his way. By using your PFC and not giving in, you are getting it back in shape, teaching your brain that you won't give in to desire instantly. Just accept that the urge is there. Don't fight it. Just experience it, fully feel it, stay with it, and it will dissolve by itself.

As you focus on the sounds and sensations of your breath, you will begin to have all kinds of thoughts and ideas. That is fine and expected. Don't think that meditation is "not thinking." This is not the case, and even if it were, we are trying to develop the PFC, not reach some kind of Zen nirvana. I don't subscribe to the "spiritual" aspects of meditation, and it is not necessary to do so to collect its benefits. If you have thoughts and lose focus of your breath, try to catch yourself doing it and bring your awareness back to your breath, over and over again. Once the alarm goes off, you can go back to your daily routine.

This simple technique can make an enormous difference in your trading. First, because it might improve your sleep (though the evidence for that is not yet broad and conclusive, personally it works for me), you will wake up more refreshed and with more willpower.

Second, because even though it takes willpower to do it, according to McGonigal, these sorts of willpower using activities "end up giving back far more willpower than they take." You will build a willpower reserve and make your PFC bigger and more effective. Meditation is like a gym for a trader.

I would recommend the reader to research about meditation, read articles and books about it, and try out different techniques to see what works best for you.

3. **Being self-critical, harsh on yourself, or feeling guilty increases the likelihood of future willpower failures.**

This is a huge one because most western societies really drill into people's mindsets that they have to be a success, make a lot of money, and achieve things; otherwise, they are losers. This can be a problem especially for males, who seem to identify themselves more with financial success than females. The result is that it can make people hard on themselves when they face setbacks, make mistakes, and don't align their behaviors with their goals.

In one interesting study it was tested whether feelings of guilt and self-criticism in dieters affected their ability to stick with a diet. The researchers gave a doughnut and lots of water (to increase the feeling of being full) to two groups of dieters, then told one group that it was okay to feel guilty, that everybody indulged once in a while, and asked them not to be hard on themselves. To the other group, nothing of this kind was said. Then the researchers put out three bowls of candy (carefully chosen to appeal to all kinds of preferences). They told the dieters that it was a "taste test" and they could eat as much as they wanted, and asked them to report on the quality of the candy. The dieters who were told that it was okay to indulge and to not to be hard on themselves ate only 40% as much candy as the dieters who didn't receive that message.

According to McGonigal, "There is abundant research that shame and guilt are the biggest triggers for further relapse". That is true in gamblers, also. "The worse they feel about losing money, the more likely they are to gamble again," she says.

As a trader, it's important to understand that when you make mistakes, such as not following your rules, overtrading, or taking bad setups, the first instinct when you lose money is to curse yourself, yell, and break things. You might feel an urge to criticize yourself, to call yourself a terrible trader or an idiot. All this does is create stress, and when the body is stressed, it will prioritize the systems that deal with short-term emergencies, and this will make you more impulsive (the System 1 brain will begin to dominate), which makes it harder to face a willpower challenge (such as following your rules or taking the day off).

Self-criticism will also make you feel bad. You'll feel an irresistible urge to try to make the money back because it will change your mood and make you feel good again. **Your dopamine receptors become more sensitive under stress**, this makes chasing good feelings more tempting, it can be quite a challenge to overcome this urge. This is a deadly combination because you will be revenge trading and operating as your impulsive self.

There is evidence that smokers who look at horrifying images on the back of cigarette packages are likely to smoke more and feel good about smoking than the ones that didn't. **Stress is the enemy of willpower and discipline.**

There is also the "what the hell" effect. If you break your rules, act undisciplined, and feel shameful and guilty about it, you might just say, "Ah, what the hell. I'm trading so badly today, I might as well just keep going and try to turn this around" which only increases the chance of further mistakes. How to deal with these urges to criticize yourself? How to deal with unwanted emotions and difficult trading days? That's where the next willpower finding comes into play.

4. **An attitude of self-acceptance decreases the likelihood of future willpower failures.**

One study mentioned by McGonigal separated smokers into two groups. One taught the technique of "surfing the urge" to deal with strong desires and temptations. The other was a control group that didn't learn it. Then they stretched out for an hour the process of picking up a pack of cigarettes, opening it, picking out a cigarette, picking up a lighter, etc. During that hour, they were not allowed to smoke. They had to deal with an unfulfilled urge throughout the whole procedure. After this procedure, they were allowed to do whatever they wanted. They went back to their lives and tracked how many cigarettes they smoked. The group that was taught to "surf the urge" ended up cutting back the amount of cigarettes they smoked by 37%, an impressive result, given that the test group was not asked to cut back on cigarettes or even to keep using the technique that they were taught!

What is the "surfing the urge" technique? They were told that urges always pass, whether or not you give in to them. When they felt a strong craving, they were supposed to imagine that desire as a wave in the ocean. It would build up, but eventually crash and disappear. They had to imagine themselves riding that wave, not fighting it, resisting it, or trying to "get rid of it," but just experience it and notice how it felt. If you apply this method to your own desires, urges, and cravings, you will notice that they will be less powerful. They tend to dissolve when you fully experience them.

I personally use a similar procedure that is described in the book *The Six-Pillars of Self-Esteem* (in the self-acceptance chapter). Here's a brief summary of how it works:

Self-Acceptance Procedure

If, during your trading session, you experience urges to average down, overtrade, criticize yourself, punish yourself, or break things, etc. First fully feel your emotions and notice how they affect you. Awareness can be very helpful. Stay with the emotions. Don't just acknowledge them and move on to other things. Take your time. Second, don't try to get rid of these emotions. Fully acknowledge that they are occurring and accept them. Accepting doesn't mean liking or being proud of them; it just means that you recognize them as expressions of yourself at this point in time. You might not particularly like them, but you recognize that it's happening and allow yourself to experience them. Third, relax your muscles, frequently when people deal with unwanted emotions they contract their body in an effort to suppress their feelings. Fourth, take a deep and slow breath while remaining aware of the emotions and not resisting them.

This simple procedure is likely to make it easier to go through the experience without letting the emotion take over your behavior. You will find that it sometimes helps a lot, sometimes just a little, but you will be relatively better off than you were before you did it.

5. **Blood sugar crashes can hurt your willpower.**

The PFC uses a lot of energy to function. It is one of the most sugar-hungry parts of the brain. According to neuroscientists, when the body's blood sugar is unstable and starts to drop, the body interprets this as a signal that you could be facing starvation or scarcity soon. As a result, it goes into conservation mode, the PFC partially shuts down. Being in a more impulsive state is more beneficial during a short-term energy crisis. This hurts your willpower and discipline.

It's important to preserve a stable blood sugar level through your trading session if you want to be at your best at all times. One of the ways that you can achieve that is to eat foods with a low "glycemic index" (GI) and avoid foods with a high GI. The GI is a measure of how quickly the blood sugar rises after ingesting a particular food. There are many free articles and books in this subject, as well as free food tables available on the internet that show what kinds of foods destabilize your blood sugar and which ones keep it stable.

The standard American diet (S.A.D.) is not very helpful for traders because it is filled with high GI foods, especially for breakfast, but at lunch, it doesn't improve much. The results of that are sugar and insulin spikes, which helps willpower in the short-term, but then the blood sugar crashes and lead to a lack of activity in the area of the brain that traders need the most, the PFC. Lunch is particularly important because right after that you face the mid-day session, where profitable opportunities are less abundant. Spending hours in that time period with an underworking PFC is not a great recipe for profits. In fact, some traders may notice that they "lose" their discipline in the afternoon and end up giving back their morning profits. Their blood sugar instability can explain why. A SAD diet also leads to diabetes and diabetes-like conditions in the long-term, which will hurt your brain's ability to use sugar. Needless to say, this will hurt your willpower.

If you want to improve your health and willpower, consider improving your diet gradually by adding low GI foods and reducing high GI foods. Your brain will thank you.

6. **Willpower can be restored through being in nature, listening to music, spending time with people you like, and exercise.**

When you use a lot of willpower regularly, sometimes you can feel "drained." The PFC consumes a lot of energy and, like a muscle, it can get fatigued. We can develop it so it gets larger and with bigger reserves, but there is still a limit on how much effort it can exert.

It's important to integrate life activities outside trading that can "recharge" your PFC, so when you are trading, your willpower is at its maximum, or close to it. According to McGonigal, activities that can restore your willpower are things like being in nature, listening to music, spending time with people that you like, watching a movie or series (for less than two hours), physical exercise (exercise is especially useful because it also builds your willpower reserve; just like meditation, it takes willpower, but it gives back far more than it took), among others,

This willpower finding also should help some traders take vacations and days off without feeling guilty about it. If you want to trade optimally, having periods where you are not trading (and using your willpower reserves) can do wonders because they will recharge you and your willpower reserves. When you come back, you will trade better than you would otherwise. Don't feel too guilty about the money you didn't make while you were on vacation because you might end up getting it anyway, due to superior decision-making when you come back.

Note:

I only wrote about some of the main ideas and methods that I have learned from these two authors, but there is a lot more in their published works that I could possibly cover in this chapter. If you are serious about improving yourself as a trader, I would encourage you to explore their work and understand their concepts more deeply.

2. Recommended Broker

Interactive Brokers – www.interactivebrokers.com

Interactive Brokers, popularly called IB, is a must-have for any day trader. Their commissions and fees are lower than most retail brokerage houses out there, these savings add up to thousands of dollars at the end of a year. They have good trading software and order types, and through their platform Trader Workstation, you can customize anything that you can imagine. They also support several types of advanced orders **and more importantly, the so-called "native" hidden orders** (Which was mentioned in this book as a way to getting around HFT tricks and advantages). If you are an IB client and don't know about native hidden orders, definitely ask them about it. It can improve your order execution and cut your costs. Their abundance of routes for listed stocks also helps when you are trying to take liquidity because you can directly route your order to an ECN or exchange. They also have great borrows for shorts and additional layers of security to make sure your account won't be hacked and your money stolen.

IB has a minimum of $10,000 for new clients ($3,000 if you are age 26 or younger), and their accounts are SIPC insured.

3. Hardware and computer technical help

You definitely need a good machine to trade with, but keep in mind that day trading is a low CPU intensive activity. If you check out your Windows Task Manager, you'll notice that even with all your trading software opened, Internet browser, news feed, etc., your CPU usage will rarely stay above 50 percent for much longer than a few seconds. What this means is that you don't need to invest in the latest generation processor (a second or third generation Intel core i3 or core i5 or an equivalent AMD chip is likely to be fine for most traders). You're better off investing in things like RAM memory and a SSD (solid state drive).

For RAM, get at least 6GB DDR3, ideally 8GB. The thing is, a lot of computer programmers and software companies get lazy with memory usage, so programs these days tend to eat up a lot of RAM, even if they don't necessarily need to use it that much if they were coded properly. Make sure you get enough, because if you don't, your Operating System will start to write data to your hard drive (or SSD) when it runs out of RAM. The speed of that operation is magnitudes lower than of RAM memory.

Along with enough RAM definitely get a SSD (and install Windows in it). A SSD is essentially a high-speed hard drive. Even if your desktop or laptop didn't come with one, you can just buy it online and install it yourself (there are plenty of videos teaching that on Youtube). A SSD, depending on the model and brand, will be about five to ten times faster than a regular hard drive, in practice this will translate to:

- All the programs you use will open much faster and some will run faster as well.

- Windows will run faster.

- Faster boot and shutdown speeds.

- Faster installation process for new software and security updates of existing software.

- Copying, editing, and moving files will take less time (for backups this is extremely useful).

A lot of computers these days are shipped with the top processors, but without a SSD, which is suboptimal to say the least, for most people the hard drive speed is the biggest bottleneck in terms of day-to-day performance, not the processor. My SSD is probably the best productivity investment I've made, it enables me to get much more work done in less time. It also helps when you have to reboot your machine and reopen all the programs during regular trading hours, that alone can save you thousands of dollars over the years.

4. How to Best Accumulate Market Knowledge — aka How to become a Student of Price Action and Market Situations

Lots of traders that I interviewed mentioned that a key element of their success was the accumulated experience of having watched the markets for a long time. They ended up building a database of charts, situations, setups, observations in their heads, which can provide them the confidence to take trades today because they have seen it all before.

One software that I've been using to speed up the process of this mental database building is the popular free program Evernote. What's nice about it is that I can quickly take a screenshot of a Level2 window or a chart, paste it to Evernote, write a small note about it, and then have it stored in the Cloud. The fact that you have to type out the lesson or observation should help increase the chance that your brain will retain that information and be able to use it in the future. You can also go to your notes database at any time and review the main lessons and charts that you have accumulated, this will further help your brain retain that information. Bellow there's an example of how I use this program:

To take a screenshot of just one specific window (like a chart window or Level 2) just hit Ctrl+PrintScreen. (The PrintScreen button without Ctrl will take a screenshot all of your workspace.) Then you just hit Ctrl+V in an Evernote note and you can write what you learned about the situation. When you close the Evernote window everything is saved and sent to the Cloud automatically.

I always try write on Evernote when I have a big loss, or make a big mistake. It isn't a loss if you learn something from it, **you're paying for an education that might make or save you ten times that amount in the future**. I'm a big fan of trading small (100 shares or even less) and writing what you learned in Evernote. I've accumulated lots of lessons and insights about how markets work and how to day trade stocks as a result of that.

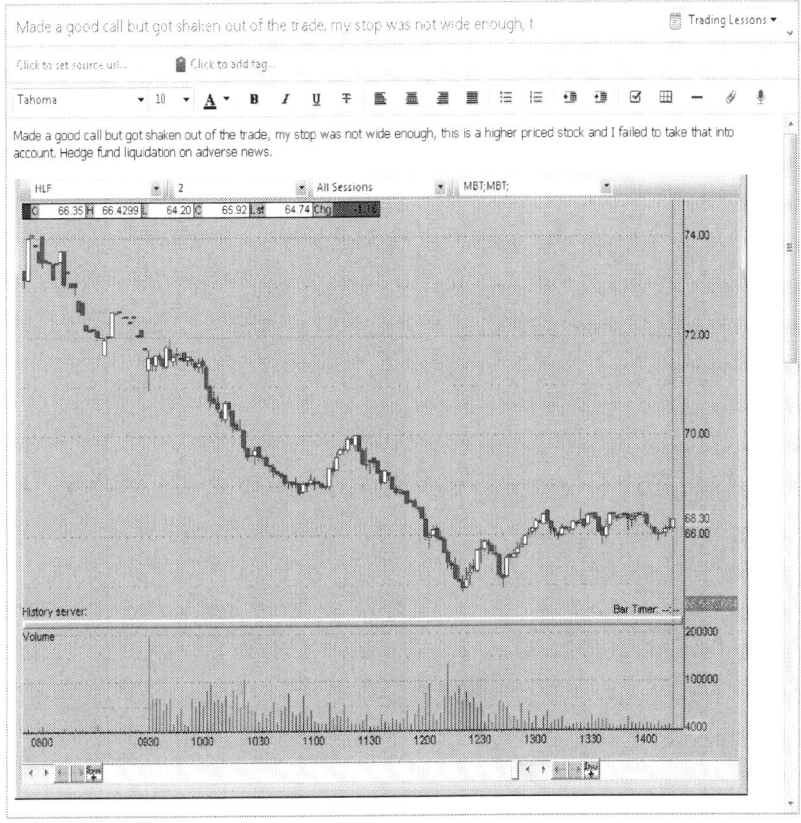

Source: Evernote and MBTrading Desktop Pro

Chapter 12

The Core Principles of Good Short-Term Trading

After conducting a lot of these interviews and analyzing my own trading results I've come up with a list that I believe are the absolute core fundamentals of short-term trading, these are principles that when I've had a losing day or I'm going through a difficult period, 80 to 90 percent of the time it's because I've violated these principles, following them can literally save you thousands of dollars. I would recommend you to print or make a copy of these principles so you can always check it back when you want to.

Think of these a simple heuristics (rules of thumb), they might not be applicable every single time but most of the time they work if you stick with them.

The core principles are:

1. Do the majority of your trading during the most profitable periods of the day, have the vast majority of your risk exposure in those periods as well.

2. Trade less or don't trade in days where you're struggling physically, emotionally or psychologically.

3. Surround yourself with great traders.

4. Have the discipline to take losses.

5. Have the patience to trade the best setups and avoid marginal setups.

6. Accumulate as much market experience as possible.

7. Avoid adverse selection, don't be a rebate sucker.

8. Do your premarket preparation work.

9. Have wide enough stops to avoid the noise.

10. Never show your hand.

11. Size your positions correctly, don't overbet, never risk your account.

12. No matter how confident you're in a specific setup, there's always at least a 10 percent chance that you're completely and utterly wrong.

13. Seek to be exposed to big gain/small loss situations and avoid exposure to small gain/big loss trades.

14. When trying to catch a bounce or "bottom pick," assume that the chance that you are right is similar to the chance that the asset will go significantly lower than you think.

1. Do the majority of your trading during the most profitable periods of the day. Have the vast majority of your risk exposure in those periods as well.

These periods are the open (up to roughly one hour and a half after the opening bell) and the close (the final hour of the day). Trading during the mid-day period is very tempting sometimes, because you'll see chart formations that probably worked for you many times. You'll start to think there's no reason not to take it since you have made lots of profits off it over the years. The thing is, in an HFT world there are simply fewer moves during that period. A decent move in any direction will frequently retrace back to the other direction as the market making algos take profits or provide support in an attempt to take profits (the stock gets stuck in "market making channel"). What gets a move following through is volume, and that is frequently absent in the mid-day session.

Lots of reliable signals, such as red to green/green to red moves, breakouts/breakdowns, and other technical patterns fail more often during mid-day than in the open and the close.

Does that mean you shouldn't trade mid-day and patterns don't work? No, it means that you need a better overall setup to trade, you don't want to take a marginal setup, because it will fail more frequently and that can upset you for later in the day (it can cost you mental capital for the close). Instead of, say, shorting a green to red play that you believe it's OK (but not great), you pass up the play and wait to see how it trades in the close. You do take plays that you believe are great setups when it starts to move (or when there's breaking news), but I can't tell you how many losses I've had simply because I wanted to trade the same patterns and setups I did at open during the mid-day but the truth is that they don't work as often.

The reliability of patterns and setups depend on the time period in which they happen, that's what a lot of technical gurus and people selling courses won't tell you, if they did their patterns and methods wouldn't look magical enough for them to get rich selling them to you.

This applies to your risk exposures as well, your larger sized positions should be in the open/close and you should cut down your size significantly in the mid-day session (unless that great setup or news play show up).

2. Trade less or don't trade in days where you're struggling physically, emotionally or psychologically.

This is another one that when I violate I will frequently face losses that I don't normally face, it happens especially when I trade on poor sleep, this hurts my decision making tremendously. I will feel more emotional about trading and get really afraid of missing out a great play, this leads to hanging on to losers due to fear of getting out right at the reversal point.

I will also feel more impulsive to put trades in, this makes my broker rich and hurts my account. If you feel that in a particular day you're struggling for any reason, immediately cut down your size dramatically, don't trade mid-day at all, and live to fight for another day. A wise trader once said: **"You have to know when to waive the white flag"**.

Sometimes I do what I call "defensive trading" days. I simply trade the open and close (the most profitable periods) and for the rest of the day I just monitor the markets, hardly putting any trades in. If you're one of those who struggle doing even defensive trading, you might be better off leaving your trading desk and doing something else.

3. Surround yourself with great traders.

Most of the traders that I interviewed stay in touch with other good traders. They learn from them by watching what they're doing, right and wrong. They can ask for advice in a private setting where it's more likely he will get a useful answer. It's very difficult to get good by being isolated and just trading by yourself. People are social creatures, and they tend to absorb beliefs, mindsets, techniques, strategies, tricks, from the people they spend most of their time with.

There are many ways you can surround yourself with great traders, some of them are: joining a trading chatroom, joining a prop firm, starting a Skype group and getting good traders in it, or getting a mentor. Also try to decrease contact with losing traders that you might be in touch with.

4. Have the discipline to take losses.

Lots of traders interviewed mentioned this one as the number one factor in their success and in the failure of others. In the previous chapter I outlined in the section "The Boost Your Discipline Mini-Guide" how can anyone can develop discipline through willpower boosting activities and mindsets. Being able to take a loss is like being able to swing at a baseball for a hitter. Without it, you can't really have a trading career.

5. Have the patience to trade the best setups and avoid marginal setups.

The thing about marginal setups and why they should be avoided is the fact that they're marginal probably due to the probability of success being lower than you're used to. As a result they'll inevitably lead you to losses. If these losses destabilize you mentally, that it will cost you money in trades later on that day. Perhaps you'll mismanage a great setup and as a result profit $1,000 less in a great trade just because you tried to make $200 in a marginal trade earlier. This math won't work out over the long-term.

Taking marginal trades will also require focus while you're in the position, this might hurt you in other positions or prevent you from seeing a potential trade that could be setting up.

Trading is different than other activities because so much depends on your mental game instead of just technical execution. It's important to take care of your mental capital just as much as you take care of your trading capital.

An idea related to this one is to put more money in the better setups and put less money in the less good ones. It's obvious, but is it violated so frequently it deserves mention. The more you like a specific setup or trade idea, the bigger you should bet, the less you like it, the less you should bet. Traders frequently violate this when they average down. They're not adding to the position because they all of a sudden they like the setup more (though they'll claim that), they do it because they don't want to take a loss in the trade. It is also violated when the trader starts to trade bigger on lower quality trade ideas in the afternoon to make it back losses from earlier in the day. The first hour is the best hour. That's the hour to make the larger bets. The mid-day period should have less size as the profit expectation and probability of the trade being a winner are lower.

They also violate it when they refuse to bet big on the rare instances where their edge is very large. "It takes courage to be a pig," and not being a pig can cost big profits.

A good tip related to this principle is to never take an overnight trade that doesn't have a significant edge. The reason is that if you do have a loss on that trade, you'll start the day with a mental capital hit. You might have to trade the most important hour of the day (the open) being upset, on tilt or in a revenge trading mindset. You might also overtrade mid-day or mismanage trades through the day. As a result, the small or marginal edge from the overnight trade will be completely wiped out when you factor in the consequences for the next day if you do take a loss (especially a big loss). If you do take it, at least go with small size.

6. Accumulate as much market experience as possible.

Lots of the traders interviewed can do amazing trades and bank huge profits not because they're superhuman but simply because they have seen that situation come up so many times that it would be unnatural not to take the trade, confidence in the setup is effortless. They can "sense" it will work. All they have to do is to size their position in and be ready to take a loss if that particular time is one of the unusual instances where the setup doesn't work.

This principle goes hand in hand with being patient regarding your trading career. Don't expect do to as well as many traders here right away. You have your whole life to get good. Focus on accumulating market knowledge and following these principles of good trading and (assuming you're disciplined) the profits will come. Using a program like Evernote to record observations and save charts and lessons learned can be very beneficial.

7. Avoid adverse selection. Don't be a rebate sucker.

Using limit orders and collecting a rebate can be very seductive, because it gives you an illusion of savings. You don't pay the spread, and you pay less in commission due to rebates, but you suffer from adverse selection (you tend to get filled when you're wrong in the short-term and not filled when you're right). Adverse selection is a hidden cost. You have to balance not paying the spread plus the rebate with the cost of suffering adverse selection.

If the security you're trading is not very liquid (and this principle does not apply to liquid issues such as SPY or big cap thick stocks), this cost can turn a profitable strategy into a losing one. Many times I fell for this trap and tried to save a few cents by using a limit order when buying a stock. This is especially a problem in larger spread stocks. I would miss lots of winning trades and wish I'd paid the spread instead. As Dennis Dick says, avoid trading larger spread and illiquid stocks, but if you can't, wait for the spread to narrow down and don't be afraid of paying it.[58]

8. Do your premarket preparation work.

If the first hour is the most important hour of the day, then being prepared for it by doing your premarket work is absolutely critical. You should know which stocks you are planning to trade or watch, setup price alerts at key levels, see what is in play, asses how you're feeling (see if principle 2 will have to be applied), find problems in your trading setup (Internet connection issues, mandatory broker software updates, etc.), among other things.

9. Have wide enough stops to avoid "the noise"

As Jeff Goldman explains and Eric Husander proves, there's a lot more noise intraday these days as a result of HFT activity. I can't tell you how many times I've made a great call in a stock but got shaken out of the trade by having too tight a stop. It's absolutely critical that you leave enough room for you to not be played in these games. It's not just that you'll be hit by small losses constantly, you'll also suffer a mental capital drawdown (you just lose confidence in what you're doing and start trading badly), which might prevent you from reentering the trade, thus missing it, and hurting your mental capital further.

10. Never show your hand.

When the HFTs or other participants see that someone wants to get size in or out they'll make that person pay. These HFT firms make millions of dollars squeezing out every cent of big orders that are trying to be worked in the markets. It's important that you learn to use hidden orders (native, not broker hidden orders), iceberg orders, and never get too big in a security. The bigger the position

---

58 In my experience, this principle applies more to NYSE, NASDAQ and AMEX securities but not as much to OTC stocks.

size mistake you make (relative to the liquidity available), the more you will be **exponentially harmed**. This is due the efficiency in which HFT firms detect big orders (the bigger the position, the more time they have to find you) that are being liquidated and the nature of auction markets (in an auction market system, such as the stock market, the price is set by the highest price someone is willing to pay and the lowest price someone is willing to offer). When your hand is exposed these HFT firms will try to milk your order for the most you are willing to pay (if you are short) and the least you are willing to offer (if you are long).

This principle also goes along with not being a rebate sucker (principle 7).

11. Size your positions correctly, don't overbet, never risk your entire account.

In chapter 7 I explained why overbetting is completely unnecessary, as it not only increases the volatility of your returns, it also decreases the returns, so it costs you money to overbet. There are also all kinds of risks when you take large leveraged positions intraday that some people forget about, such as trading halts, merger and acquisitions news, bankruptcy filling news, etc. Betting too much also hurts your returns because losses will decrease your mental capital and lead to inferior trading decisions later in that day.

12. No matter how confident you are in a specific setup, there's always at least a 10 percent chance that you're completely and utterly wrong.

Several times in my trading career, I've been completely convinced of a certain outcome. I'd done my analysis, seen the numbers, and simply didn't see how I could not be correct. The market then, of course, proceeded to show me that I was completely and utterly wrong. The result was a loss in my trade. It's a very useful risk management guideline to have to believe that there's always a 10 percent chance that you're completely wrong. Is 10 percent a magic number? No, but it helps you satisfy the human tendency of wanting to be right (after all, there's a 90 percent chance that you're correct), but at the same time keeps your risk management alert system in check, because you know there's a chance you'll have to face a big loss. This prevents you from overbetting, ignoring price action, refusing to take a loss, not reassessing a trade based on the news, etc.

The truth is that when you have a position in the markets, you're always exposed to black swans, fat tails and unlikely events, by assuming that a certain percentage of the time you'll be hit by something unexpected, you ensure that you won't blow your account up one day by being too confident.

13. Seek to be exposed to big gain/small loss situations and avoid exposure to small gain/big loss ones.

Nassim Taleb, in his magnificent book, *Antifragile*, talks about how there can be two types of exposures that people typically are exposed to, one where people make or lose small amounts and then make it big when an expected event occurs, and one where they make small amounts for a long time and then face a huge loss when an expected event occurs. Perhaps a graphical display of this idea can help the reader understand:

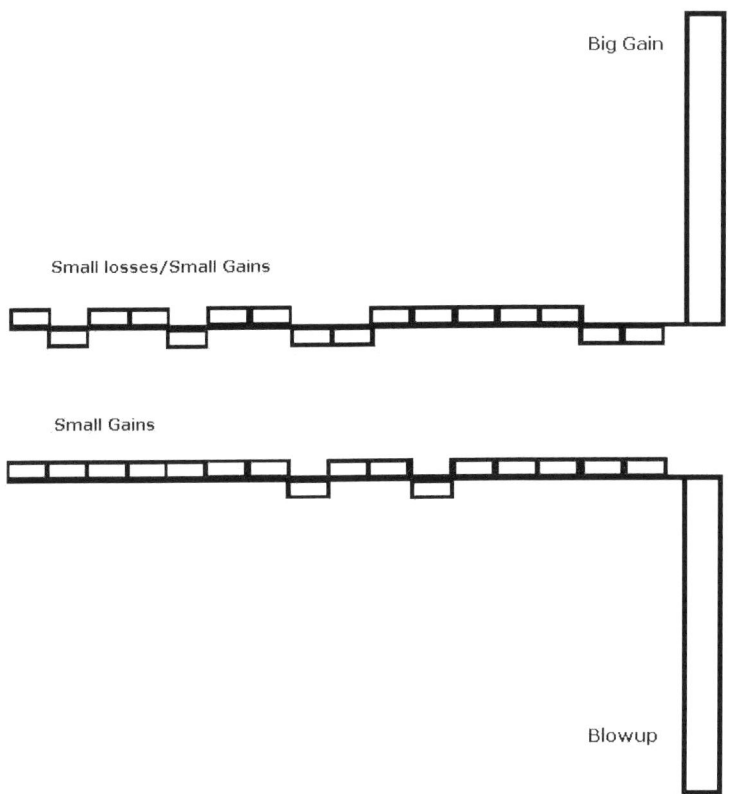

Big Gain

Small losses/Small Gains

Small Gains

Blowup

The second exposure model is dangerous because you never know how big that loss is. Recall from Chapter 8, Lesson 1, that if you go a lot above your Kelly size, you are expected to have long-term negative returns, even if you are trading a system with overall positive expectation. This model is the most seductive because psychologically, it is the easiest to trade. You keep making small amounts every day, you get more reinforcement that you are a good trader, but then one day, the "system" doesn't work and you give back all you made and then some, perhaps even go into debt with the broker. What are ways you can be exposed to the first model and avoid the second? Here is a quick list:

- Trade the best day trade setups. They are the ones with the best risk/reward ratio due inefficiencies in intraday asset pricing. They usually happen at key support/resistance levels, when news is fresh, when momentum starts shifting, etc. The more you accumulate market experience, the more you will notice these inefficiencies.

- Buy OTM (Out of the Money) options in situations where there is a potential for a big move. You can be exposed to extremely asymmetrical payoffs by doing so.

- Be careful with overnight trades (in particular, big positions with leverage). The additional risks will prevent you from controlling the loss size and expose you to bigger, unexpected losses. You will populate your trade results distribution with additional big losses that wouldn't be there otherwise.

- Be very careful with short selling. Short selling, by its very structure, is a small gain/ big loss trade. The most you can make is 100%, but the loss is unlimited. This doesn't mean that you shouldn't short; it means that when you do, controlling your risk is the number one factor that you should pay attention to, especially if you are carrying a trade overnight. A big (say 25-50% of your net worth) overnight short is one of the riskiest positions you can possibly have because in a fat tail/short squeeze scenario, you could literally lose everything and then some. Volkswagen stock, for instance, closed at around €210 the day before its big squeeze. It opened at €350 the next day and rallied all the way to €1000 over the course of the squeeze (btw, the stock looked awfully weak before all of this). Anyone carrying a big overnight short was forced to take a large loss as the gap up prevented any risk control. The US stock Medbox (MDBX), made an even more amazing squeeze in 2012, going from $40s all the way up to $210 in one day (and most of it was in a gap up).

These types of black swans are unpredictable (don't kid yourself thinking you can dodge them by good analysis, you only have to be wrong once to lose everything), so cutting down the size of overnight shorts is a necessity because you never know when you will be caught on the wrong side of one. Of course, it doesn't pay to insure yourself against an event that will happen once, say, every 10,000 years, but for one that could happen once or twice in your lifetime, it definitely pays. As a rule of thumb, assume that one day, you will short a stock overnight, and it will open up 300% against you (similarly to the two previous stocks mentioned), and then size your position accordingly (a loss of anything more than 30% of your net worth, in the mega-squeeze scenario, is probably too large). Of course, always get out when a stock is making huge moves against you, no matter how painful.

• Don't average down or up. This is what blow ups are made of because you are increasing your risk exposure in a low quality trade (because you are going against the momentum, which is very dangerous in a HFT world because the algos exacerbate these trends) while your mental capital is getting depleted. You will end up having a lot of capital at risk while making poor decisions and the computers pounding the trend against you. All it takes is one trade where you keep adding into for you to lose everything in a gigantic loss. Remember the Kelly chart.

• Stick with your stops. If you frequently let your losses ride, some of your small losses will turn into bigger ones. . You will populate your trade results distribution with additional big losses that wouldn't be there if you stuck with your stops.

• Avoid shorting OTM options unless you are experienced and have rock solid discipline when it comes to bet sizing. Selling OTM options can yield small gains for a long time, and then lead to a huge loss when an expected event occurs. People are seduced by these gains, and they will frequently look at historical data to find comfort in running this strategy. The issue is that there are always new things that "never happened before" so historical data can lead you to a trap. The reader might recall that the Options Expert from Chapter 10 engages in some option selling in his speculative activities. The difference is that he will also buy way OTM "garbage" options to lock in a maximum loss in the trade. He also understands bet sizing more than does the average trader.

14. When trying to catch a bounce or "bottom pick," assume that the chance that you are right is similar to the chance that the asset will go significantly lower than you think.

Bottom picking is a quite risky and difficult strategy to execute. It requires experience and risk control to be successful. Some of my largest losses and from a lot of traders have come from trying to catch a bounce too early. Frequently, things go much lower because of the momentum and panic. In October of 2008, no one would have imagined that the S&P500 could go down so much in a single week. As a result, many people blew up.

As a rule of thumb, always assume that the chance that you are correct and the bottom will start is similar to the chance that the selling will take the asset significantly lower than you think. This doesn't mean don't take the trade; it means that if you do take it, get out as soon as it looks like you are wrong (asset makes new lows or breaks below a key level).

Another way that some traders play it is by scaling in. When things look oversold, they start to buy it a small position and add when they look even more oversold. If the bounce happens, great, they will ride for a while and sell. If it doesn't happen, they have an "uncle point," a point where they will be out, no matter what. Why should they be getting out at that point? Because the chance of a bounce is similar to the chance that it will go significantly lower than they think, and it might very well stay there. This is a point that some traders might not realize. Sure, it might bounce, but it still might not make the trader even in the trade because it went significantly lower than what he thought.

Realizing that you are just as likely to be right as you are to be wrong will force you to think in terms of reward to risk ratios and protecting your account instead of trusting that the bounce will come.

The rule might not be completely accurate statistically, but as a risk management heuristic, it works.[59]

---

[59] This principle can also be applied to picking tops and/or shorting parabolic up moves. Always assume that the chance it will go quite a bit higher is similar to the chance that you will get the top.

Conclusion

I hope that through this book you were able to improve your trading results by learning from the experience and wisdom of other traders. Trading has gotten more difficult in recent years, but so has virtually every other area in finance. In this book there is a lot of knowledge, advice, and tips on how to adapt to these changing conditions and be successful. I encourage the reader to re-read the chapters from time to time.

Writing this book was a hard task for me, mainly due to lack of time, but somehow I was able to pull it off. When I started the interviews back in August of 2012, I'd just decided to start to day trade actively. I had no idea what was going to happen. But I knew I had no choice, because I had bills to pay and really didn't want to get a "real" job. The uncertainty of what kind of result I would get, combined with the need to pay my lousy bills, made me work really hard to learn from the best guys I could find. The result of this journey is this book.

Society frequently looks down on this profession and links it to gambling (sometimes rightly so), but the truth is that being trader, having the freedom of working when you want, taking vacations at any time you want, and having your results depend entirely on you is one of the best feelings a person can have. You feel like you have destiny in your hands and are free to enjoy your life.

If you're willing to work hard and be disciplined, trading is and always will be one of the best jobs on earth.

About the Author

Fernando Oliveira is a full-time trader who was born and resides in São Paulo, Brazil. He made a living off poker and online casinos from 2004 to 2012. In 2012 he transitioned to day trading US stocks and futures. He holds a Technical High School diploma in IT and is a college graduate in Financial Management.

He can be reached at contact@neweradaytrading.com

On Twitter @neweratrades

His website is www.neweradaytrading.com

Printed in Great Britain
by Amazon.co.uk, Ltd.,
Marston Gate.